First things first: yes I am very tall, no the weather isn't different up here, and no I don't play basketball. Glad that's out the way.

I've been a professional footballer for 20 years, have 42 England caps, have scored over 100 Premier League goals and hold the record for the most headed goals in Premier League history.

I've been at a fair few clubs too, including Queens Park Rangers, Portsmouth, Aston Villa, Norwich, Southampton, Liverpool, Portsmouth, Tottenham Hotspur, Stoke and England.

In my time I've been promoted, relegated, won trophies, gone months without scoring, been bought, sold, loaned and abused - and I've loved almost every moment of it.

How to be a Footballer

PETER CROUCH
WITH TOM FORDYCE

EBURY
PRESS

5 7 9 10 8 6

Ebury Press, an imprint of Ebury Publishing
20 Vauxhall Bridge Road
London SW1V 2SA

Ebury Press is part of the Penguin Random House Group of companies
whose addresses can be found at global.penguinrandomhouse.com

Penguin
Random House
UK

First published by Ebury Press in 2018
This edition published in 2019

www.penguin.co.uk

A CIP catalogue record for this book is available
from the British Library

ISBN 9781785039782

Printed and bound in Great Britain by Clays Ltd, Elcograf S.p.A.

MIX
Paper from
responsible sources
FSC® C018179
FSC
www.fsc.org

Penguin Random House is committed to a
sustainable future for our business, our readers
and our planet. This book is made from Forest
Stewardship Council® certified paper.

CONTENTS

PROLOGUE

I always wanted to be a footballer. Of course I did. Not a basketball player, as I get asked on a daily basis, or a roofer who doesn't need to use a ladder, or a zookeeper who can talk to the giraffes face to face. We'll get on to all that business in a while. In the meantime, no, the weather isn't different up here, thanks for asking.

Glad we've got that out of the way. Now. You become a footballer because you love football, because you spent your childhood doing overhead kicks against the fencing round the tennis courts in the local park, because you watched the World Cup on telly and fell in love with the goals and the kits and the passion and the excitement and the team song with the rap bit in it. You become a footballer because you keep going, even when a director of football keeps sending you out on loan to non-league clubs, when your early appearances are greeted by laughter and chants of 'Freak! Freak! Freak!' and 'Does the circus know you're here?' and you walk off at half-time to see your dad wrestling with a load of fans who've been abusing his son in front of his face. You become a footballer because you can trap a ball much better than anyone expects of a bloke your shape, and volley it in a way that confuses people who have set ideas about what a player your size is for, and then learn to head it as well

1

as everyone assumes you could anyway. You become a footballer because you love football.

And then you are a footballer, and you're suddenly in the strangest, funniest, most baffling world of all. A world where one team-mate comes to training in a bright-red suit with matching top hat and cane and glasses without any glass in them, and another spends his evening hiring a Ferrari, parking it outside a nightclub and then lying on the bonnet directly in the eyeline of all the girls coming out. A world where players buy cars so big they can't park them or become so blasé about how many sports cars they own that they forget they have left a Porsche at the train station. Even when their surname is incorporated in the registration plate.

You look around you, and you try to make sense of it all. The player who gets a tattoo of a chimpanzee wearing glasses and Beats by Dre headphones and kissing the barrel of a gun. The team-mate whose preparation for a big game is turning up with a Tesco's bag containing the same four items of food every single time. The fellow striker who sends a tweet and then replies to it as if it's a text message from a stranger, starting a conversation with himself that the whole world can see.

I've seen football change over the past 20 years. I've been promoted, relegated, won big trophies, gone months without scoring, played for my country at World Cups, been bought, sold, loaned and abused. I think I have a good understanding now of how it works: the tactics, the transfers, the endorsements and the nights out, the glory nights, the wild celebrations, the times when you can't score even when you're two yards out and the goalkeeper is lying on his back behind you.

I've made my own mistakes. I don't have any tattoos, but that's mainly because none of my limbs are wide enough to support a visible image. I have owned ridiculous cars, at least until an infamous run-in with Roy Keane put me right. I have stood in terrible nightclubs listening to music I hated, at least until ten days in Ayia Napa taught me a lesson I could never forget. There have been clothes I have bought that cost more than the industrial sewing machines on which they were made. I have never carried a Louis Vuitton man-bag which contains nothing but my own personal hairdryer, but it was close.

And so the time feels right to take you inside this world – past the bouncers, round the velvet rope, into the madness and fun and weirdness of life as a footballer. To take you with me onto the team bus and show you how the rules work on who can sit where and with whom, to open the door on footballers' houses and try to understand when an orangery became a must-have accessory. To come with me on a night out, where I will be badgered by strangers to do the Robot and fellow players will walk around in caps, despite caps being banned, and sunglasses, despite the fact that it's a nightclub and thus already very dark.

Walk with me into the dressing-room, to find out which players refuse to touch a football before a game, to discover why a load of millionaires never have any shower gel, to hear what Cristiano Ronaldo says when he looks at himself in the mirror. Lurk on the back post to understand the perfect technique for heading that incoming cross into the top corner or cracking it on the volley with the outside of your foot if it swings behind you. Listen to the stories about how to beat that particular defender there and why the full-back charging in at you is not to be messed with and why that goalkeeper is quite honestly the strangest person you will ever share a penalty area with.

We will go into post-match interviews, make fools of ourselves on social media and try to ensure that we never again pay £250 for a haircut that should have cost a tenner. We'll be coached and cajoled by Harry Redknapp, upset Rafa Benítez with an ill-judged leather jacket and be soothed by the sound of an accordion played by Tord Grip. There will be some very bad music and some very bad decisions.

But it will be fun, all of it, and like nothing you have seen or read before. I am Peter Crouch. This is *How to Be a Footballer*. Shall we?

DRESSING-ROOMS

Come with me inside football. Come with me into the inner sanctum, and to all the other secret places in football too.

The dressing-room. Sixteen players, the manager, all the assistants, the medical staff. And yet the man who has all the power is the kitman.

Once the kitman has chosen a peg for you, that's it. Every home match you will be given the same spot. In every away dressing-room the order of players will be the same. Try and sit in a different place and there will be uproar: why are you doing this, and why are you doing this now, just before kick-off in a game we have to win?

There will be method behind his system. You might be put in a little row of mates, or grouped together by position. Striker with strike partner, central defender with central defender, goalkeeper on the end by himself. At home your locker will be numbered, with a framed photo of you in action by your spot. Ideally with you looking dominant, or scoring a goal, or generally looking heroic. A little glance at it just before you head out onto the pitch, like a visual pat on the back, a fist-pump, a 'you've got this, big man'.

The dressing-room at the stadium is a different place to the training ground. They might serve the same purpose but the vibe is

5

far more serious. You meet before matches at the training ground, take the coach to the stadium, and the fun stops. You walk into the dressing-room and think, this is what it's all about, all the hard work in the rain and cold all week, all the hours of practice in the park after school as a kid, all the good eating and stretching and gym-work and early nights. Early-ish nights. On weekdays.

You arrive at 1.30pm for a 3pm kick-off. Some of the lads will be having a last massage, some listening to their music. I'll read the programme from cover to cover and try to find something amusing from within its pages to read to the lads. 'Hey, fellas, listen to what the captain's written in his column this week! Oh – you're getting a massage. And I forgot – no one talks to each other in here any more.' There are tables of drinks, water, caffeine shots, energy gels, cans of Red Bull, packs of chewing gum. Jelly Babies get shared out. Get your hands off the black ones, you know they're my favourite.

The best dressing-room in the old days was at Highbury. The famous marble halls amazed. Then you walked into the away dressing-room for your first ever experience of underfloor heating. When you've never tried it before it blows your mind. 'Oh my God! Lads! The floor is actually hot!' We'd be tossing our club-issue flip-flops to one side and strolling about in bare feet with wonder on our faces. Now, of course, it's standard issue in most footballers' bathrooms. It's just how you heat rooms. Back then it was the eighth wonder of professional football. 'So this is Arsenal . . .'

The Emirates now is great. The home dressing-room at Wembley is huge. You can tell that Aston Villa are still a big club by the size of theirs. There's carpet everywhere.

The old stadiums hold the strange ones – Fulham, the away one in the cottage at the corner of the ground, a listed building, so small; Anfield, where they were so compact you could hear the other team shouting, poky old showers; QPR's Loftus Road, squashed and leaking noise from the stands all around. At Anfield I used to look around and wonder which legends of the past had sat where I was sitting, whose coat had hung on my peg, and wished that they had carved their initials into the woodwork, as if you were at school. In England's dressing-room at Twickenham each individual place has a list of notable players from the past who starred in your position. I would have loved having that over my shoulder. St John. Keegan. Dalglish. Rush. Voronin.

They had character. Too many of the new ones are smart but bland. The ones we used in the new stadiums built in Germany for the 2006 World Cup were comfortable but soulless, and difficult to distinguish from one another. The benchmark had been set for me when I made my England debut the summer before at Giants Stadium in New Jersey. Each player had their own booth the size of a comfortable bathroom, complete with La-Z-Boy recliner. At the end of the match you didn't want to leave. You just wanted some popcorn and the highlights of your 3–2 win over Colombia on a flatscreen.

The big ones in the Champions League can make you feel like a gladiator. The San Siro, the Bernabéu, the Camp Nou – at all of them the dressing-room is underground, and you can feel the noise above you as you get changed, hear all the whistling as you jog out to warm up, feel that you're climbing up into a cauldron of hate as you walk out slowly a few minutes later for kick-off. I remember looking down and seeing the hairs on my legs standing up. The bouncing of the fans in the stands disturbing the water in the cups on the table, your shirt shaking in your hands as you pull it on.

When it goes wrong it's a horrible place to be. When I was sent off at the Bernabéu after 14 minutes of Spurs' Champions League tie with Real Madrid in April 2011, I walked back to the dressing-room from all that ear-ripping noise to the eeriest silence. Eighty thousand shouting and screaming outside, me entirely on my own, the loneliest man in the busiest part of the entire city. Too much time to gather your thoughts, too many echoes, no one to apologise to or put their arm round you. The same thought on a loop going round your brain: what the hell was I doing? A huge roar up above you: that's a goal, shit, that was too loud to be one of ours. Shit again, it's all my fault ...

When it goes right, it's instead the best bar in town, a pop-up club where everyone is on the same vibe and everyone is suddenly best mates. The party we had at the San Siro when I scored the winner for Spurs against Milan in the Champions League of 2011, the Anfield dressing-room after we beat Chelsea on penalties to win the Champions League semi-final of 2007 ... these are among the best nights out you will ever have, and they're nights in, surrounded by dirty shorts and muddy socks and shirts that stink of sweat, beers being shaken and sprayed everywhere, food being lobbed, dancing and jumping and singing and whoa, there's no way we're sleeping tonight until the sun has popped its head back up.

About the only silver lining to Liverpool's defeat by Milan in the final of 2007 was that I got taken for a drugs test immediately after the final whistle. It meant that I had to walk straight past the dressing-room and into a small cubicle, where I sat for what seemed like an age trying to summon up a wee having been running around on a hot Athens evening. Had we won, the greatest football-related party I'd have ever experienced would have been going on, the culmination not only of so much collective effort that season but all my hopes and dreams and hard work from the age of five onwards. I'm not sure I could have missed it. I might

8

have just taken the six-month ban and explained myself afterwards: look at my physique, it's clear this is all natural, I needed to spray beer at Steven Gerrard and dump a bin of cold water all over Rafa Benítez. Otherwise, what are you left with? 'Daddy what's your overriding memory of the night you won the greatest trophy in club football?' 'Sitting with my penis in my hand, while being watched by a stranger with a clipboard, trying desperately to think of running water.'

You'll be familiar with the tales of how teams used to try to ruin opposition teams by monkeying with the away dressing-room. It certainly used to go on – turning the heating up so much that you were falling asleep before kick-off, cutting off the hot water so that the showers were freezing, bringing you the usual pots of tea but lacing it with so much sugar that you were either unable to drink it or required immediate dental surgery. At Rotherham you used to get changed in a Portakabin and then walk across to the actual ground. These days they instead try to kill you with comfort. Palatial rooms, every seat padded, delightful showers, Molton Brown toiletries if you're at Stamford Bridge. It's like visiting an all-male spa. Just when you feel ready for your facial peel you realise you've got Gary Cahill trying to tread on your ankles.

I still find it strange that the communal bath has gone for ever. When I began it was an absolute staple of the game – all of you piling in, naked and covered in mud, a good old splash about and then climbing out with things winking in all directions. And then time passes without them, and you think, what a very strange vibe that was. Sitting in dirty water. Plasters bobbing about. Bits of grass and mud sticking to you, whether you had brought it in or not. Imagine trying to introduce the concept to the young lads now. They'd think you were insane, or predatory.

It was sports science that killed them. The heat was bad for your legs. Ice-baths were supposed to significantly speed up your recovery post-match. But there was something I quite liked about them. They were deep, the deepest bath you'd ever had. All of you in there together, a camaraderie about it all. There's a reason the Roman Empire was founded on the collective bath experience. They bring you together. All are equal in a bath built for all.

It's the classic FA Cup final celebration shot: 13 men covered in dirty water, half of them smoking, the rest drinking milk straight from the glass pint bottle. When you see Bobby Charlton and Bobby Moore in there, bottles of bitter in hand, it looks tremendous fun. It's like a wet pub. From the nipples up it's a stag-do, from the nipples down it's a very weird nightclub.

Now, of course, it's all about the shower. In the biggest dressing-rooms, like Wembley, there will be 15 showers. It's all open-plan rather than individual cubicles like a posh gym. Neither are there any shower-gel dispensers on the wall. You're expected to bring your own, which because we're footballers and have almost everything else done for us, means we always forget. We always seem to end up sharing one tiny hotel shower gel that someone has nicked, all passing it round and squeezing increasingly insubstantial amounts out of the bottle. The exception is when the team has stayed at a Malmaison. As you'll know if you've had the pleasure of the Malmaison experience, the free shower gels and shampoos are at least a seven-day size. They must lose so many. The day after a Malmaison we're mob-handed. 'Anyone need conditioner? No?'

Towels are once again the responsibility of the kitman. It will have your squad number on for identification, although this also means you can get stuck with the same ropey old thing for too many seasons. My last one at Stoke had been in circulation for six years. It was more rip than material, stringy where it wasn't hole. I had to pull our man up on it. I'm not a diva, but I do like to be dry after a shower.

A downside of dressing-rooms: the toilets. Think about it. If it's a morning meet, you've got thirty blokes who've come straight from home and then had a coffee. At Stoke there are three toilets. That's an ugly equation. There's also the location; they open directly into the dressing-room. The aroma is barbaric. There's not even a small antechamber or hall that can act as an airlock. That scenario is the only reason I'm glad Robert Huth left. He's a big German, he has big German appetites. That's all I can say on the matter. It's so bad that I sometimes go upstairs to use the single toilet on the nice corridor. A small oasis amid so much heinous pollution.

An upside: the food. After an away match you will always have stuff brought into the dressing-room, and once again it's Arsenal leading the way. Pizzas are standard wherever you go but the Arsenal standard is that little bit higher than everyone else's. They're virtually artisan. There will be chicken wings, potato wedges, all the sort of stuff that you might consider forbidden but which in that critical hour window after a game are fine, because you just need to get something down you, and what the something is matters less than you eating it. The tastier the food, the easier it is to get down. If you've played the full 90 minutes you can often feel a little queasy. You need all the help you can get. If you've been on the bench and not got on, you can actually feel hungrier, because you've gone the same five hours without eating but you haven't had the intense exercise to churn your guts. You'll see the strange sight of three blokes who have been sitting on their backsides all day absolutely inhaling a series of family-sized margheritas.

You'll get fights, not over the last slice but at half-time if someone's made a bad mistake or hasn't tracked back with his runner. It's not actually a bad thing. It can be a safe space to work out all that anger before the second half begins. I once saw Steven Nzonzi and Jon Walters have a full-on punch-up, then go out and play brilliantly together in the second half. They both got good digs in, but it showed that they cared. Far worse is a dressing-room where no one is talking when you're 2–0 down at the break, when you can tell that to some players it doesn't make enough of a difference if you win or lose.

They will be the stage for comedy acts. While at Spurs we had a pre-season game against Brighton. On the way down there our young midfielder Jamie O'Hara had been telling us all about his new contract – £15,000 a week, a decent amount for a player making his name. In the first half we were awful. We trooped into the dressing-room and Harry Redknapp absolutely hammered us. 'You f***ing shambles! You useless bunch of wasters!' A finger jabbed at O'Hara. 'This kid is the only one putting it in. You lot getting paid x, y and z, and he's only on five grand a week!'

On poured the rant, everyone head down, no one wanting to meet his eye. Eventually he ran dry and stormed back out of the dressing-room. A long silence. And then the ice was broken by Jonathan Woodgate. I peeked up and saw him grinning and thought, how can he be laughing after that? And then he pointed his finger at Jamie. 'You little liar! You told us you were on fifteen grand a week ...' It wasn't the amount we were bothered about. It was the fact he was telling every man and his dog a load of porkies the week before.

The dressing-room was always a sanctuary, a place where no one outside the team would ever know about those fights and japes.

The assistant manager would be stationed at the door, using his arm to keep it shut if the referee was coming in and the manager was still telling the team to kick the hell out of the opposition's main man, blocking off the tea-man if two players were at each other's throats. That'll change. Manchester City have the Tunnel Club at the Etihad; the natural progression, for the media organisation that bumps the next television rights deal up even further, will be to demand access even closer to home.

I can understand that. As a fan your greatest dream is to be let into that final sanctum. Even with the best-planned pitch invasion after a promotion or trophy win you can't get into the dressing-room. And they are special places. I played in a Unicef game at Old Trafford, my side containing half the United treble winners of 1999, the manager Sir Alex Ferguson. On one side of me were Ryan Giggs, both the Nevilles, Paul Scholes and David Beckham. As Sir Alex gave us his team talk I deliberately turned my shoulders so that I could only see the United boys, and for a moment I allowed myself to imagine that I was there with them in '99, maybe before extra time in the FA Cup semi-final against Arsenal, maybe before the Champions League final against Bayern Munich at the Camp Nou.

I'm not a United fan at all. I never have been. But you have to respect what they did as a team. And so I sat there, thinking: this is so weird, but mad in a beautiful way, because this is what they went through. And I'm experiencing it too, and so few others ever will.

SUPERSTITIONS

I was told once that multiple Grand Slam winner Serena Williams, arguably the greatest tennis player of all time, the epitome of cool talent and excellence under pressure, has one illogical fixation: she will not change her socks once during a tournament.

Across two weeks and seven matches of a Slam that's a lot of work for a sock to do. It scarcely seems believable, which perversely makes people much more likely to believe it. Superstitions by definition don't make sense, so why should this not be true?

A cautionary tale. There's a story doing the rounds – I say story, it's got to the point now where it's almost a meme, definitely a banner and a T-shirt and the source of endless enquiries on social media – that we can refer to as Crouchie's Having His Nachos.

It goes like this. I'm at the cinema, and there is a long queue at the food concession. Undeterred, I push straight to the front, look at the bloke behind the counter and bark the word 'Nachos' – no please, no apology to all those hungry punters left in my wake. There's also a version where I don't pay for them, but anyway. Having been served I turn to the queue and then stand there, putting nacho after nacho into my mouth, munching away expressionless. A shout goes up from the back – 'What you doing, Crouchie?' – and I deliver the fateful line: 'Crouchie's having his nachos!'

Now I don't mind a nacho. If on a visit to the cinema I might occasionally partake of some. But push in? Never. Eat them while blocking the queue? No. The whole point of buying food in the cinema is to take it into the screening. Who smashes down a whole box of nachos in the foyer? And then – greatest sin of all – refer to myself in the third person? Get out of it.

Unfortunately none of that seems to matter. I've been sent photos of people wearing 'Crouchie's having his nachos' as a slogan. It's been held up in stadiums. A week seldom passes without someone tweeting me a picture of them with nachos and a knowing grin.

Maybe it's the same with Serena. She wears the same brand of sock in every match; sometimes they get clay dust or grass stains on them. Before you know it there are photos doing the rounds of her with dirty socks and someone's decided she hasn't washed them since seeing off the world No. 112 in straight sets ten days before. And so when we discuss the superstitions of footballers, I have to begin with those I have witnessed with my own eyes. Or, in the case of Shaun Derry, heard with my own ears and smelled with my own nose.

Derry would insist on being sick before every game. By which I mean, if the nerves hadn't naturally made him sick, he would stick his fingers down his throat and do the job himself.

At the risk of stating the obvious, it really killed the Portsmouth dressing-room vibe. Graham Rix or Harry Redknapp would be knee-deep in their big motivational rant, tension building, the rest of us sitting there in rapt silence, and suddenly from the toilets would come an ear-splitting, 'UURRGHH …'

You learned to anticipate it – 'Where's Dezza?' – and suddenly what sounded like a motorbike roaring through twin exhausts. I'm a broad-minded man; whatever works for you, you do it. Personally if I threw up before a game I'd be weak as a kitten for hours afterwards. But you get discreet pukers, the apologetic ones who take themselves off into a quiet corner, and you get the opposite, which was Shaun Derry.

Harry himself was more about ties. If we won, the same tie would make an appearance for the following match. If we then lost, he would recycle to a previously unlucky one and try again. You had to admire his perseverance.

There was a period at Southampton where the tie in question was a shocker – dark background, images of red dogs all over it. We had a few good results, so he kept going with it, and as I recall it was worn while we were beating Liverpool at home and Middlesbrough away. Could the tie take any credit? At one stage one of the lads took a glance and told Harry that it was horrendous. Harry, his face going red with fury, replied that his grandson had given it to him. So even if it was lucky for the team it was seriously unlucky for that player, who spent the rest of the week very much keeping out of Harry's way.

Ultimately the tie's power must have been limited; we were relegated that season. Neither did its earlier success buy it any credit. As soon as we started losing, Harry ditched it. Maybe it came back at future clubs. Harry has surely had more teams than he has ties. Recycling would be a practical necessity.

Superstitions aren't designed to make sense. Before England games, John Terry would refuse to touch a ball with his feet in the dressing-room. Every time a ball came near him he'd freak out. A rolling ball would see him lift both feet off the floor, like an old dear with a mouse. Let's underline the madness of this: he was a footballer. His career, his essence, his entire life was about the interface between his feet and a ball. You'd find yourself deliberately rolling one at him just to see his reaction.

I have my own. In the early days I was far worse than I am now, but I had to cut back. It was getting stupid. There were so many that I struggled to remember what I was supposed to do next. Even now there are plenty: always a long-sleeved shirt, regardless of the weather (on a hot day, at a summer tournament, roll up the sleeves); when we do the handshakes pre-match, jump as high as I can and head thin air, do a little sprint and then bend down to do up the laces of my right boot. At the same time my dad will be doing his own: same coffee from the same café, same pre-match lunch, at least until it goes wrong. Should we lose or I miss a chance, he'll blame himself. I'll hear it from my mum afterwards – 'Sorry, Peter, he says he went to the wrong van for a burger at half-time.'

Deep down with these things there's often a seed of logic. The shoelace thing began with the thought, what happens if my boot flies off when I'm having a shot? So you start retying the laces, and you're playing well and scoring goals, and suddenly it seems too much of a risk to ditch it. Footballers are creatures of habit. If you've played 600 games, spent the last decade in the Premier League, scored goals in World Cup finals, why would you jeopardise it?

I console myself with the thought that mine are at least practical. My former team-mate at Spurs, Benoît Assou-Ekotto, was always a man apart. Think of the stereotypical modern player: tattoos, Drake on his MP3 player, obsessed with the game and the fame it brings. Benoît was not only not interested in football, he genuinely didn't like it. He didn't know many footballers – and I mean didn't know who they were, rather than not know them socially. When you sat down with him at White Hart Lane at 1.30pm on a Saturday, he'd have no idea which team you were playing in an hour and a half. 'But Benoît, we've been talking about them in training all week ...'

And so to his pre-match meal, the one he would have before every single game. Now none of us are adventurous. It's pasta, chicken, no sauce, and has been for the past 20 years. It's pure fuel rather than enjoyment. Get it down you, get on with it. Benoît wouldn't bother with any of that. Instead he'd turn up with a Tesco's bag containing the same four items every single time: a croissant, a hot chocolate, a full-fat Coke and a packet of crisps.

The croissant I could understand. He is French-Cameroonian. The hot chocolate: same cultural backstory. He used to dip the first into the second. But the crisps, and the Coke – it was like two discrete lunches, one belonging to a middle-aged Parisian and the other a 12-year-old on the Seven Sisters Road.

And it worked. He was always in great physical shape, and only very rarely injured. We accepted it, along with all the other weirdness: the random cars he would turn up to training in, sometimes a Smart car, then a Lamborghini, then a Ford Focus, then an old Cadillac with big rear fins; the way he would refuse to take ice-baths for recovery, on the rather basic premise that they were 'too cold'.

When Benoît was on international duty, legendary Cameroonian striker Samuel Eto'o decided to mark their qualification for the 2010 World Cup by buying every one of his fellow players an expensive watch. Benoît refused to accept it. 'No one buys me a watch. If I want a watch I can buy my own.'

I like to picture the look on Samuel's face when Benoît came out with that. The confusion, the disbelief. The thoughtfulness of the original idea, the generosity of the gift, the anger with which

Benoît greeted it. 'You what? Don't insult me, I'm not taking this nonsense …'

I refuse to stretch my calves before a match. It started when I was a teenager, taking creatine in an attempt to add some bulk to my lean physique. Creatine dehydrates you, so come 70, 80 minutes, my calves would be cramping something terrible. Rather than blame the creatine, I put it down to the fact that I was stretching my calves. The exact thing that stops you getting cramp. So I thought, do you know what, I'll stop stretching my calves.

At exactly the same time I stopped taking creatine. I haven't had a moment's cramp since. To be fair, I haven't got the biggest of calves. But I haven't had any injures since either. So why risk it? When we're told to stretch our calves, I do my hamstrings instead. Footballers' logic.

I once had some lucky pants that my wife Abbey got me for Christmas. A classic Y-front, green, the words 'LUCKY PANTS' across the business end. Can pants decide on their own if they're lucky, or is it up to the pant wearer? Either way, these ones were – I scored for Liverpool in the first match I wore them, and then kept wearing them, and kept scoring. And then one week I forgot them, left scrabbling desperately in my bag for the flash of green before the match, and suddenly I stopped scoring.

I'd been really worried about one of the players in the dressing-room spotting them. I'd wanted to keep them hush-hush. In retrospect I think I should have been more open about them. The mistake may have been in washing them. Perhaps a little bit of the luck leached off every time they went in the washing machine. What they needed was the low-temperature silks wash, or doing by hand. Maybe they came pre-loaded with six slices of luck, like a pay-as-you-go sim. I'm sure they're still at home somewhere, but they've lost their grip on me. Neither did I ever find out where Abbey got them from, so I could source another pair. I like to think she bought them from a mysterious old woman dressed in a black cloak and pointed hat. Either that or the novelty gift items aisle at M&S.

Abbey was unaware of the magic effect of those pants. Her lack of interest in football is stark, despite her dad being a lifelong Liverpool fan who's been to all five European Cup final wins; it's not unknown for her to text me at 2.45pm on a Saturday and ask me where I am.

I rather like it that way. It means I can switch off when I get home. I once hit the crossbar with a shot from two yards out. After the game I was obviously a little down on myself. Abbey asked me what was up; when I told her, she was genuinely impressed. 'The crossbar? But that's such a small target. Anyone could have hit the net – that's easy, it's right in front of you. But you managed to hit something right up above your head, and first time. That's amazing!'

Contrast that with the fate of a former team-mate of mine, who returned home after giving away a penalty to find his wife waiting for him in the kitchen with fists on hips and a look of fury on her face. 'What were you thinking, you idiot? How many times have I told you – stay on your feet! Show him out wide, don't dive in!' And she grabbed him and started demonstrating what the correct body position would have been, and where he should have put himself, and pushing him past the kitchen table and into the hall.

It's harder for supporters than players when it comes to superstitions. At least as a player you can influence the game. As a fan you can wear all the lucky pants you like, but you can't have a ball hit you on the backside and go in. And they blame themselves – 'I knew I should have stayed standing up rather than sitting on the sofa, it worked in the first half,' or 'If I hadn't lost that scarf then none of this would have happened ...'

The foreign influx into the British game has changed things a little. There is more pointing at the sky now when running onto the pitch or celebrating a goal, which you'd assume is more to do with where players think heaven might be rather than a love for cumulonimbus or passing jet passengers. Even those who aren't religious like to narrow the odds sometimes. At Portsmouth Linvoy Primus and Darren Moore were committed Christians. They would pray before games, and had a prayer room installed at Fratton Park. And then suddenly Jermain Defoe was joining in, much to the surprise of those of us who had never heard him mention any religious affiliations before. But when you start doing something and goals and success follow, you convince yourself that it might be helping, even if there's also a chance it's doing nothing, and before you know it you can't leave it behind.

Player: Laurent Blanc

Superstition: Before matches at the 1998 World Cup, kissing the bald head of his French team-mate and goalkeeper Fabien Barthez.

Verdict: According to legend, this superstition won France the World Cup. And you can understand its genesis – Barthez has the most kissable head in the team, at an almost perfect height for the slightly taller Blanc to kiss. He's tried it once, a struggling team has won the subsequent match, it's then too risky at a home World Cup to ditch it.

But here's the thing. It's non-transferable. It worked brilliantly in that combo, but I can't see Ryan Shawcross kissing

Jack Butland, let alone the other way round. Harry Maguire and Jordan Pickford? I don't think so. It's classically Gallic; French men kiss each other anyway. The English game has changed greatly over the last 20 years, but it's still different.

Player: Tommy Elphick
Superstition: The former Brighton, Bournemouth and then Villa defender holds on to the goalpost before each game.
Verdict: Why? And for how long?

Player: Paul Ince
Superstition: Last man out of the tunnel before a pitch, not putting his shirt on until reaching the pitch.
Verdict: I can understand the whole last-man thing. It's the cool thing to do. It makes you look in charge. 'You kids go ahead, I'll check for danger at the rear.' Traditionally the best player, or at least the one who thinks he's the best, will always come out last. The skipper leads you out. What else of note are you left with? No one remembers the bloke who came out fourth or ninth. You just have to be careful; Arsenal's Kolo Touré once missed the start of the second half in a Champions League match against Roma because he was waiting for William Gallas to leave so he could be last one out. Gallas was already on the pitch. Awkward.

The shirt-off thing: to pull it off, you have to be in good shape. If you're not in good shape, you're not doing it. Then your superstition becomes, I'm not leaving this dressing-room until I'm fully clothed. And with a loose bib, and possibly a generously fitting subs coat on as well. While breathing in.

23

Player: Gary Lineker

Superstition: Refusing to take any shots during the warm-up.

Verdict: You might want to mock Gary's reasoning, which was apparently based on a fear of wasting goals, as if as a striker you have a finite number of goals in your body. To which I would say, he didn't waste any goals, did he? Forty-eight of them for England, the country's record goal-scorer until overtaken by Wayne Rooney, 238 in his league career at home and abroad, the first Englishman in history to win the Golden Boot as the top scorer at a World Cup. Something's working there. Why criticise?

Player: Andy Cole

Superstition: Refusing to warm up on the pitch.

Verdict: When I was a ball-boy at Chelsea as a kid, I used to study every player obsessively to see what pearls I could take from them. Whenever Manchester United came to Stamford Bridge, I would look for Cole and yet never spot him until kick-off. So when former United midfielder Darren Fletcher joined Stoke, I asked him about it. Apparently Cole would refuse to touch a ball before the whistle went. He would stay in the dressing-room, doing a few drills in there – fast feet, jumps, stretches.

Andy Cole scored 293 goals over his career. He won the Champions League with United, five Premier League titles and two FA Cups. Would he have done better had he taken a few pot-shots before matches? A golfer might say so. Before every round a pro will be on the driving range and putting green, grooving their swing. I think of Frank Lampard, taking ten penalties at the end of every training session. I think of David Beckham, able to score that sensational last-minute free-kick against Greece in 2001 because he had done it day after day in training. But that's training. Cole was as obsessive as they came in training. By the time he got to match-day, his work was done.

Player: Johan Cruyff

Superstition: While a player at Ajax, Cruyff would slap his goalkeeper Gert Bals in the stomach before matches. And then spit his chewing-gum into the opposition half.

Verdict: Sometimes you wonder how these things start. Former Wales and Lions second row Delme Thomas used to knock back a schooner of sherry before games – with two raw eggs cracked into it. Who first thinks about adding a raw egg to sherry? Wind it back further – who decides to take a bottle of sherry to a game in the first place? Did he go straight to the two eggs, or start with one and think, I liked it, but it just needs a little more egg?

Same goes for Cruyff. What does Gert think the first time the most creative footballer of all time trots up to him and cracks him in the guts? Bent over double, a look of surprise and pain on his face, just managing to gasp the words: 'Johan ... why?'

The chewing-gum: I get that. It's territorial. He's a cat marking his territory. A mountain lion. This is my half. Stay out of it. And check the bottom of your boots afterwards.

Player: Pelé

Superstition: Edson Arantes do Nascimento, to give him his full, glorious name, once gave his shirt to a fan. When his goal-scoring form dried up, he then sent a friend off in search of said fan to retrieve the lucky top. His mate couldn't find it, so gave him back the same shirt he'd worn in the non-scoring match, telling him it was the lucky one. None the wiser, a happy Pelé went back to banging in a few more of his 1,283 career goals.

Verdict: I can sympathise. I used to feel the same way about a pair of boots, but that one went south when boot sponsors decided you should have a fresh pair for every match. I'm old-school. I liked to have one pair for the season. I've had to adapt, but it's not easy scoring in one pair and then immediately ditching them.

Our team socks now come in a left and a right. On the sole of one will be an 'L', on the other an 'R'. You make sure you put the correct one on each foot. And then you come in from a match where you've played particularly well, and you pull your socks off to find that you've inadvertently been wearing two 'L's. You've had two left feet, and it's rather suited you.

They changed it again last season. The same 'L' on the bottom, another 'L' now to signify large. It messes with my mind. Have I got two lefts again? Was that lucky for me or disastrous? Am I a large or an extra-large? In all this messing about, have I done a Kolo and missed the kick-off?

You might not think a pair of socks could make any difference. But just as snooker players have only one cue that works for them, so a footballer can feel the difference. If I had to wear a pair of boots half a size too small, I'd feel that my touch wasn't as good. Some kids in my youth team used to wear two pairs of socks. I tried it, but it felt as if it made my touch too bouncy. I couldn't control the ball quite as well.

Player: Sergio Goycochea
Superstition: Urinating on the pitch.
Verdict: This reputedly began when the Argentina goalkeeper got caught short before a penalty shoot-out against Yugoslavia in the quarter-finals of the 1990 World Cup. Desperate to go

after 90 minutes of normal time and an additional half-hour of extra time, he discreetly watered the pitch before becoming the hero of the shoot-out. Come another shoot-out against Italy in the semis, he did it again. Another Argentina win. And so from that point on, before every penalty shoot-out, he would reach down his shorts once again.

There is no footage of Goycochea actually performing the Sergio Sprinkler, which leaves significant room for speculation. For some reason it's hard for a man to urinate against nothing, just as if you drive your car into an otherwise empty car-park containing one other vehicle, you always end up parking pretty much next to each other. So I can't see him standing brazenly on the D of the penalty box and doing it, just as I can't see him doing it on the goal-line that he will shortly be diving along. The goalpost makes a certain sense – it's the closest he's going to have found to the classic lamppost set-up – and the corner flag even more, because there is absolutely no chance of him having to roll about in the grass near the corner flag.

Maybe he sprayed it everywhere, like a cat marking its territory, like a Dutch legend spitting his gum. Once again, critically, it appears to have worked. Two penalty shoot-outs won at a World Cup, within a few millimetres of saving the Andreas Brehme penalty which won Germany the final, voted goalkeeper of the tournament. There's always logic to superstitions, if you look hard enough.

Player: Gary Neville
Superstition: Always wore the same aftershave while Man United were winning.

Verdict: This was away from the pitch, of course. One of the lads I've played with recently has taken to spraying aftershave on his kit before a match. We've hammered him for it, of course. If you are going to smell on the pitch, you want it to be unpleasant so that no one will want to come close enough to mark you. But apparently an opposition player came up to him at a corner, sniffed the air and then nodded approvingly. 'Cor, you smell nice, what are you wearing?'

That's when I realised the game I play and love is evolving. I don't even think it was that pleasant cologne. You could smell it on the team bus for hours afterwards. I don't wear the stuff myself. I prefer the scent of a man.

CARS

I'm 24 years old, I've just been signed by the reigning European champions, and it's gone to my head. Specifically, I've bought myself an Aston Martin, and I'm driving round Hale Barns in Manchester with the windows down, sunglasses on, elbow resting on the sill, steering with two fingers, speed garage blasting out of the stereo.

I don't even like speed garage, as we will discuss later. I'm certainly not sure I like this car. A little voice deep down keeps telling me that an Aston Martin really isn't me, but a louder voice is telling me that as an England international playing up front for Liverpool the old rules no longer apply. Big voice: Peter, you've never looked cooler. Little voice: Peter, you're a monstrous bell-end. And so I'm cruising around, trying to convince myself I look like Steve McQueen or Daniel Craig, ignoring the old Peter telling me I've become everything I swore I wouldn't, and I pull up at a set of traffic lights and there's Roy Keane in his car right next to me.

Ah, there's a man who understands my vibe. Fantastic footballer, winner of multiple league titles and FA Cups and League Cups and the Champions League, captain and heartbeat of Manchester United through the most successful period in their history. I give him a nod. I give him a wink. I may even point my index finger at him and make a clicking sound at the same time. All of it saying, you and me, eh, Roy? Same game, same level. In it together. Rivals yet friends who just haven't met before. Alright, Roy?

He looks back at me. Even through my shades I cannot miss the disgust on his face. It's like he's looking at something which has just curled out of the backside of his dog Triggs. He shakes his head and stares back at the road ahead. I'm frozen in my pose, grin slipping off my face, and when the lights change and he drives off without a backward glance I'm left there with the handbrake on and an awful realisation: oh my God, I've become one of those twats.

I sold the Aston Martin the next day. A £25,000 hit on it, and I considered myself lucky. All because of Roy Keane – Roy, as my absent conscience, Roy as a modern-day footballer's spiritual guide.

That moment at that set of traffic lights was the best thing that ever happened to me. Had I kept the car I would have hated myself a little bit more every day. Even in the brief period of ownership I didn't want to drive it to Liverpool's training ground, because it felt obscene gunning it through the struggling areas around Melwood, waving under the noses of all those Liverpool fans how much money I was making compared to them. Taking it to the shops I felt like a fool, because who goes to pick up some milk and a loaf of sliced bread in a sports car that can do 0–60mph quicker than you can swipe your loyalty card?

It was like buying a very flash new shirt from the sort of shop where the prices are so high that each item of clothing has its own shelf: you know deep down it's not you, and you try to pretend otherwise, that's it's actually a new and better you, but you don't want to wear the shirt on the first big night out that comes up, except you do anyway because it cost so much money, and when you're out it not only feels uncomfortable but makes you feel incredibly self-conscious, and when you glance in the mirror you see a man even you want to punch, and all the time you're wishing you'd actually worn that old jumper with the hole under the arm that has done a perfectly acceptable job for the last four years.

I hadn't realised how quickly I had reached Peak Footballer. I see it now with some of the young lads coming through at Stoke, making the first team and within a week getting the hat-trick of tattoo sleeve, sports car and Beats by Dre headphones. You should never get ahead of yourself car-wise; no Merc when you're still in the youth team, no Porsche unless you're a Premier League regular. But it sneaks up on you. One minute you're a nice bloke who just happens to play football. The next minute you're buying a car that gets stuck on speed-bumps and costs as much to fill up as a fighter jet.

The relationship between footballers and cars has always been open to heinous error. I think of Stephen Ireland, who while at Manchester City had an Audi R8 with a trim the same red as the colour of Manchester United's home shirt. You could call that unfortunate, and to give Steve his due he did get all the red bits redone in a more appropriate sky-blue. But what would you call the black Range Rover he then bowled about in which had a pink trim, or the convertible Bentley which looked like he'd borrowed it from a peak-era Snoop video?

We don't always help ourselves as footballers. There should be no stage in a man's development where he considers a Bentley with red wheels to be an attractive reflection of the man he has become. Still, Stevie's matured. By 2018 he was driving an Audi again – admittedly again with a trim, this time a slightly more muted yellow, but you have to consider the journey he'd been on. One man's nightmare is another man's refuge.

Others are still waiting for the scales to fall from their eyes. I think of Mario Balotelli, former Manchester City, Liverpool and Italy striker, and the Bentley Continental GT he decided to have repainted in green and brown camouflage colours while living in Alderley Edge, just south-west of Manchester. The purpose of camouflage as I have always understood it is to offer an element of disguise by allowing you to blend in with your background surroundings, in which case Mario's Bentley would have been ideal had he habitually been parked in front of woodland, or axle-deep in a grassy field. The fact that it was usually parked outside Panacea bar and nightclub rather spoiled the idea; he would have been better off having it painted with images of half-cut revellers, muscular bouncers and bollards. Because no one else in the north-west of England had a camouflage-painted Bentley Continental GT, it actually worked as the least camouflaged vehicle imaginable. As soon as you saw it, you knew Mario was close. Neither was it practical. Mario's entourage was so large he would have been more suited to a minibus. You'd be in Panacea and it would be empty; within seconds it would be rammed, all because Mario had turned up. When he left an hour later, so did 95 per cent of the crowd.

He hasn't changed. My former Stoke team-mate Marko Arnautović was friends with Mario when the two of them were at Inter Milan. Marko had a beautiful Rolls-Royce Wraith – classy, understated, timeless. Falling under the influence of Mario, he then had it wrapped in chrome. I think I spoke for many when I laid eyes upon it: 'Marko, you had a beautiful car there, why did you ruin it?'

Then there is the case of Nile Ranger, the former Newcastle and England under-19 striker, who bought himself a Range Rover and then had another letter 'r' added to the marque on the bonnet. You'd think that having the only Ranger Rover on the streets of

Britain would be enough, but that would be until you saw the rear of the car, where he added the word 'Power' too. Power Ranger Rover. Thank you, football. There are times when I think, why didn't I just go and be a postman?

My own stable began with a mixture of pride and the prosaic. It was a Volkswagen Polo, bright green, £5,000, only a year old. It was green because the ones which were a normal colour were £8,000. When you're 17 years old, on a YTS scheme and living at home, bright green makes a lot of sense. I spent a small portion of the money I saved on a stereo so flash that the front of it flicked up when you wanted to put a CD on. When you're driving five lads from Ealing over to Spurs and back for training every day, these things matter.

I was so excited when I first passed my test that I took all the boys out as soon as I got home. Because I thought all footballers went to Hollywoods nightclub in Romford, I drove everyone all the way from the western suburbs to the east and didn't even pause to question my thinking.

You may be familiar with *The Inbetweeners* and the infamous incident of the bus wankers. Years before that sitcom was written we experienced a very similar humiliation, cruising back from Romford in the bright-green Polo. This time it was a group of lads already on a bus, us winding the window down and making clear with shouts and gestures our superiority in actually owning and piloting a vehicle. We didn't even need to mention the fact that we'd been to Hollywoods. It was 2am, they were on a night-bus, we were in a one-year-old second-hand Polo.

Amusing? I was laughing so hard I drove straight into the kerb, burst the front near-side tyre and wrecked the wheel. I'm not sure what the worst bit was: the bus slowly pulling level with us, the fear that the bus wankers were getting off ready to kick the hell out of us, the hour on the pavement trying to fit the spare wheel or the eventual 4am arrival back home in Ealing, all the other lads asleep, me coming to the realisation that I had just taxied all my mates the length of London without having got so much as a single drink out of it.

I loved that car. Unlike the Aston Martin, it suited who I was and where I was at that time. When a few months later I went on loan from Spurs to non-league Dulwich Hamlet, there would be no team coach. It would be a case of, this is the address of the club we're playing this afternoon, who's got a car? My dad would drive me. That doesn't happen in the Premier League.

You have your role models and you accept the influence they have on you. At Spurs, Les Ferdinand used to arrive for training in a silver Ferrari. It was entirely in keeping for a man so continually classy he fully deserved his title of Sir Les. He was the only player I've ever known who would neatly fold his dirty training kit each day and leave it in a squared-off pile under his peg in the dressing-room rather than lobbing it on the floor for the weary kitman to pick up. When word got around that I was off to Dulwich, Les made a point of buttonholing director of football David Pleat, within my earshot, in the training ground car-park: 'Now listen – Crouchie's too good for that level.' Imagine hearing that, at 17 years old, having done nothing in the game – an England international, a Spurs legend, being thoughtful enough to say something like that. I remember looking at him all starry-eyed as he climbed into that Ferrari and roared off in a cloud of dust. 'Dulwich first, but one day, Peter, one day . . .'

Us YTS lads had a rule: if you missed a penalty in our little competition at the end of training, there would be no lift home in the green Polo. Instead you had to take public transport – a long walk from Spurs Lodge up Luxborough Lane, across the M11 bridge and up to Chigwell tube station, and then the hour-long underground journey back to Ealing if you got lucky with the timings on the Central line. It was a horror, except for one occasion: the four of us in the car, chugging back round the North Circular, hearing a distinctive roar in the lane outside us and seeing a silver Ferrari cruising past, the lad who we'd left behind grinning at us from the passenger seat and flicking us a distinctive hand gesture to indicate his delight. Classic Sir Les.

It's a rare thing to go straight from green Polo to silver Ferrari. And so when I broke into the first team at QPR I took a trip with my dad to the Renault garage on the A40 at Park Royal and went big on a Mégane. I wanted to go bigger – 'Dad, I'm getting the convertible' – but was told it would be too flash. It was good to be there when history was made by the words 'Mégane' and 'too flash' first being uttered together in the same sentence. Don't go mad son, get the coupé, yeah?

A few months later, having been named player of the season, I felt I had earned my go-faster stripes. And so I did get the Mégane convertible, silver with a blue roof. I suppose I must have thought of myself as a Mégane man by that stage. I can't explain it any other way.

Not every footballer is obsessed with cars. We had a journeyman Aussie lad at QPR at that time named George Kulcsar. He drove a second-hand Mini Metro. The back of it was like a skip: footballs, old trainers, empty packets and cans where he'd eaten something at the wheel and just lobbed the rest over his shoulder. You'd ask him about it and he'd just shrug. 'I don't give a monkey's, mate.' I liked George, almost enough to get in his car with him.

Then there was Robert Huth, the big German defender we had at Stoke who went on to win the title with Leicester. When Tony Pulis was manager, training was more about team shape than personal fitness. He wasn't keen on you doing any extra work. Huth, who has the build and the brow of a Terminator, felt he wasn't doing enough – so opted to cycle in from Hale to Stoke for training. Even on the A50 that's getting on for 40 miles one way. If he went there and back on B roads to avoid the big lorries he'll have been close to riding a Tour de France stage. I shall never forget him swooping into the car-park on his carbon-fibre racer. Hugely impressive.

Fashions change. When I began at QPR a big Premier League player might drive a Mercedes, the next rung down a BMW. While I was at Portsmouth the SUV came in. By the time I'd moved to Aston Villa, always at least one style behind Lee Hendrie, Darius Vassell and Jlloyd Samuel, Gareth Barry was in a Jag. It looked like a bullet. When he turned the engine on, the radio aerial would rise silently from the bonnet. I was fascinated by it like I'd just time-travelled from the eighteenth century.

Sometimes cars suit the individual character. My one-time team-mate at Liverpool Djibril Cissé used to bowl about in an airbrushed Chrysler with a huge black-and-white image of his daughter sprayed across the bonnet. Another time he turned up in an old-school 1960s Cadillac, as if he were off to a high school prom in small-town America. But you have to bear in mind that this was a man who used to plug a modern copy of a 1920s candlestick phone into the hands-free socket of his mobile phone when he wanted to make a call. He would hold the receiver in one hand, unhook the ear-piece and talk away as if it were perfectly normal. It wasn't like he was showing off; it was only him and me in the dressing-room when I witnessed it. There are few men in this world who could take a hands-free option and turn it into something that actually required two hands. Djibril is one of them.

Ironically, given the average footballer's wages, you're often given a car for free. In his early days at Everton Wayne Rooney was pictured by a blue Ford Ka with the registration plate ROO NI. He looked delighted at the time. On international duty with England, a photo-shoot with team sponsors Hyundai saw me given one of their top-of-the-range jeeps on long-term loan. The best thing about it was a dashboard feature called a concierge button. You'd press it and be connected to a real person who could help you with anything you required. 'Good morning, Mr Crouch, are you well today?'

It used to astound me every day, even though it was probably just a woman in a call centre in Chennai with Google open on her laptop. When anyone got in the car I would say, right, get on this: 'Yeah, hi there, what's the weather going to be like today?' and do an amazed face at my passenger.

In retrospect I never really made the most of it. A good concierge can sort you out with anything – the name of the best tailor in town, a pair of tickets for the most in-demand show. I would usually ask it for the nearest McDonald's.

Its complementary successor was a Volkswagen Phaeton. It was far from the classic footballer look: a sensible saloon with all the exterior flair of Robert Huth. Immediately I was hammered by my team-mates for looking like a posh dad, or a bloke going out to Heathrow to pick up a German businessman. But what a car! So light to steer, so effortless on the motorway. I was distraught to have to hand it back. You're beginning to see now why I might have felt uneasy in that Aston Martin.

At least I could fit my 6'7" frame comfortably within its understated interior. At Portsmouth our 6'3" defender Alessandro Zamperini used to give me a lift to training in his Smart car. Our knees went past our ears and bumped gently against the roof. This at a time when 5'5" Shaun Wright-Phillips was driving a Cadillac Escalade, the lowest ratio of body-size to car ever recorded until Robert Earnshaw turned up at Nottingham Forest in a Hummer.

A Hummer is not a practical car in the UK even for a big man. It's left-hand drive. It's too big for an ordinary parking space and impossible to get into a multi-storey. At Southampton our Belgian defender Jelle Van Damme had one; it was much too large to fit into the underground garage at the apartment block we both lived in, so he had to get special permission from the council to park it on the road round the corner.

Who else in any other walk of life except football would buy a car you can't drive and a car you can't park? Hummers weren't even nice inside. They were designed for war-zones, not Ocean Village marina in Southampton. They can withstand IEDs but you can't get to Sainsbury's in them. They were uncomfortable to sit in, and only had the most basic radios – understandably so, because they were supposed to be used to ferry troops around occupied territories, and soldiers are less bothered about sub-woofers and heated seats than footballers.

Madness, everywhere you look. I think of Jermaine Pennant, banned from driving, deciding regardless to go for a spin round town, thinking the police would assume it was one of the other people in Stoke who drives a chrome-wrapped Aston Martin. Maybe he thought his Aston Martin had the same function as James Bond's in *Die Another Day*, with adaptive camouflage to make it invisible to the naked eye. Then again, Jermaine had been in Stoke for several weeks when he got a call from his previous club, Real Zaragoza, asking if he knew that he'd left his sports car parked outside the city's train station. Only a footballer could forget that he was missing a Porsche. Particularly one with the registration plate P33NNT. I doubt he caught a train either.

Generally speaking, footballers are terrible drivers. Testosterone, youth, a car that needs a spoiler to stop it from simply taking off into the sky. As kids at Spurs during pre-season we would have races from the training ground to Epping Forest. First one there wins ... hang on, is that one of the lads' Escort wrapped around a lamppost? The examples being set to us were similarly poor; José Dominguez, always late for training, everyone else out on the pitches when he came slaloming down the road in his Porsche, wheels spinning, parking it sideways, engine revving and then ticking as he abandoned it and ran for the changing-rooms. It's why the insurance premiums are so high. At 17, my yearly quote was almost twice the cost of the green Polo itself. In an attempt to bring it down, I went on an advanced driving course. I still have the certificate that came through, emblazoned with the words, 'You are now a master driver.' I bring it into play when Abbey is in the car and criticises my skills. 'You can't talk to me! You don't understand what I'm doing, because I'm so far ahead of you. It's official: you're not on my technical level.'

There are certain unwritten vehicle/football rules for me. A manager cannot drive a players' car. No Porsches, no silver Ferraris. Instead, the sort of car where you'd expect to see a chauffeur behind the wheel. If a player drives one of those, it looks like they're the help. Wrong again.

Secondly, no one should buy a flash car when either they're playing badly or their team is. Steven Fletcher posted photos of him and his new Lamborghini Aventador when Sunderland were in the relegation zone. Poor form. You shouldn't be ashamed of doing well for yourself, but you have to consider the supporters. When Joleon Lescott followed a 6–0 defeat for his Aston Villa side with a tweet of a £120,000 silver Mercedes, he claimed that his phone had done it from his pocket without his knowledge. To which I would say: that is a very smart smartphone, or a very strange pocket. Turns itself on, opens its own camera app, frames and captures the image perfectly, loads it to Twitter, posts the tweet. I wish I had pockets as intelligent as that.

Three. Think practicality over posing. When I went back to Spurs under Harry Redknapp, the drive round to Chigwell from my home in Surrey was taking me three hours each way round the M25 and destroying my back in the meantime. The purchase of a Mercedes Viano – bed in the back to sleep in, television overhead to pass the time – plus the hire of an excellent driver made perfect sense, and several other players have now gone the same way.

Then there is the personalised plate. I've been offered loads down the years, and at one stage I was going to splash out on TA11 1. But I realised the foolishness of it and pulled back just in time. Why would you want everyone to know who you are and where you're going? There is a limited resale value if you get one that is genuinely specific to you; were I to buy P CR0UCH 1, I could only sell it on if Paul or Phil Crouch were feeling particularly flush. And if you get one so obtuse that you have to explain it ('Yeah, the 8 is a B, the 1 is an L and the 4 is an E, except the second one which is still a 4') then it doesn't work in any case.

My all-time favourite footballing car? The three-wheeler Robin Reliant that the squad at Portsmouth purchased when Tony Adams was in charge. The player voted the worst in training not only had to drive it home – picture David James in a car that size – but had to add a new feature before they returned it too. By the end it had been stretched to a five-seater, had speakers fitted in the boot, wore alloy hubs, had a megaphone on the roof wired to the stereo and pulled a trailer. Sean Davis used to drive it round the pitch. Good times.

I much preferred the Reliant to the Aston Martin. That single glance from Roy Keane was in retrospect a turning point for me; without that, I may have gone the same way as Pennant and Cissé and Ranger. Well, maybe not Ranger, but still. Instead I came crashing back to earth. Thank you, Roy.

Maybe he's still cruising round Hale Barns, stopping at lights, policing the young flash footballers and their outrageous vehicles. Maybe it wasn't him at all, but a manifestation of my dying consciousness. Maybe multiple footballers have imagined seeing Roy Keane at traffic lights.

Maybe he didn't even know it was me. He just thought, there's a twat. And who could have argued with him?

DEFENDERS

I love football. I love playing it, I love watching it. And I cannot for the life of me work out why anyone would want to be a defender.

Midfielders create chances. Strikers make things happen. Being a defender is all about stopping stuff. It's fundamentally negative. You get in the way of other people being creative. You stop the fun stuff.

It's a different mentality in every possible way. How strange to not want to go forward. How boring to stay mainly in your own half. Imagine standing there watching other players do the fun stuff.

I used to glance over at the defenders working under Tony Pulis at Stoke. Cold mornings, the balls heavy and wet, Pulis lobbing them in the air, the defenders jumping for headers, the midfielders battling to pick up the scraps. I had one overriding thought: thank God I'm not a defender. And then a second: what they're doing is not why you become a footballer.

When I first started playing first-team football, the old-school defenders were nightmarish characters. They would smash you all over the place just because you were there. You didn't have to play against Chris Morgan for more than a few minutes to work out why he got sent off six times for Barnsley and the same at

Sheffield United. Neil Warnock's United team used to double-team you. If it wasn't Morgan it was Shaun Derry. If it wasn't Derry it was Paul Devlin, who once spotted me with the ball by the corner flag and went straight down the back of both my Achilles. Today it would be a straight red. It would be three reds. Back then it was a yellow and a little laugh in your face as he ran off.

You know when you look into someone's eyes, and you don't see anything there? That was Kevin Muscat. I was 19, playing for QPR away at Millwall, Sean Dyche already tenderising any bit of my body he could reach. And then Muscat came over, smashed me with a couple of elbows, got in my ear and told me he was going to break my legs. I looked back at him and realised, oh my good God, it's Kevin Muscat. He will break my legs if he gets the chance.

Muscat finished his career with 123 yellow cards and 12 red cards. He finished a few other players' careers too. I got away lightly. But that sort of intimidation used to work. Glen Johnson told me that in one of his first training sessions with West Ham, Stuart Pearce came straight through the back of him. It used to be that defenders would whack you to see if you could handle it, to see if you fancied what professional football really was about. And British crowds responded to it. We all cheer a last-ditch tackle. In Italy they consider that same act a failure: why didn't you stop the move earlier? When a defender boots the ball into row Z, we love it. Jamie Carragher used to come across and clear the ball into the back of the stand when he quite possibly could have taken a touch, and the Anfield crowd were delighted. You do the same thing in Spain and you'll be jeered for not keeping possession. Which other nation cheers corners? On average a top team will score a goal from a corner once every ten games. But we don't care. We love them.

So I am not a defender and I would rather retire than have to become one. But you need players who love being defenders and you need defenders who have the exact strange mentality that makes no sense to me. Stop people. Be negative. Take pride in destruction. Have fun ruining everyone else's.

Defending is an art. It's a brutal, ugly art, but it is a gift all the same. My first game against Premier League defenders came when QPR drew Arsenal in the FA Cup. The difference in class between what I had been facing in the Championship, then known as the First Division, and what Tony Adams could do was terrifying. He was strong. He was good in the air. By this stage of his career he was comfortable on the ball too. I'd pull on to him, ball at my feet, him behind me, waiting for him to come too tight so I could roll off him and away. One moment he was there at your back and suddenly he was gone, round the other side of you and taking the ball off your toes before you had worked out where he was. I'd had a header cleared off the line by Ashley Cole at 0–0. This is okay, this level, I thought. And then Adams got stuck into me, and we ended up losing 6–0. That was when I realised: ah, this is the Premier League. This is what an international defender does to you.

Adams had charisma. He usually had Martin Keown alongside him too, which was similarly useful. Keown would be all over you like a rash. Pull on to him and he'd rattle you like a bull running into a fencepost. There would be very little chat, just lots of aggression. When that Arsenal team had finished with you it felt as if you'd fallen under a steamroller; for all the talent they had strutting up front – Thierry Henry, Dennis Bergkamp, Freddie Ljungberg – it was that defence that won titles and doubles for them. Only with the signing of Sol Campbell later that summer did they ever really follow like with like. I watched Sulzeer come through at Spurs when I was a kid, went to one of his first games, when he came on up front and scored, and when I played against him as a man he had the strength of Adams and the awkwardness of Keown. He held that Arsenal team together when the men alongside him were significant step-downs on what had come before: Pascal Cygan, Philippe Senderos, Igors Stepanovs, Emmanuel Eboué, Oleh Luzhny. You would look at Arsenal and wonder if defenders were appreciated any more, when they turned down the chance to buy a young Phil Jagielka or mature Ashley Williams. You don't have to want to be a defender to understand that you can be nothing without them.

In the early part of the 2000s English football was blessed with so many world-class centre-backs. In another era Jamie Carragher would have won double the 38 caps he did for England. But he had Sol ahead of him, Rio Ferdinand, John Terry, Jonathan Woodgate, Ledley King, all of them special players, maybe none of them quite as underappreciated as the last.

I came through the Spurs system with Ledley. We used to play little games of five-a-side on the ancient ball-court at White Hart Lane on Tuesdays and Thursdays. Small-sided games on tight pitches find players out. They're unforgiving. And yet Ledley ran them from centre-back. He barely made a tackle because he seldom had to. At a time when we were familiar with the virtues of the English way, he was a continental cruiserweight, a defender who could do all the traditional stuff and things we'd never imagined on top. We played together for England under-18s at a youth tournament in Spain. When it finished both Barcelona and Real Madrid tried to sign him on the spot. As a home boy he preferred to stay in London. It's hard not to wonder how different his career may have been had he taken either offer.

Because it was injuries that wrecked him, and injuries that prevented him from being a player the whole nation knew and appreciated rather than just the insiders at Spurs. And I still believe I was there when his problems began.

The Spurs youth team had been sent to the British Army's Bovington Camp in Dorset for a week of toughening up. It was brutal stuff – sleeping in tents, up at 5am, long runs when you were already exhausted, relentless numbers of sit-ups. We were sent off on another endless yomp despite Ledley complaining quietly that his hip was in bits. None of us wanted to give up. We thought we just had to get through it. And so afterwards Ledley – always muscular, never a Mo Farah – had a problem that wouldn't go away. The wear on his joints from that week, at that stage of our physical development, was a crazy thing to inflict.

He still played, and he played like Franco Baresi, a man from an alien football culture, a man who could defend like a broken-nosed bruiser but bring the ball out and start attacks like a midfield playmaker. I left Spurs. I went west to QPR, to the south coast with Portsmouth, to the Midlands with Aston Villa and to East Anglia on loan with Norwich. I went to the north-west with Liverpool and I went back to the south coast – twice – with Southampton and Portsmouth. And when I eventually fetched up back in north London with Spurs, Ledley was still there, still endlessly classy, still permanently injured.

It was sad to see. No football for him each week, just the pool, and an exercise bike, and a warm coat so he could walk through our defensive shape on a Friday. Forced to retire early, finishing with only 21 England caps when he could have had as many as Rio, picked for two World Cups but forgotten at both.

Rio? His gift was calmness on the ball. Calmness on the ball and a total refusal to maintain any of our friendship from England camps when we came up against each other in club football. We were up against each other when I scored the winner for Liverpool against Manchester United in the FA Cup; there's one photo where it looks like I'm going to lamp him. You had to be aggressive playing Rio to get yourself any sort of space. Same as John Terry. All he wanted to do was grab you. So you went looking for the other centre-back, the one you think you can bully, the one you don't mind having a battle with. The good ones you don't want to battle, because as soon as that's happening they've got you.

As a ball-boy at Chelsea I remember watching an ageing Glenn Hoddle playing sweeper and spraying these incredible passes about. It was so unusual then. Since then we've had plenty of central defenders who like coming forward or passing, but not so many who are content living out the basics. If you have two centre-halves who are happy to stay as pure defenders, who will win everything that comes their way, who won't give the strikers an inch without a lump to go with it, you have the foundations for a successful team. I'll always believe that Stoke lost something essential when Robert Huth was allowed to leave. Maybe the management became too obsessed with the idea of a defender who could knock Hoddle-style quarterback passes around. And so Huth went to Leicester, paired with Wes Morgan, and did all the basics to perfection. Cross the ball all you want, we'll head it clear. Run at us, we'll tackle you. Try to turn us, we'll block you. Those two were the building blocks on which Leicester's extraordinary Premier League win was constructed.

Huth is a classic of the genre. He's not well in the head; he loves to defend, he loves hurting people. When I first saw him at

Chelsea, lumbering around, I said to Glen Johnson, 'Who's this clown?' Glen shook his head. 'Watch yourself. He's a total nutcase.'

If you play against Huth in training he'll smash you and get to his feet grinning. If you play against him in a match he'll stand on your feet at corners and elbow you if you do get off the ground. He's broken my nose at least a couple of times. If you ever smashed him you'd know you were getting at least one back. And that's fine. That's what you want from a proper defender. Don't dream of being a striker. Mess things up for them instead. Just stop goals.

Pep Guardiola has a wonderful way of playing football. His Manchester City team have so much going forward that they probably don't need to worry about defending. They also have Vincent Kompany at the back, which means it will happen anyway. Kompany is the best defender of the modern era. He has it all: pace, strength, aggression, dominance in the air. Put it this way, if you're playing against a partnership of him and Nicolás Otamendi, as a striker you pull on to Otamendi every time.

English football tests defenders. Javier Mascherano won four La Liga titles and two Champions Leagues playing centre-back for Barcelona. He basically did what he'd done so well at Liverpool – sweeping up the mess left by others around him, making sure he was always on the spot if something went wrong. But at centre-back? I'd have given my skinny left arm to pull on him. He's 5'8". In the Premier League he would have been bombarded.

It may sound counter-intuitive, but I actually found it easier playing against ball-playing international centre-backs in the Champions League than I did those less acclaimed, lumpy English defenders. They showed me more respect. I didn't get kicked as much. You could jump all over them. Alessandro Nesta was a fabulous player. He won two Champions Leagues and the World

Cup. Yet playing against him in the San Siro for Spurs was almost fun. It was like pulling on to Ricardo Carvalho at Chelsea. When they signed Gary Cahill it was like having Terry on both sides. Much less enjoyable.

The Premier League makes you tough. One look at Nemanja Vidić told you he wasn't going to ask you if you were okay after clattering you. Sami Hyypiä you could imagine in the Finnish Army in the Second World War, marching through the frozen sub-Arctic wastes without a word of complaint, collar of his greatcoat turned up, showing minimal fear in the face of the Russian advance. Even when you played on the same team as him his chat was monotone. He spoke like the Terminator. We would go on pre-match walks as a team and he would keep his headphones on. Autograph hunters would come over, smile, and ask for his signature. He'd look at them expressionless and reply with the same total absence of emotion. No. I am not signing that. And walk on.

Martin Škrtel. Look at the shape of his head. Look into his eyes. It's not normal. Playing against him for England against Slovakia, a few days after sharing pleasantries in training for Liverpool, he would challenge for the same aerial ball as you but do so by jumping off your thigh. The referee would never spot it; his attention would be on the ball. You'd look down to see red stud-marks all over your leg. You'd say, 'Oi, Martin, what the hell you doing?' He'd say, 'Oh, it's Crouchie, sorry, sorry.' And then the next ball would come in and he'd do it again. I was his team-mate. You can imagine what he was like with someone he didn't know.

I don't want to ignore full-backs. They haven't ignored me. Some of them have been the source of my most important goals. Steve Finnan, Glen Johnson, Fabio Aurelio, Graeme Le Saux, Gary Neville. Others have been the stooges as I've scored from those crosses, the smallest man on the pitch with the tallest coming over the top of them, the injured wildebeest to my cantering giraffe.

As kids we were all familiar with the old 'left back in the changing-room' gag. But there is glamour in every position now. No longer is the full-back the one whose sole tasks are to take throw-ins and raise his arm for offside. They are wingers, they are sprinters, they are creators. They are big, like Kyle Walker, and they are as strong as the men inside them. They'll run further than any other man on the pitch.

You have the understated ones, like Finnan. In our time at Liverpool not once did I see anyone get the better of him, and I include on that list Cristiano Ronaldo. He would also provide assists for me off the pitch; when we went out in town, I would drink and he would not, so he would drive us everywhere. Ideal.

There are the ones who don't need to rely on pace, who put style before the windmilling of arms and legs, the Paulo Maldinis. And there are the glamorous attacking ones, the ones who can score from all sorts of unlikely angles like Maicon, at least until Gareth Bale totally destroys them in their own stadium and they go from 4–0 up at half-time to clinging on at 4–3 and the full-back not knowing which way is up. The making of Bale and the finishing of Maicon.

I was always an admirer of Denis Irwin, both for his defensive skills at left-back for Manchester United and his free-kicks and penalties. Because defenders, even those who concentrate on defending, can score goals that change matches and championships. Think of Steve Bould in that Arsenal team and his flick-ons, of Stuart Pearce and his free-kicks. Terry against Manchester United in 2009, Kompany against United in 2012, critical to the Premier League title in both seasons. Adams against Spurs in the FA Cup semi-final of 1993,

Andy Lineghan in the final replay, Carles Puyol in the 2010 World Cup semi. Huth scored nine goals one season for Stoke. That was only three less than the two strikers. I arrived the following summer.

There are some things you can rely on a defender for. They are less likely to have flash cars than strikers. The further towards goal you start, the more you are attracted to bright shiny things. On a team night out it will be the defenders in an average shirt and bog-standard pair of jeans and trainers. Only a very few – John Scales, Ramon Vega – looked better off the pitch than on it.

And yet they also make superior managers. It must be something about being organised, seeing the game spread out in front of you. Mauricio Pochettino was a defender. Guardiola sat in front of the back four as a defensive shield. It makes sense. How could a flair player, one who had never tracked back in his own playing career, persuade others to do what they could not be bothered with? David Ginola is much better as a TV presenter and occasional actor than a manager. Not convinced? I give you the lovely Ossie Ardiles, brilliant creative midfielder for Spurs, a manager best remembered at the club for picking five forwards in the same team. While relying on Kevin Scott and Colin Calderwood at the back.

TATTOOS

A few years ago I received a tweet from a Sheffield United fan named @Smiggy. 'If Stoke beat Chelsea today I'll get a tattoo of Peter Crouch's arse on my face on my 17th birthday.'

The thing that puzzled me was less his certainty that we would lose to a team who had at that stage of the season been beaten seven times in their first fifteen matches, and who would shortly be sacking manager José Mourinho for the second time. It was the fact that he seemed to think my arse was distinctive enough to make a tattoo, whether on his face or elsewhere. My arse just looks like an arse. If I were shown it out of a line-up of ten arses belonging to men of my height, I'm not sure I could pick it out. It would just look like a bum on his face – a conversation-starter for sure, but a conversation more likely to start with, 'Is that a tattoo of a bum on your face?' than 'Does that bum belong to Peter Crouch?'

I think he probably meant to say he'd get a tattoo of my face on his arse. That way at least you'd recognise me in the showers, assuming the tattoo artist did a decent rendering. More importantly, we did beat Chelsea. On penalties, admittedly, but they were reigning holders of the League Cup and we put them out. Which obviously meant I had to reply to my new correspondent Smiggy.

'When's your birthday, my friend?'

I mention this not to humiliate Smiggy, who with that sort of public pronouncement has probably got that area covered, and more to highlight the madness of the mindless tattoos. There are many reasons why I have no ink, but the greatest involves regret. I look back at haircuts I have had in the past, and my first thought is usually 'What the hell was I doing?' I look back at the jeans I was wearing and the trainers I thought were cool and I think, 'What the hell did I think cool was?' Men have beards and then a few years later are very glad they no longer have them. A moustache that looks magnificent at one age looks absolutely appalling shortly afterwards.

So it is with tattoos. Whether it's my arse on your face or your face on my arse, how can you genuinely be confident that you will always like it? Celtic bands around the bicep. Barbed wire around the same area. For a brief period in 1997 both looked fine. By the start of 1998 they looked a bit dated. By 1999 they looked unfortunate, by 2000 they looked laughable, and by 2001 they looked like they were hidden by longer sleeves as often as possible.

What if you have a liver bird done on your shoulder and then sign for Everton? Robbie Savage had the Armani logo tattooed on his arm. He then had to go through hell to have it removed. I rest my case.

My next reason for not having a tattoo. If you've got big arms, if you have muscles that ripple, a tattoo in that area draws the eye to it and magnifies the girth and sinew on display. Maybe it even acts as motivation to work out and keep that arm big, because if you get old and get fat arms with it, the image not only distends but now draws attention only to a bingo-wing.

Either way, the related question for me is simple: which part of my body do I actually want to draw attention to? There's not a great deal there to work with. My biceps are not humungous. My pecs ... not great. Calves? Not huge ... I've got nice hands, I reckon. They're not bad.

I could probably get quite a bit of writing down my thigh. It would have to be a short font, but the sentence could be a long one. I could get every team I've ever played for down my arm: Spurs, rendered as Tottenham Hotspur; QPR, as Queens Park Rangers; Portsmouth, twice; Aston Villa; Norwich City, with 'loan' in brackets.

And yet for the modern footballer the tattoo has become a staple. It's as if you can't be a professional player unless you have them. One minute you're coming through the youth system with your skin all your own. Next week you break into the first team, and before your second match you have a full sleeve done.

One young lad at Stoke had a huge work done when he signed his first pro contract. It was him, standing by a wall, holding a football and a pen, his mum and dad next to him, his squad number and the date he signed all there. All mapped out – but what if he doesn't make it? Signing a contract doesn't mean you'll make the first team, stay in the first team or have a career in football. What if he ends up working in a bank? Maybe he'll get a tat of him shaking hands with the bank's HR officer on his stomach.

I'm okay with having the names of your kids written on your boots. But why do you need them on your body? If you need a reminder of the name of your own kids you've got bigger issues. 'Oh, wotshisface, the one I've brought up and loved and cherished for seven years ... oh, I know, I'll just look at my arse in the mirror and check.' What if you have four or five kids?

You'll start big and then start running out of room, the names getting progressively smaller, the fourth kid miffed because his name is half the size of his older sister's. The fifth is even less happy. 'How come my brother's on your biceps and I'm on your little finger?'

It appears to be an addiction. You get one, you get two. You get two, you get a sleeve. You get one sleeve, you get the other. No space left on the arms? Go round the back. Then spend most of your afternoon rubbing moisturising cream into them when you should be chatting to your team-mates.

The irony is that tattoos were supposed to be rebellious. They were supposed to make you look different. Now you're different if you don't have any. We've gone from the only tattoos you might see being the occasional sailor-style one – a snake around a shield, a Union flag fluttering – to them being so popular that you don't even notice them. By being everywhere they've almost become invisible. Different but the same as every other player, just like the Louboutin trainers with low-hanging designer tracksuit bottoms that everyone wears.

Almost. I played with a lad at Portsmouth who began by having the words 'Different breed' tattooed inside his bottom lip. He followed that up by having 'Pure guns' tattooed on his biceps, with some tattoo bullet-holes to match. You'd think that would be hard to top, but then you wouldn't think about marking your friend Leon's stag-do by having the letters 'L' and 'E' tattooed on your left buttock and 'N' on your right buttock, with the 'O' being formed by … well, you don't need me to tell you how the 'O' was formed.

The catastrophe, it seems, is only ever a misunderstanding or a pint too many away. I have a mate who was born on 11 October.

He decided to mark this auspicious date by having it tattooed in numerals on his arm. Unfortunately the tattooist got it wrong, so that it reads 9/11. His tattoo is literally a disaster.

Even David Beckham, as responsible as any footballer for this insane craze, has had issues; he got his wife's name done in Sanskrit, except the artist rendered it as 'Vihctoria'. I suppose it's okay if you don't speak Sanskrit. Footballers, as a rule, don't speak Sanskrit. Maybe that's where the problem started.

Player: Nile Ranger

Tattoo: 'Ranger', written across his own face.

Verdict: Yes, it's Nile once again. And once again I don't understand this one. Is it for him or a stranger? Surely he's not going to need reminding of his own name. It also looks so painful. I wouldn't have 'Crouch' inked on my head. For starters, people might not know if it was my name or an instruction.

Player: Mario Balotelli

Tattoo: 'I am the punishment of God. If you had not committed great sins, God would not have sent a punishment like me upon you.'

Verdict: So he's got this written in four lines across his left pec. Apparently it's a quote from Genghis Khan, one of the original big-name foreign stars to make an impact in Europe. I think Mario's being harsh on himself; I know his record for Liverpool was poor, only 4 goals in 28 appearances, and he cost them £16m and left on a free, but I'm sure God's got worse in his locker. And blaming it all on Brendan Rodgers's great sins seems a bit harsh.

Maybe it looks cooler to an Italian who has English as a second language, a bit like average French words look glamorous to us. It's like those players who get Chinese writing down the inside of their forearms. They've got no idea what it actually says. It might be the full menu. I heard about one bloke who asked the tattooist to 'put my name here'. He ended up with a tattoo of 'my name'. I've got no sympathy.

Player: John Carew
Tattoo: 'Ma Vie, Mes Régles'.
Verdict: I think the big former Villa striker wanted to make a simple point: 'My life, my rules'. Unfortunately, he got the accent wrong on the final word. It should have read 'règles'. So instead it translates as 'My life, my menstruation'. On his neck!

Only in football. Only in football could this happen.

Player: Artur Boruc
Tattoo: There's no easy way of saying this. It's a monkey, drawn on his stomach, with its bottom-hole where his belly-button is.
Verdict: It looks like it's been drawn with a pen. It's a monkey with its bottom out. On his stomach. But I'm sure he loves it. Goalkeepers in a nutshell.

Player: Alberto Moreno
Tattoo: Buckle yourself in for this one. It's a chimp, but a chimp wearing glasses, and Beats by Dre style headphones, kissing the barrel of a gun.
Verdict: You're playing full-back for Liverpool and Spain. You're bored, you decide to get a tattoo. Maybe you really like

chimps. You sit down with your tattoo artist. Just the chimp, sir? No, hang on. Can you do a chimp, but in a suit? Yeah, nice shout, what about sticking a pair of glasses on him too? Love it, let's have him holding a gun as well. Hold on, will he be allowed a gun if he's short-sighted? Good question, but let's not forget the bigger issue here: he's a monkey.

Player: Andre Gray

Tattoo: Famous figures from Black history.

Verdict: You can dislike tattoos as a concept but still admire the artist's work. On Andre's back you can spot Martin Luther King, Bob Marley, Malcolm X, Muhammad Ali knocking out Sonny Liston, Rosa Parks, Nelson Mandela, athletes Tommie Smith and John Carlos doing the Black Power salute. I can't imagine how much it hurt, but the detail is magnificent.

There are, of course, some tattoos that are impossible to resist. A few pundits criticised Raheem Sterling for getting a machine-gun done down the outside of his leg. That was before someone on Twitter pointed out that it was actually clearly me doing the Robot. It's always nice when talented young English strikers pay tribute to the heroes that inspired them, and 5'7" Raheem, with his electrifying pace and movement, deserves every credit for doing the same.

TRAINING GROUNDS

Ah, the glamour of life as a professional football player. When I joined Portsmouth from QPR, I drove to my first training session and thought I had inadvertently enlisted for service on the high seas.

There was nothing bespoke about the Pompey training ground. It was the HMS *Collingwood* naval base, named after a nineteenth-century admiral and apparently left exactly how he had known it as some kind of tribute. The pitches had once seen grass but now had only a vague memory of it. They were as windy and exposed as the deck of an aircraft carrier.

We got changed in some old Portakabins and had to take our own kit home to wash it. When it came to lunch we drove across the road to the barracks and ate alongside the sailors. They hated us – screeching into the car-park in our sports cars and 4x4s, us in shorts and expensive trainers, them about to spend a year on a ship with only other men for company. Food was served on a prison-style tray. The base was the home of the Maritime Warfare School, and every time we got out of there without battle breaking out I gave a sigh of relief.

It was always cold. The rain came in sideways. The base had a Latin motto, *Ferar unus et idem*. It translated as 'I shall carry on regardless' and that's what we had to do.

That's how training grounds were in those days: quirky. At QPR we had used the old British Gas sports grounds in Acton, which being only ten minutes away from my mum and dad's house made a pleasant commute. The changing-rooms there weren't Portakabins but they were unusual in their own way. There were eight of them, but you could only fit six men into each one. It felt a bit like being back at school, and it meant you never really saw anyone who wasn't in your little clique. I was in with the other young lads, Richard Langley and Sammy Koejoe, all the older lads a few blocks down. I have no idea why they were designed like that. Maybe British Gas fitters preferred six-a-side to full matches.

The way to judge how much training grounds have changed since then is the fact that at Stoke's Clayton Wood you can both ask for a cappuccino without someone wanting to punch you and receive one which is very pleasant to drink. That didn't happen in Stoke a decade ago. It's now standard to have swimming pools, ice-baths, hydrotherapy suites and anti-gravity treadmills. No more sessions slogging it up some random hill to get fit; at Liverpool they have a specially designed incline area where the slope is the absolute ideal angle. I looked round Sunderland's Academy of Light before moving from Liverpool to Spurs. There is an actual hairdresser's on site, a full barber shop with the right chairs, mirrors and equipment. It's left unstaffed, so that lads can summon their own hairdresser and have them come in and do their hair whenever they want.

There are meeting suites at most complexes, as if you're at the HQ of a major tech firm. There is so much money in football that players, agents and staff want a space where they can do deals. There is table-tennis, massage, a chef and a restaurant. You can stay over. It's like a hotel with the most expensively filled car-park in the country.

No more food served on metal prison trays. No more glancing across the room to be met with a terrifying glare from a bloke with a crew-cut, unless you happen to have offended Ryan Shawcross. It's like eating in a very nice restaurant with a limited menu. The trends move on. Protein shakes superseded by beetroot juice, red meat cut back and vegetables boosted, green juices on hand where there used to be creatine. There is always a fresh soup no matter where you go, which with the number of clubs I have had has turned me into something of a connoisseur: broccoli, chicken, Chinese sweet and sour. The only one I'll turn my nose up at is a gazpacho. Not in an English winter.

It used to feel as if you were eating only to refuel, like sticking petrol in a car. Chicken or steak, boiled potatoes, pasta. Minimal sauce, because sauce was considered to be a bad thing. It's improved since then. You are now allowed flavour. Under the no-sauce regime you would just cover everything in ketchup, which they realised was slightly self-defeating.

The early overseas stars were horrified by what they first found. Gianfranco Zola and Ruud Gullit would apparently look at what was on offer and push it away in disgust. What is this filth? Even now I'm yet to meet a well-travelled foreign talent who doesn't consider our food the worst in Europe. Quite a few refuse to eat at the training ground. They'll go home and expect their partner to rustle something better up, leaving the rest of us in our tracksuits. 'Stefano! Jean! Where you going? They've got mulligatawny on!'

There is always a set time that you need to arrive by. It might be 10am arrival for 11am start, but wherever you are there will always be the same groups. There is the phone gang, on their mobiles doing deals or talking to the partners they last saw about 20 minutes earlier. There are the gym-heads, pumping iron before training proper has begun, and there are the massage boys, keen on a deep-tissue fascial release before they dare to start jogging.

Then there is the coffee and chat club. Absolutely my scene. Robert Huth would be in the gym, flicking enormous weights around as if they were made of balsa wood, working so hard he would need to change his kit because the initial one was drenched in sweat; other lads rushing around barking instructions into their smartphones. And the coffee club just sits there, feet up, enjoying a little conversation, watching all the madness going on around and thinking, what's the rush?

Each man has his own routine. At my age it is all about being able to get out on the training pitch, and I know exactly what I need to do. At Liverpool I was encouraged to do deadlifts and squats before training, but it was getting me injured. Look at my physique. I'm not built for heavy metal. I might have a few muscles released and my back loosened up, but weights are reserved for after the main session, and even then strictly rationed. And I'll never do any weights after a Wednesday when we've got a game on the Saturday. It stays in your legs. It takes away the immense explosiveness and raw pace for which I'm famed.

At Portsmouth, Sol Campbell used to get a two-hour massage. He would get in at 8am and be flat out on the padded table until two minutes before we were due to begin. We had two masseurs. Sol would hog them both: the first working one of his enormous legs, the second kneading furiously at the other. We'd throw him abuse as we walked past the physios' room in our boots and training tops. 'Bloody hell, any chance, Sol?' He'd raise his head briefly from the circular hole cut out of the table for your face and look at us expressionlessly. 'When you've got seventy caps for England, come back and talk to me again.'

Sometimes clubs will run tests before you go out. There was a phase at Spurs where they became obsessed with our hydration levels. You would have to urinate in a cup and measure the pH level. That's now been overtaken by the jump test, designed to measure your fatigue levels. You do a vertical jump. They record how high and how explosive it was. If you're below your average you might be told to do a little less running in training. If you're like Zebedee they might add a few extra shuttles on. Not everyone has worked out what it means, which at least means that not too many try to game the system by pretending to be unable to leave the ground.

There will be rows. When the team for Saturday's game is announced on the Friday lunchtime, there will always be a player hammering on the door of the manager's office, fuming that they haven't been picked. Lots of coaches now reveal the team on Saturday morning so they can avoid the scenes. All that has done is shifted the strops to the start of the following week. Come Monday morning the coffee, gym and massage table are ignored in favour of a red face and the smashing of fists against doors.

Steven Gerrard was a regular complainer, not because *he* was ever left out but because of the strange decisions that Rafa Benítez would sometimes make. The team-sheet would go up, without Xabi Alonso's name on it. Stevie would go bananas. 'Why the f*** has he done that?' Straight to Rafa's door, bang-bang-bang. You know you're at a club that's in trouble when you come out of the manager's office having let off steam to find a long queue of your team-mates stretching down the corridor waiting for their own turn. Not all managers will allow it. No one was brave enough to confront Alex Ferguson. No one was allowed to approach Fabio Capello. You could only speak to him if he spoke to you first. Others are more relaxed. Harry

Redknapp could open up on you if you did something he didn't like, but you could also talk to him. Sven was calm when all around were losing their heads. Rows, tabloid stings, headlines about affairs – he could never understand what all the fuss was about.

Outside every training ground will be the autograph hunters. At least, they used to be autograph hunters. Fans waited by the gates, you signed the headshots of you they'd brought with them, everyone was happy. They're now autograph sellers. Grown men carrying a suitcase of shirts, wanting each of them signed so they can frame them, stick them on eBay and make a load of money. Players noticed that and no longer wanted to stop as they drove out, which spoiled things for genuine fans twice – once at the gate, again online when some shyster was offering signed kit for £500 a pop. So the charlatans wised up to that, and they started bringing kids to do the dirty work for them, either their own or paying someone else's. So you stop, and a bloke in the bushes pushes forward a kid who should be at school. The kids will be in the team kit, freezing cold. They will also already have been at Liverpool, Manchester United and City that same day, working like Victorian street urchins. So now you have to drive past the kids, which just feels so wrong.

We used to go for walks as a team before games. Now you can't, because you're badgered not by real fans but by people using you to make themselves a dodgy fortune. I must have done 100 autographs in a single sitting for one chap. After ten minutes of non-stop signing I confronted him. 'You got a hundred signed posters on your wall, have you?' 'Nope.' 'What are you doing with them then?' Silence. Not least because if he'd answered, yes, I do have 100 signed photos of your face on my bedroom wall, I would have been even more scared.

There will be the odd strange person, often carrying a plastic carrier bag full of bits of string and broken biscuits, who will flag you down to ask you exactly what is going on with an arcane aspect of the club. There will be old fellas with their Rothman's football annuals who have collected every one and would like them signed. That's great. It's the bad guys who are exploiting those real ones. And all the time us teetering along a line, knowing it only takes one of the villains to say, 'Ah, that Peter Crouch is nasty piece of work – wouldn't stop for us, thinks he's better than the fans,' and suddenly it's everywhere, and people think you're a person that you absolutely are not.

The sanctum for all of us is the physios' room. It's the hub of the entire training ground. There's nothing like it. In theory you only go in there if you're struggling with an injury, but the theory doesn't take into account the gossip that's shared in there, the stories and jokes. You'll talk about weekend plans. You'll talk about transfer rumours. You'll wind up the physios by asking which one is actually in charge and does the other one know. We could all quite happily spend all morning in there. You have to remember that footballers never have to grow up. They come straight out of school into football, which has half as many rules and twice as many characters. You never have to grow up. We're children with advanced physical skills.

You try to avoid the kitmen. They are notoriously miserable individuals. Gaz at Stoke is a good lad, Graham Carter at Liverpool another one, but they are always tight with the kit, as if it is either theirs or they have to pay for it. You ask them for an extra top. 'Why?' 'I've forgotten my hoodie.' Disbelief, arms thrown out. 'You've forgotten your hoodie?'

Should you give away your shirt after a game they'll be narked and you'll be charged. It's £50 a shirt, straight out of your wages.

That's what you'd pay in the club shop. Where's the staff discount? Where's the wholesale price? You play a lower division club in the FA Cup and a young lad asks in the tunnel if he can have your shirt after the game. You're not going to say, no, not unless you give me 50 quid. So you hand it over at the end, forced smile in place, thinking, argh, just done another 50 sheets ...

The kitmen are always locals. Perhaps the moodiness comes from the demands of the players and the fact they're often supporters of the club too, so would take it personally if their failure to remember that a particular player insists on blades on his boots and another moulded studs led to a poor performance and dropped points. Their day-to-day existence is based around picking up dirty clothes belonging to other men, and they will let you know. If someone takes off a sock and leaves it balled up they will berate you. There aren't many like Les Ferdinand who will fold all their used kit up as carefully as if it were a freshly laundered Armani shirt.

All these hard-working staff around the training ground have a role to play in the success of the team. Supporters always assume the stadium is the heart of a club. It is on alternate Saturdays. For the vast majority of time it's the training ground. It's where everyone is every day. It's where the characters who define a club do their work, like Ange, the secretary at Stoke, who has printed off more documents from my email and posted more letters for me than a secretary I could employ myself. It's like having your own PA. There are the security men, again always locals, who as a result are the conscience of the fans in your ears. 'Hey, Crouchie, we getting a result on Saturday?' If you're snubbed by the security men you know your reputation with the supporters is in trouble. There is the caretaker, always fixing things players have broken, the cleaners who have to make good the mess we casually leave around the place before heading off for a free soup. The groundsmen appear friendly until you do a knee-slide celebrating a goal, the leaving of two long muddy grooves in their precious pitch being treated the same way as if you had left a dirty protest on their bathroom walls.

There is a comforting routine to the actual training you do. Assuming you have one game that week and it falls on a Saturday, you'll have Sunday off or as a light recovery, train Monday, do a horrific day of intense physical work on Tuesday, have Wednesday off, work on tactics on Thursday and then set-pieces and a focus on the next day's opposition on Friday.

You can fear the hard days. At QPR, manager Gerry Francis instigated what he called Terror Tuesday. It was a double session, intense games so relentless that you couldn't move on the Wednesday. So you made sure you didn't try, by going straight out afterwards. Jono's Irish bar on the Uxbridge Road for a few looseners, then hopping on the Central line into London proper to paint the town blue and white hoops. The Tuesday session died a long time ago, victim of football's great overseas enlightenment, but it was marvellous while it lasted.

All footballers love a five-a-side. It's the ideal showcase for all the touches and tricks you have without actually requiring too much running. Working on the shape of the team is far less enjoyable, although it's arguably more important. At Liverpool Rafa Benítez would set the 11 players out exactly where he wanted, pick the ball up and run to a different place on the pitch, and we'd all have to shuffle over to our new positions. Then he'd move again, and we would shuffle into a new shape. It would go on for 15 minutes, a pain in the backside but absolutely essential to the success of the club under him.

Harry Redknapp would leave the hands-on stuff to his coaches but step in when it was needed, a kick up the backside or a pat on the back. I knew he rated me and it gave me such confidence. I'd walk out onto the pitch before a match thinking, we'll smash this lot.

And it was always fun – lots of time with the ball, lots of five-a-sides. At Spurs, Robbie Keane would sometimes complain that we should be doing more work on team shape and tactical patterns. Harry would give him a dirty look and launch into one. 'What the f*** would I want to do that for? You want me to tell Gareth Bale where to run? Eh? You want me to tell Luka where he should pass it? Huh? These are top players, Robbie, top players!'

He made you feel like the best in the world. His tactical understanding of the game was excellent, but that ability to simplify it was the key to us winning so many games. Players don't like being deluged with information. They don't like being given jobs they can't do. Get the good ones doing what they're great at, get the steady ones supporting the good ones.

His instructions to our Honduran midfielder Wilson Palacios were uncomplicated. Give to Modrić. I don't care if he's a foot away from you. Pass it. Tackle, hunt the ball down, give it.

It made Palacios one of the most effective midfielders in the Premier League. When he moved to Stoke he wasn't half the player, because he was trying to do twice as much – long-range passing, goal-scoring, little dinks and flicks. Roll it to Luka. Straightforward but perfect.

I'd been at Liverpool, where Rafa Benítez was all tactics and drills. As a kid he had loved to play a Spanish version of the game Risk, which was all about strategies and schemes. You could see that on the training ground, and he was amazing at it. The perfect manager would be half Redknapp and half Rafa.

Harry could make you laugh, whether he was trying to or not. When he was angry it was nightmarish, because the part of you that wasn't scared was trying desperately hard not to laugh. You'll be familiar with the clip when he's being interviewed on camera and gets hit by a stray ball hit by one of his own players. That sums him up. He goes bananas, and then just when you think he's over it, he comes back for a second charge. He can't let it go, even when he's back talking to the interviewer. 'No wonder he's in the f***ing reserves ...'

Because of his public persona, because of the stereotypes that come with him, I don't think he gets the credit he deserves. He gets called a wheeler-dealer, which he hates, but he's never been at a club where they've just handed him £200m. He has usually had to work within certain parameters and make the best of the assets he might be able to sell and those he can bring in with the proceeds. When he sees a situation, whether it's a tactical problem or one of man-management, he simplifies it. That's how he gets the best out of his resources.

The warm-up, however, whoever does it, is seldom much fun. I wish you could just take a pill and be done. Over hurdles, under hurdles, stepping in and out of ladders ... I preferred the days of a jog round the pitch and an easy group stretch. The best are boxes, essentially a big game of piggy-in-the-middle, ten players in a circle, two others trying to chase the ball down. Twenty completed passes and the two in the middle stay in, intercept a pass and you switch with the bloke who made it. Get nutmegged and you stay in. Go aerial if you like, go out of the circle as long as you can volley the ball back before it touches the ground. It's always seen as just a bit of fun, but it sharpens your mind, tests your touch and works you hard if you're in the middle. Stick someone in a box and you can tell straight away if they're a player.

The possession game is another classic. Three teams of eight playing in half a pitch, one of them standing on the boundary lines like a human wall. The team in possession has to hang on to the ball, the other has to win it back. You can use the players on the touchline to bounce the ball off, but you can't let it go out of play. Losing team stays on, winning team steps off for a rest. Relentless physical work, constant pressure, lots of competition. Those two games on their own are a great day.

Each manager likes to add on their own specifics to get you ready for each match. Tony Pulis was about team shape first, shape second and shape third. There was no room for free-flowing football or anything off the cuff where you razz the ball about. Harry Redknapp would do shape only if he had to. He trusted the players and tried to set them free. Fabio Capello loved his shape and he loved his discipline; Sven could not have been more relaxed. Graham Taylor liked his training as he liked his playing, direct and hard-working. Graham Rix was all passing, Mark Hughes was all passing. For me the best managers avoid getting stuck in a stylistic rut and instead tailor their own preferences to the resources they have at their disposal. Round pegs do not fit in square holes no matter how hard you push.

There are some managers, the ones who used to be great players, who cannot help but show off their own skills. Glenn Hoddle used to do it, Gianfranco Zola used to do it. When Zola was at West Ham it was embarrassing for the players; he was the best one on the pitch, and he was wearing brogues. Craig Bellamy had to have a word. 'You're popping free-kicks into the top corner from thirty yards, and all it's doing is destroying our confidence. Not least because you're also wearing a suit and tie.' Mark Hughes at Stoke would restrict himself to the occasional amazing volley for the same reason. I can understand it's difficult; if I ever become a manager, I'd find it impossible not to join in, at least until I became rubbish. But you are not one of the players, and you cannot train like one. If you want to stay fit, do your work once the players have gone. And do not be like one manager I had, who would work out in the club gym wearing a singlet and fingerless weightlifting gloves, two players ready to grab the barbell off him, looking at himself in the mirror as he lifted, feeling his muscles ostentatiously afterwards.

You have players whose dedication at the training ground explains perfectly their performances when it matters. David Beckham would stay behind as the rest of the England team went in for lunch so he could take ten free-kicks. Frank Lampard couldn't call it quits until he had struck ten perfect penalties. It's not a complicated equation; the best players put the most into training. Frank's attitude and his desire were the best I have ever seen, and they brought their fair rewards.

That's the good stuff. There are also fabulous players who don't lift a toe in training and yet somehow perform like world-beaters in matches. I was told Carlos Tevez looked like a bag of spanners away from the big stadium. He wouldn't move and you wouldn't see a sniff of those skills. Had you only watched him in a fluorescent bib you'd never have signed him in a million years. And then under the lights he would run himself into the ground, a non-stop ball of energy and commitment and naked pleasure in the sheer fun of it all. Maybe he was just conserving energy. Ledley King at Spurs couldn't train, because after every session both his knees would swell up like he'd injected them with water. All he could manage was a spin on the exercise bike, a little pool work and then stroll out slowly in a big warm coat to walk through a few shape drills. Come matches he would somehow have the ability to glide. It was like he was running without trying. I think he was as good as Rio Ferdinand.

There are also those players who look outstanding on the training pitches but simply cannot produce it in matches. At Portsmouth we had some world-class talents: Lassana Diarra, Niko Kranjčar, Jermain Defoe, Glen Johnson. The best by far, Monday to Friday, was Arnold Mvuemba. He was sensational. But you've never heard of him, because on Saturday afternoons he would be a bag of nerves. A genius midfield playmaker who could turn invisible at the sound of a referee's whistle.

Those open pitches can be a lonely place. When you're in form, when you're being picked, when you're playing two games a week, it's all fun. The rest of it is recovery. But when you're not playing, when the first team are inside getting rub-downs and you're outside in the cold and the rain, trying to top up your fitness by training with the kids, trying to get up for it while some mouthy 17-year-old is attempting to boot you around to prove his manhood, you can lose your head. That's when the nasty tackles come in. That's when the fights happen. Arguments and rows, shoving and finger-pointing, always the coaches left to sort it out, never the manager.

You try to find your own little amusements. Mock punishments for the worst player, little humiliations to keep standards up. From Burnley the lads at Stoke borrowed the idea of a wheel of misfortune. A spinning arrow, a circle split into segments, some good, most bad. If you are late to training, you have the choice: accept the standard £250 fine, or go to the wheel. One segment will get the fine cancelled. The adjoining one will double it, the next one round triple it. You might hit the jackpot, which is to receive £500 instead. Or you might have to clean a team-mate's car by hand, or make tea for everyone in the squad.

I'm an instinctive wheel man. I take it on every time. When it's done properly it's a joy: Charlie Adam coming in wearing his best suit, as if he were going into court, Jack Butland acting as the stern judge. 'How do you plead?' 'Not guilty, your honour.' 'Then I sentence you to one spin of the wheel ...'

He got a stinker. A meal for the entire team, paid for out of his own pocket. We filled our boots. Starters, drinks, complicated puddings. A bill as long as my arm, and that's saying something.

CLOTHES

It's always been the way. Footballers love clothes. They have the money, they have the youth, they usually have the body. And yet so many still seem to manage to get it so wrong.

Wrong, yet think that they are so right. For Djibril Cissé, a bright-red suit with top hat and cane was only the start of it. He would wear glasses that had no lenses in them. Not just clear lenses, which anyway serve no corrective purpose, but frames without anything in them. You could push your finger straight through and tickle his eyelashes.

It was around that time that I felt I had lost a handle on what was cool. You wear glasses for fashion. Right. But everyone knows they're not glasses. Mainly because they're not glasses, on account of not having glass in them. Rewind it a fraction more. At what stage does pretending to have an impairment become cool? Would he have worn a large hearing-aid even though his hearing was perfect? Cissé was the sort of dresser to consider all those options. Bear in mind, as I said earlier, that this was a man who used a 1920s telephone as a hands-free mobile attachment.

He once came along on a night out with a robotic metal covering on his right hand and forearm designed to make him look like the

Terminator. He started his own label, called Klubb 9, and then another called Mr Lenoir. He's worn a man-skirt and an actual skirt. Now I've worn one myself, but that was for charity, and I went the whole hog – granny skirt, tights, cardigan, David Walliams hanging off my arm ... But Cissé wore them for real and pulled it off. And he used to get changed in the same Liverpool dressing-room as Didi Hamann, who would be wearing dirty old trainers, stonewashed jeans and an unironed baggy T-shirt. Not only did these men share the same profession. They got dressed next to each other.

I hold my hand up. I've had some bad fails. In those dark days as a youth team player when I found myself in the garage clubs of Ayia Napa, all the lads were in sleeveless tops paired with baggy Maharishi pants. The sleeveless top requires a set of big guns to carry it off. I couldn't carry it off. I would look at my arms, which looked like pieces of wet spaghetti, and lament the cruel gap in the market for men of my build.

Before I had a few quid, the choices were awful. You could either pay a fortune – a fortune you were not earning – to have a bloke make you something bespoke that actually fitted you, or you could wear affordable stuff that made you look like a sapling.

If anything the trousers were worse than the sleeveless tops. I either had to attempt to wear shorts every day, including through the winter, or accept that my ankles were a public viewing gallery. If you have a 44-inch waist you can get jeans that fit without a problem. If you have a 26-inch waist you're laughing. But if you're slim and tall you're lost. My sleeve lengths were always too short, unless I bought an extra-large shirt, in which case it would hang off me like a five-man tent. A medium in torso would be fine across the shoulders but finish on my belly-button. I looked like Britney

Spears, or a 1980s fitness instructor. Every shirt I had I would have to wear with sleeves rolled up, to at least disguise one aspect of its ill-fittingness.

Before I met Abbey I used to style myself. And that was horrific. I look back now on my early days, at my look during my time at Villa, even early Liverpool, and none of it fits. My jeans were pulled too high. My jumpers were too baggy. My shirts were draped over my shoulders like ponchos. My trainers were white and bad.

She has helped me. A gentle hand, polishing me up a little. But before then came the biggest disaster of all, a Prada jumper from Harrods that even now makes me both angry and upset. By this stage I was doing alright financially. I could walk into a menswear department with optimism. And so when I saw this top with standard woollen arms but some weird half-cashmere, half-camelhair body, I thought, maybe, and when I tried it on and it fitted I thought, why not?

To the till, a pleasant conversation ongoing with the shop assistant. Barcode under the scanner, a beep and a smile. 'That will be £800, please.'

Eight hundred pounds! I was furious, first with the assistant and then myself. Why had there been no price on it? Actually that bit made sense. But why had he not warned me? Even worse, why did I then hand over my credit card, smoke coming out of my ears, rather than throwing the jumper in his face and the hanger on the floor?

Instantly I resented the jumper too. I knew I had never been a shopping natural, that allowing me to roam a retail environment without a wingman or woman was potentially disastrous. I was no David Bentley, who would finish training at Blackburn and drive straight to the Trafford Centre off the M60 in south Manchester to browse for hours and just soak in the vibes. But now I was at war with myself too.

Right, you've paid for this horror, you're going to have to wear it now.
But I don't even like it any more.
I don't care. £800! You're going to get value out of this if it kills you.
But it looks like I'm wearing an ordinary jumper with a camelhair bib over it.
Don't blame me, you bought it.
Yeah, cheers.

It was horrible too. It wasn't even a nice colour. It was cream. At home I twitched about it for a while and then decided I simply had to crack on. It wasn't going to get any cheaper or more attractive sitting in my wardrobe. I went out. I drank a Guinness. I bought another, leaned back in my chair and dropped the entire pint all down myself.

It was ruined. Dead. Finished. I attempted to wash it, and it simply became a grey crop-top instead. I've wondered subsequently if my subconscious made me spill that pint as a deliberate act of self-sabotage so I would never have to wear it ever again. Maybe my subconscious was at work in ordering a Guinness in the first place, the darkest, most stain-heavy beverage available, rather than something washable like a gin and tonic. It was probably the worst purchase of my entire career, clothing or otherwise.

I like to think I'm a better, more confident man these days. If I were to find myself back at Harrods with the same top and the same display on the till, I'd like to think I'd react with an 'Eight hundred pounds! You having a laugh?'

I picked up a jacket in a store recently and this time asked how much it was before trying it on. The assistant kept a straight face. 'Five thousand five hundred pounds.'

I couldn't help myself. 'Five grand? You're f***ing joking!' He tried to have a chuckle about it. I could sense it was forced.

Since reaching my late thirties I've adjusted my look and tactics. I'm no longer a tracksuit and trainers man. I've smartened myself up a fraction: a variation on a shoe, rather than a trainer; a black or dark jumper, possibly a jacket. It feels like I've finally found myself. Or my wife has.

Football, however, is still exploring flashier avenues. There is a new dress-code in the Premier League that begins with Louboutin trainers, the ones with uppers covered in small studs or spikes. They'll only set you back £650 a pair. Those are paired with the low-hanging tracksuit bottom, the gusset at least as low as mid-hamstring, so it appears as if you're carrying a bag of potatoes in your smalls, or that you're a toddler in the early stages of going nappy-free who's done a poo in his romper-suit. A baseball cap at all times, sunglasses even when indoors. Around the swimming pool in summer it is now the cropped short, of the type first popularised by Cristiano Ronaldo. It's absolutely not for me, in the same way that I simply could not have played football in the late 1980s when the standard football short ended just shy of your unmentionables. I know Ian Ormondroyd tried it, but he was a mere 6'5". Had I been Cameroonian when they introduced that figure-hugging one-piece in 2004 I would have had no choice but to announce my international retirement.

The game does attempt to self-police. You will have the toes cut off your socks or your new boxer-shorts covered in Deep

Heat three days in a row. It's standard practice when a player comes into training in something horrific that another player will wait until they have left the room and then put it all on and go into the gym to do weights, or jog out onto the pitches for a muddy warm-up. I once had a pair of zip-up boots that I cherished at the time but could never risk wearing in the football part of my life. I have a secret yearning for an Ugg boot (So warm! So cosy!) but I know that on feet the size of mine not only would I look like the Abominable Snowman but I would see them again on our goalkeeper as he booted a load of muddy balls at the halfway line.

It can get serious. There was a dark period at Stoke in 2013 that began innocently enough with Matty Etherington getting his new leather jacket flushed down the training-ground toilets. Quickly, however, it got out of hand. Etherington decided to take his revenge by taking a load of mouldy fish-bits, like old kipper heads, and putting them in the shoes and car of Jon Walters, who he suspected of the jacket theft. Walters then escalated it at pace by getting a severed pig's head from a local butcher's – still covered in blood, dried and otherwise – wrapping it in Matty's jeans and putting it in his locker. Matty found it and put it in Glenn Whelan's, except rather than Glenn Whelan's he accidentally put it in Kenwyne Jones's. Before you know it, Kenwyne has lost the plot and is putting a brick through Glenn Whelan's car window, and Glenn is threatening to go round Kenwyne's house, which we all knew was a bad idea, because Kenwyne was a well-built individual. It became quite a big thing in the dressing-room, unsurprisingly. We looked back at the time a few weeks before when we had covered Michael Owen's car in flour and eggs to mark his retirement as almost a halcyon period, a time of innocence and wholesomeness.

If it sounds like a dangerous world, there is always the safe bet of the tracksuit. The only stick you might attract for that will be if it's clear it's a club one you haven't paid for or a freebie from your sponsor. There will be a freebie merchant in every dressing-room, the one who refuses to spend a penny when they can wear something gratis. Ryan Shawcross, do not try to hide at the back. On a night out the scrutiny will rise another notch. Every element of your outfit will be examined. There have been at least two occasions when Glenn has come as a geography teacher, I would guess inadvertently: dull shirt with jumper, chinos, shiny shoes.

It's rare for a lumpy, uncompromising defender to wear extravagant clothes. A boring player equals boring clothes; you wouldn't get a broken-nosed centre-back bowling about with Djibril's cane. It's also unusual to find a continental player who doesn't come to training far smarter than his English equivalent. Beni Carbone would, I'm told, wear a suit every day at Aston Villa, Dimitar Berbatov the same at Spurs and Manchester United. As a man from Bulgaria that could have gone either way, but he represented a fresher, more clean-cut side of his nation's image. I bumped into Gianluigi Buffon on holiday one summer; he was miles ahead of where we were.

The first British player to really catch up was David Beckham. Even so, he has not been immune from the ghastly mistake. The sarong was outrageous for the time. The matching leather suits he and Victoria sported around the same time made them look like sex tourists. If you're going to be a style icon, you will take a few gambles that simply do not pay off.

Maybe that's why Wilfried Bony will post a photo on Instagram most mornings of himself in one of his outfits. He's checking that he's gambled right. He's checking that he hasn't made the same mistake as the wife of former Liverpool striker Andriy Voronin, who used to wear leopard-print on pretty much every occasion she left the house. I asked him about it once. What's the thing about the leopard-print? He told me that in his native Ukraine it was considered a sign of prosperity, because it was unavailable for purchase. You'd think a Kiev version of Del Boy would import a van-load of knock-off stuff, but no. And so the two of them used to walk around the middle of Liverpool, her in a flared leopard-skin jumpsuit with heels, him in shiny silver tracksuit bottoms; if you search on Google, she is the first result for worst-dressed WAG in history. The internet can be a cruel place.

A friend of my mum's was selling her large house in Leeds many years ago. A youngish bloke wearing ripped jeans, trainers and a T-shirt came round to view it. She binned him off, on the basis that there was clearly no way he could afford it. It turned out to be Gary Speed, who could have afforded it three times over.

So you should never judge a footballer on his appearance, unless they are one of the following, in which case you should.

Stephen Ireland, photographed wearing what looks like a waistcoat from a wedding he went to when he was 15, a far larger man's shirt, bad stonewashed jeans from a 16-stone American builder and a cap. His wife's in a cocktail dress. What does that combination mean? What social occasion is he off to?

Gerard Piqué, pictured leaving a game wearing a knitted and hooded jumper with a stitching pattern that makes it look like chain-mail armour. He looks like he's off to war. And that he's baking. He's holding a mobile phone when the accessory he actually needs is a sword.

Lionel Messi in a red crushed velvet suit at the FIFA Ballon d'Or awards, a few seats along from Ronaldo looking amazing in a traditional dinner jacket. Charles N'Zogbia wearing a suit that looks to have been made out of my mum's shower curtain. Mario Balotelli (why always him?) in a woollen hat in various shades of brown and with five bits sticking up like a fingered glove. He looks like the gangster penguin in Wallace and Gromit's *The Wrong Trousers* when he's disguised as a rooster with a rubber glove on his head. Ashley Cole and Cheryl in their matching white suits, fixed grins in place, having obviously signed a contract for a few quid. I know Ashley. I think he'd be dying inside.

There are certain clothes shops that all footballers go to. They're the type of places that have doorbells to press before they'll let you in, where you walk in and think, hmm, it's a bit sparse in here, and then realise that's because each individual item costs as much as a rack of standard-issue clothing. In the north-west it's Flannels in Manchester, on Crown Square in Spinningfields, and Cricket on Mathew Street in Liverpool. All the players go there so all the players look the same: the same shoes, the same shirt. I got caught up in all that at one stage – buying expensive clothes I didn't really like, because you feel you have to fit in. When you're young and impressionable it's easily done. Thankfully I came out the other side unscathed, except for the occasional £800 camelhair crop-top. Player liaison officers will also come to the training ground with gear, setting up a little shop in the dressing-room, a tailor with him to measure a few of the lads up for suits, percentages being taken all over the place.

I remember when my mates were starting work for the first time, the pain of having to buy suits when you wanted to spend your money on anything else, of having to wear a shirt and tie every day of the week. And so I never forget that one of greatest things about being a footballer is that you can go to work wearing whatever you like. Free tracksuits. Shorts in summer. Flip-flops. You have a shower and come home to stick whatever else you like on. When we do get told to wear suits it signifies something special: an FA Cup final, a place in England's World Cup squad. Armani with the national side in 2006, M&S when a little of the glamour had faded in 2010. White Armani for Liverpool at the 1996 Cup final, perhaps the most famous suits in English football history; Gazza gabbing in his post-match interview after his free-kick had won the 1991 semi-final for Spurs against Arsenal, 'I'm now away to get ma suit measured. YES!' I loved Gazza so much I even loved him in a shell suit. I was desperate to have the Umbro one he wore at Italia 90, but my mum and dad couldn't source one. Others decry the elasticated ankle cuff on a shell suit. I loved it. My ankle was going to be sticking out no matter what the cuff was like. At least with the shell suit passers-by were thinking it was the fault of the elastic rather than the wearer's 6'7" lanky frame.

It matters for managers too. As with so many areas of football, Pep Guardiola has changed the rules. He can stand on a touchline in suit trousers, trainers and a black jumper, and he pulls it off. He tucks his shirt into his trousers, a huge no-no since the days of Britpop, and it looks amazing. This in a managerial world where fans sing about Tony Pulis wearing the club shop, where Arsène Wenger sported his famous sleeping-bag padded coat, where Ron Atkinson was defined by his shades and Jim Smith by his flat cap. If I were a manager and opened my wardrobe at home on the morning of my first match in charge, tracksuits to one side, suits to the left, I'd go left. Worn with proper shoes. It just brings you that little extra respect. Plus, should a high ball come your way and you still kill it dead in your polished brogues, you look like a superstar.

You might recall the period at Liverpool when Rafa Benítez started wearing a leather jacket. It was around the same time as the emergence of his goatee, of the Doc Marten shoes with the suit trousers. There was a theory in the dressing-room that he was trying to compete with José Mourinho, at the time considered the coolest, most stylish man in the Premier League. The Liverpool/Chelsea rivalry was a big thing on the pitch, with those three Champions League semi-finals in four years, and we felt that Rafa was attempting to open a new sartorial front too.

The leather jacket was never him. Word was his wife had pushed him in that direction, that he was never happy wearing it. So that Christmas, when we had a Secret Santa and I drew Rafa, I got him two things: Mourinho's biography, and a new leather jacket.

You should have seen his expression when he opened the gifts. His face just fell. Oh no, I thought. I've actually offended him. It's all gone wrong.

I never told him it was from me. Until now. Sorry, Rafa.

VOLLEYS

It may just be that there is nothing better in football than an overhead volleyed goal.

So elaborate, so ridiculous, so spectacular. Someone who could quite easily head the ball instead deciding to throw themselves into the air, turn themselves upside down and attempt to make contact with a ball flying towards them at 60 miles an hour. It's insane. And the insanity of it is precisely why it's so sweet.

The cross has to be the right height. The ball has to be slightly behind you. You need to be travelling so you can get up and meet it with perfect timing. If all that is happening, the adrenaline will start fizzing through you as soon as the possibility presents itself. Your eyes light up. Yes! I don't have to head it. Yes! I can have a go at it. Most of the time you land on your arse and the ball lands anywhere but the net. But when it goes right – oh, what a feeling!

I've always loved volleying. It was something I used to practise naturally as a kid, on the rock-hard ground of the school playground, landing my bony bits on the rough concrete, running over every evening to Pitshanger Park in Ealing, using the sections of fence by the tennis courts as our goal, one of the lads with the ball out wide, pretending to beat their full-back, deliberately dinking the cross too far back for a header, me jumping up and hammering it with a fantastic pinging sound against the fence. We would do it until dark, finish school the next afternoon and head straight out again, compiling our own lists of the greatest volleys and volleyers we had seen – Hugo Sánchez at Real Madrid, Mark Hughes, Luca Vialli; Tony Yeboah's two for Leeds, Matt Le Tissier's loads for Southampton, David Platt against Belgium, Marco van Basten against Russia.

All that obsession, all that practising, means that I find it easier volleying a ball than I do striking one on the deck. David Beckham was such a clean striker of a dead ball. Charlie Adam could do it all day long. I can get more pace, accuracy and direction on a volley. And that's why I could score that famous goal for Stoke against Manchester City: I used to do it lots. I'd practised the flick-up off instep and volley with the outside of my foot thousands of times. I'd even tried the exact same shot at Blackburn the week before, and the goalkeeper had saved it.

Had I trapped the knock-down, as most footballers instinctively would, it would have been so much harder to get the dip needed to get the ball up and over Joe Hart. I knew that it needed the pop-up for the power and the placement. It was a weird thing to do by conventional standards but it was almost second nature for me, and that was why I'd probably have to call it as my best goal ever: past England's first-choice 'keeper, against the team who would be crowned champions a few months later, the opening goal in a match that would prove critical to our season.

And yet. The number of fans who've asked me if that goal was meant to be a cross ... I understand the disputes over certain goals. The Ronaldinho one for Brazil against England in 2002 was 100 per cent a cross; we only think otherwise because he was such a genius in everything else he did. Had Terry Butcher taken it, or Phil Stamp, we never would have considered it as anything other than a mis-hit cross. Look at where his eyes are aiming. Look at the shape of his foot.

But mine? Why would you smash a cross in as hard as you can? Why would you aim it directly at the goal? Why would you hit one when there wasn't a single team-mate in the penalty box? I'm a relaxed man. I enjoy talking to supporters of all clubs. But it's hard not to lose your rag when someone who has never played professional football tries to tell you that a skill you've practised thousands of times that has resulted in the best goal you've ever scored a week after you nearly scored the exact same goal is actually a fluke.

When you hit a volley properly it's impossible to forget, unless it happened in the brief period when Setanta had the rights to some Premier League matches, in which case no one can remember it at all. I scored a scissor-kick for Portsmouth against Stoke from a Jermain Defoe chipped cross that was as sweet as anything, but even Jermain is only hazy about it now. I had one for Stoke against Birmingham that almost broke the crossbar, but that has to be a footnote too.

Context makes a difference. The overhead kick I scored for Liverpool against Galatasaray might almost wriggle past the Man City one in my personal all-time list because of all the detail around it: a Champions League tie en route to the final, a Tuesday night at Anfield, the goal going in at the Kop end; Steve Finnan's little push past his man and first-time cross, the shape I inadvertently made in the air, Steven Gerrard jumping on my back as we celebrated, Luis García putting his hand over his mouth in faux-shock. I knew the moment I connected with that one that it was in. A few weeks later

I got another, this time against Bolton, from almost exactly the same place by the penalty spot, right foot overhead into the bottom right-hand corner.

And then there are the ones that don't come off. My build works both ways on an overhead kick. When they come off they look more remarkable for the length of the limbs going four different ways in the air. When they go wrong my arms and legs seem to send out a different message: why on earth are you trying that?

I had one against Trinidad in the 2006 World Cup: 0–0, my eyes lighting up as the ball came in, launching myself into the air for the scissor-kick, thinking, bang, this is what I do.

I made contact alright. Straight back to the crosser. Thankfully it all worked out in the end; I scored from that late header before Gerrard added another to send us through. But the aftermath wasn't pretty. A photo emerged of me midair, right leg going left, left leg going right, right arm straight up above my head, left arm curved down by my right leg. Quickly it became a meme, that image Photoshopped onto hundreds of others: Peter Crouch Can Do Anything. Me as a synchronised swimmer. Me as a jockey, down low over a stallion's neck in a thrilling finish. Me as a clockface, as a fast bowler, surfing a big wave, doing sprint hurdles, slam-dunking. Me as the propeller of an airplane, as a wind turbine, as a swastika on the wall behind Adolf Hitler. They were everywhere. They went on for ever.

I kept faith in my technique, even if it's a little different to the standard, even if it annoyed Fabio Capello when he was England manager. I hit a scissor-kick with my laces, but if the ball was off the ground or I was volleying first time, I would always use the outside of my foot. I just feel the surface area is bigger and it comes more naturally to me.

Playing for Spurs against Inter Milan in the Champions League at White Hart Lane, I missed with a volley at the far post that I really should have scored. Capello pulled me aside at the next England training camp. Great result, Crouch, but your technique for volleys is wrong. You must change.

I realised then that he had never seen me hit a volley before. I realised that he could thus have barely seen me play. If he had he would have seen the result of all that childhood and adult practice. Volleying was arguably my best skill. Why should I change my entire approach since the age of nine? I thanked him, nodded my head and thought, right, I'm going to have to politely totally ignore him.

It's the seeming impossibility of the best volleyed goals that make them contenders for your all-time favourites, whether it's the overhead, the scissors, the chest-down and thump or the run on to it and crack it. I'd have the half-volley in its own character, the sort of beauty Gerrard used to specialise in, sprinting on to a bouncing ball and belting it hard and low, and I wouldn't give it half-marks either, the bounce in many ways making it harder to hit than a full volley.

You try to narrow it down to a top five and it's so hard. You have to love Alan Shearer's for Newcastle against Everton, because it's in before the 'keeper moves. Pure laces. Pure venom. Paolo Di Canio's jumping one against Wimbledon seems impossible – scissors midair, rolled off his toes, hit with the outside of his foot – and it sums up the man that he would even try. He's playing well, he's a confident man anyway, and he goes with total instinct. Delightful.

Zinedine Zidane for Real Madrid in the Champions League final of 2002. Mind-blowing. The ball has gone so high. He's not been able to run on to it. He has to swivel to hit it, and it's on his weaker foot. He's beyond the near post and has a postage-stamp-sized portion of the goal to aim at. And it's the Champions League final!

Philippe Mexès in the Milan derby of 2015. That volley is a scandal. He shouldn't even contemplate it. James Rodríguez in the World Cup for Colombia – right off the laces, the pop-up off his chest so nice, a lively turn as he strikes it, a kiss of the crossbar as an extra treat. Dejan Stanković from near the halfway line to lob Manuel Neuer in the Champions League quarter-finals of 2011, hit with the outside of his foot as I favour, the thought popping into his head swiftly followed by a 'Why not?'

Robin van Persie's for Arsenal against Charlton, for the fact he's running on to it. The sweetest timing you can imagine. Wayne Rooney's for Manchester United against Newcastle always gives me extra pleasure for the strop he's in before he hits it. He's ranting at the referee, giving him earfuls on both sides, then just jogs in and smashes it as if to deliver the angriest of eff-offs. Even his celebration is smashing the ball back into the net. He's still fuming. Rio has to have a word. It doesn't help.

Marco van Basten at Euro 88. To return to the subject of disputed goals, he's meant that all the way. It's never a cross. If he had given up football immediately after that hit the net he would still never be forgotten. Partly because a player has never retired in the middle of a major final, but still. Next time you watch it, see how baffled the Russian 'keeper Rinat Dasayev is. He's setting himself for a cross, thinking, Ruud Gullit's going to come in again, and he's on fire, and the next thing he knows this missile has rocketed over him and he almost falls over in its slipstream.

I played golf with van Basten once in Mallorca. A nice man. All I wanted to do was recreate that goal with him on one of the greens.

Danny Rose for Spurs against Arsenal. That game was actually Danny's debut. I was on the bench that night, and as the ball came down I thought, no, just pass it. And then he finds so much power that he doesn't even need to hit the corner. It's almost straight at Manuel Almunia, but it's travelling so fast he may as well be trying to stop an invisible ball. It's the perfect illustration that the key to great volleying is not to rush it. Don't hit it on the way up, wait until it's at its lowest point. That's key. It's all about the wait.

Olivier Giroud and his scorpion one. It's unreal. He hasn't floated it in. He's smashed it off his studs. You could argue there's some luck in it; he's swung a leg at it, and with the trajectory of the cross he can't do anything else or score any other way. But the power! And it came so soon after Henrikh Mkhitaryan's own scorpion, when from a team perspective he shouldn't even be in the box, he should be tracking back. Mkhitaryan has options. He could stop and swivel. But the Giroud goal has to be better because he's further out. I only wish I'd seen them both as a kid. I would have practised them every day. The Mkh Flick I would have tried every evening in Pitshanger Park. The G-Spot I'm not sure I was ready to find while I was still at school.

And so my top five? Zidane. Van Persie against Charlton. Giroud, although that's harsh on Mexès. Di Canio. And van Basten, of all of them the one I would most like to have scored myself. Imagine winning the European Championship for England with a goal like that. Knowing the Dutch, they probably had a massive row about it afterwards. Hey, Marco! Why did you not cross it? I was at the back post? Shut up, stupid, he should have laid it off, I had run 50 yards to be in support. But guys, I scored! You scored, sure, but you meant to cross it, didn't you? Didn't you?

TEAM BUS

So much about football has stayed the same, so much has changed. When I first broke into the first team at QPR, way back at the start of the century, the highlight of most away matches was the journey back on the team bus. As you climbed on board, someone would hand you a can of lager. From under the seats a big slab of cans would be pulled out. An hour or so in, you'd pull up outside a fish and chip shop. The kitman would hop off and return with 20 portions. You'd wash it down with another Foster's, play some half-cut cards, be dropped back at the training ground in Ealing and then go straight to Jono's, the Irish bar on the Uxbridge Road near Ealing Common, for a few more.

Now? Now there's a chef on board and a kitchen at the back. It's a recovery shake as you step on board and a little tray of sushi when you're seated. The card schools have broken up, their pupils ageing and scattered round the country: Jon Walters, Charlie Adam, Glenn Whelan. The closest you get to the blackjack battles of old is when a few of the overseas players like Mame Biram Diouf and Jean-Eric Maxim Choupo-Moting bring out Uno. Uno is a card game for children. Its rules, skill level and potential for gambling reflect that. The iPad dominates where the conversation and jokes used to flow.

I know the world has moved on. Raw fish is better for you than fried fish. The chip is less mighty than the compacted rice. Foster's can only be classed as a recovery drink if the cans that precede it are Special Brew. The iPads haven't entirely killed the games, as long as you don't mind losing to Walters on his Scrabble app.

But it used to be so sociable. Watching films together, taking it in turns to bring one along, getting absolutely hammered if yours was voted to be rubbish. It wasn't just the players. Staff might make a choice too. At Portsmouth our kitman Kev let slip that he used to be a boxer, and that he had some footage of his best fights. We were on at him for weeks. 'Come on, Kev, bring some along, we'd love to see it. Huge boxing fans, all of us.' And then he did, and we piled in barely before he'd swung a grainy punch. 'Oh dear, look at his footwork!' 'What, is that meant to be a punch?' 'Kev, who's this fat oaf? He looks familiar.' Forty minutes of it, he endured. And he still had to get the fish and chips.

The films we did watch weren't high-brow. It was not the target market for French arthouse or anything in the native tongue of one of the few foreign players at that time. During that same spell at Portsmouth, our maverick Croatian playmaker Robert Prosinečki could barely make a phone call, let alone work the DVD player on the bus. Instead he would content himself with smoking heavily before and after each journey. It was often in the dressing-room showers, and always the hard stuff too, Marlboro Reds as a minimum. His English skills would come and go. He could tell you exactly where he was going to put the ball for you, but he was suddenly all shrugs and cupped ears when it came to films. Or also being told to track back.

So much has changed, so much has stayed the same. There are still and there always will be strict rules about who sits where.

1. **Always sit in the same seat.** You are like a commuter of old, a creature of habit. You are there for a reason. You have earned it, either through your seniority, your conversational skills or a combination of both.

2. **New signings must ask where they should sit.** Nothing is more guaranteed to make the wrong impression than plopping yourself down where the club captain sits, or breaking up a four-man table that has been the absolute cornerstone of that bus for the past two seasons.

3. **The correct protocol if you are unsure is to ask the most senior player, 'Is that seat free?'** The correct protocol if you are the senior player is to respond, 'What the hell?' You have to work your way up. Start in the no-man's land in the middle of the bus. Prove your credentials with incidental banter. Quite literally, what are you bringing to the table?

4. **If someone is sold, the pecking-order shifts.** All players can in theory move up one square. Players whose chat has proved outstanding may leapfrog another who has consistently offered too little. Do not complain. You had your chance.

5. **If there is a row, expect the other players to stir.** I've seen it kicking off over seats on the bus. 'What do you think *you're* doing?' 'Whatever. I'm not moving.' 'Well, that's my seat.' And the rest of us in both their ears – 'Oh, he'll move, he's bricking himself …' so that the man in question definitely can't move, because he doesn't want to look scared, and then some feigned outrage to the one whose seat has been squatted – 'I wouldn't take that from him, that's a disgrace …' I've seen proper fights. And felt slightly guilty afterwards.

6. **Young lads: go where you're told.** All in good time. Don't force it. Your chance will come. Tom Edwards at Stoke

started out on the margins, but he's worked up onto a good table now.

7. **Players in charge of music at the back, remnants of card schools in the middle, readers at the front.** There's a reader in every team. Jamie Carragher loved a footballer's autobiography. Guardiola, Wenger, Maradona, Cruyff – he would work through a different one every week. Rob Green would not only read on the bus but would go to his local in Hampstead and read there too. He had his own mug behind the bar, would get them to make him a tea, and then sit by the fire reading. Classic goalkeeper's move. I have no idea what he used to read when we were on England duty because I never got that far down the wrong end of the bus. Also I was too busy throwing stuff at him. We are 20- and 30-year-old men with kids. I know.

8. **Staff always at the front.** It's just like a school trip. Teachers in the first two rows, don't look back if you're not going to like what you see. It totally unsettles everyone when a member of staff even tries to sit in the middle. If the manager came to sit at the back it would blow my mind.

You have to be open to change in this game. At Stoke, our diminutive former Barcelona and Milan midfielder Bojan was responsible for starting a bus-based *Mario Kart* school. He was unbeatable, Joselu the only man who could hang on to his bumper. It developed into a nice little league, eight players strong, with relegation for those who finished the season in the bottom two. We tried poker a few times, but there were issues with the chips on the polished table-top when taking bends or braking at pace, and the rules were a little daunting to one or two.

And there is always a sleeper on every bus, none of them more effective than Sandro when we were together at Spurs. It sort of made sense; as I'll explain in more detail later, this was a man who had his entire house sound-proofed so he could party longer, later and louder. The man could sleep anywhere. Give him two minutes and he would be gone – in the dressing-room before games, after games, in the lull in the middle of an afternoon. Most bus sleepers get woken up. Something bounces off their head. Sandro could sleep through bricks.

There are certain no-no's. I'm aware everyone else does it, but for me the fashion of disembarking at the ground while wearing headphones is a crime. This is the moment when you should be thrilling to the roar of the home support, or at opposition grounds reeling at the horrendous and clichéd comments about your body shape. Embrace it. Don't shun the very people who pay your wages and send you vitriolic abuse via social media. It seems to have become a competition as to who can sport the largest headphones. When I was growing up it was all about how small they were. Out of principle I don't own a pair. I want to hear the world around me. At least some of it.

Headphones on the bus I'm fine with. Carlo Nash, veteran reserve goalkeeper at Stoke, used to play his iPad at full blast without any plugged in. Racing games, all screaming exhausts and squealing tyres. He would have the whole bus shouting the most straightforward of chants: 'NO HEADPHONES!' He was 38 by then. It was unbecoming.

Another unspoken rule. Never be late for the bus. Managers have left players stranded, hundreds of miles from home, for not being on board when they should be. Roy Keane did it at Sunderland and Ipswich, and he has my backing. It's rude. It's saying that your time is more important than the team's. Even if the bus waits for you it's a brutal gauntlet to run. You get ironic cheers as you climb the stairs. The first person you see is the furious manager. As you walk down the aisle it's boos. Fabio Capello wouldn't even look at you. He would just wave a dismissive hand in your face and let the consequences follow.

There are toilets on today's buses, naturally, but they are strictly for number ones only. I've never seen anyone attempt a number two on the bus. The circumstances under which it would be permissible would have to be so severe that you wouldn't be allowed to travel in the first place. Even the overseas players know it's a no-no. It's universal across all team sports.

My dream line-up, if I could choose any three players from my career to join me in the classic four-man table set-up, would be Wayne Rooney (always entertaining), Didi Hamann (liked his gambling, much more amusing man than his public persona would suggest) and Lee Hendrie (always funny, always liable to do something daft).

You don't want non-stop chat. Make it discerning. Leave pauses for reflection and the chat of your team-mates. David James was king of the monologues. At Stoke Geoff Cameron cannot go a day without telling you why the US is superior to England, either in a general sense or via a specific anecdote. 'There was this one time, back in Houston ...' One lad at Portsmouth couldn't stop talking about football, even when we all needed a breather. We nicknamed him Mark Pougatch, in honour of the radio and television presenter who loves his football and talks enthusiastically about it. The lad would come over on the bus, and someone would say, 'Watch out, boys, here comes Pougatch ...' We used to pretend to be asleep.

The bus can be a place to release all the tension that has built up over the course of the week. Tony Pulis wasn't shy about letting people know who his favourites were. He used to love Matty Etherington. He would take him aside on a Friday morning when the rest of us were running around in the rain. 'Don't train today, son, just get a big coat on and watch. You're too important.' Our stand-in goalkeeper Lee Grant would get it from Mark Hughes. 'This lad's attitude is first class. Jack Butland's come back in, he's taken it on the chin and cracked on, wishing Jack the best of luck. Why can't you all be like him?'

We would wait until we were at the back of the bus and then let rip. 'Matty, don't you move, let us pick your nose for you. You're too important.' 'Whoa, whoa, don't go tying your own shoelaces just because the rest of us have to. Just get a nice warm coat on and watch.' For Lee it was more forthright. 'Oh, that is disgusting.' 'That's sick.' 'Up his backside again, are we?' All for having the correct, professional attitude. The bus can be a cruel place.

The ultimate arbiter of on-bus behaviour is the driver, although of course to them it's never a bus but a coach. It's their domain. They almost feel like part of the team, and some of them actually have joined the staff, usually as kitmen. It's a short step from standing by the bus with the keys to loading a few trunks into the luggage compartment so well that everyone takes it for granted that that's what you do.

The slightest bit of traffic and they get hammered from those at the back. 'What are you doing?' 'Haven't you got satnav?' 'Is this your first time on a bus?' You find these days that most work for an outsourced company rather than one club, although you'll usually have the same man for each of your journeys for the same team.

When you move clubs and see them behind the wheel on a different bus it almost feels like they're cheating on you.

It's not an easy gig. You'll see them out in the car-park cleaning the bus/coach while you're inside enjoying a buffet breakfast. Coming back from distant destinations like Newcastle they'll drop you off at the airport and then head off into the night for the long slog home while you speed through the skies above. The compensation comes in the form of tickets. You can always sneak the driver into a game. That and the parking. The only people except the chairman who can drive to a match and know there's a guaranteed parking spot for them under the main stand.

And the bus can be your lightning rod for all the electricity that's in the air on the biggest nights. Driving to Anfield for Champions League games, the supporters would get there early to see the bus and players arrive. There would be flares going off, palms slapping on the bodywork, chants shaking the windows. Sometimes it felt like the whole of Liverpool was waiting for you to get off. Your bus had become a chariot to the coliseum, a magic carpet taking you somewhere you'd always dreamed of going. As long as no one was sitting in your seat, of course.

DROUGHTS

You join a new club as a striker, you want to score in your first game. If not the first game, the second. If not the second then a couple in your third, and away you go. You want to get off the mark like Alan Shearer did for Blackburn after his record transfer from Southampton, with two absolute beauties, or Wayne Rooney with a hat-trick in the Champions League for Manchester United.

I joined Liverpool in the summer of 2005 knowing they were the biggest club I'd played at so far. They had just won the Champions League. I'd been on a wonderful goal-scoring run at Southampton and I was breaking into the England team. In training I was flying. I couldn't stop scoring. I wasn't even thinking about it. The ball would arrive, the ball would be dispatched. Easy and natural and no doubts and all well in the world.

I arrived at Anfield and had a quiet word with myself. Just get going here, get an early goal and settle down. The first game came and went. Then the second. Then the third. No need to panic here, Peter. You're playing in a slightly different role, a little deeper than you're used to. You're not in the box so much, but that's what Rafa Benítez wants. He's happy with what you're doing. It'll come.

Four games. Five games. Suddenly aware that the scrutiny at a club like Liverpool is of a magnitude you've never experienced before. Six games. Seven games. Songs coming from the opposition supporters. Eight games, nine, ten. Articles in newspapers, doubt in my mind, trouble getting off to sleep. Eleven games, twelve games. Nothing. Nothing.

Everywhere I went they seemed to be talking on the television about my lack of goals. I would walk into a room and have to switch the TV off. I had to stop buying newspapers. My parents had to stop buying newspapers. I found myself thinking, I should have stayed at Southampton. I'm not good enough for this level. I'm out of my depth.

Thirteen games. Fourteen games. I started drinking after matches. It was the only way I could get off to sleep. My dad would take me out after games. Come on, have a few beers. It used to relax me a little. It meant I could go back into training on the Monday morning and feel like I was starting again.

Fifteen games. A special double-page spread in one of the tabloid football pull-outs, done in the style of Kiefer Sutherland's *24*, in honour of the 24 hours of football I had gone without a goal. That familiar split-screen graphic, a photo of me pulling a different anguished face in every one. Sixteen games. Watching the FIFA World Player of Year awards, and the presenter using me as the big joke in his opening lines – 'Is Peter Crouch not here?'

It followed me everywhere I went. You try to tell yourself that bigger names have gone through the same thing. Shearer might have started like a train for Blackburn but he later went 12 games scoreless for England as Euro 96 approached. He got through it because manager Terry Venables told him he would stay in the team regardless. It almost cheered me up. I felt like I had to score in every game I played for England or I would be out.

You tell yourself that other players have been through worse. Danny Graham, scoring one in 42 games for Sunderland. Garry Birtles, signing for Manchester United from Nottingham Forest and going goalless for 30 games.

You hang on to what you can. The Liverpool supporters were incredible. Not once did they stop singing my name or turn their backs on me. The city can have a siege mentality sometimes, after all it has been through, and the fans took me in as one of their own. Everyone else in the country was having a go, and they wouldn't have it. He's one of ours. We're standing by him. Then there was the power that Steven Gerrard and Jamie Carragher wielded in the city. Word appeared to get around from them that I was a good lad. The Kop saw the hard work I was putting in during games. The fans heard about the effort I was putting in during training.

That was all wonderful. But maybe it all came down to a night I had in Carra's local.

The pub was known as the Solly, a classic pre-match and post-match boozer for both Reds and Evertonians. Carra took me aside after training one afternoon. You'll have to come down the Solly. Everyone's done it. Michael Owen's done it. It's a great night. It'll take your mind off things.

We'd been there about an hour, the place absolutely packed out, when I found out about the karaoke. Come on, Crouchie, we all do it. No, no, I can't. I've only been here a couple of months. Come on, la, choose your song, let's crack on.

I went for 'Hey Jude'. Local band, local favourite. Silence, as I began, standing up on the stage, looking out at this great sea of Scouse faces. Through the first verse, a few nodding heads. Plugging on, getting into my groove now. Hitting the big finale, the *na na na na-na-na na* ... and suddenly all the arms in front of me are up in the air, and they're waving from side to side like a field of wheat in the wind, and everyone's singing it back to me, and my arm is waving around too. *Na na na na-na-na na* ... little Scouse fellas swinging off the chandeliers, the whole pub singing in unison, me feeling like a rock star, all my worries forgotten, not even thinking about goals and missed chances. And that night, and everywhere I went afterwards, random Liverpudlians I'd never met before would start singing 'Hey Jude' when they spotted me. The bloke who looked after the car-park at the training ground, the security men, pedestrians in the city centre, store assistants when I popped to the shops. A glance at my face, the recognition, a smile, and then the song – *na na na na-na-na na* ...

It wasn't the end of my problems. Against Portsmouth, with us leading, we won a penalty. Gerrard picked up the ball to take the spot-kick, and I intervened. I took the ball off him, off our captain and regular, near-flawless penalty taker. I just thought, I've got to get this done.

It was saved. It was a good save, and Bolo Zenden popped in the rebound, but it almost killed me. I barely felt I could celebrate with the rest of the team as they piled on top of Bolo. I trotted over and stood nearby sheepishly.

It helped that we were flying as a team. It helped that everyone at Anfield and in the squad were willing me to score. You'll have one go in off your arse, I was told. Get in the six-yard box, a shot will hit you in the face and wrong-foot the 'keeper. It was all much appreciated, but strip it all away and a striker has to score goals. And I couldn't.

After 1,229 minutes of barren football, it happened. Wigan at home, running at their defence, Kop end at my back. Defenders retreating, crowd screaming – a shot from outside the box, looping up off the centre-back's leg, high over goalkeeper Mike Pollitt, dropping down, the 'keeper backpedalling and flapping at it and the ball at last – at last! – nestling in the net.

I went bananas. Arms out like an airplane, sprinting down the left touchline, Carra jumping all over me, the whole of Anfield bouncing. They initially had it down as an own-goal. Nonsense. Just to be sure, I then ran on to a long ball from the back and popped that one over Pollitt and into the net too. This time it was Stevie who was first to catch up with me as I hared off.

I was away. Goals coming thick and fast suddenly, scoring in the World Club Championship, in the Merseyside derby, against Manchester United. Repaying a little of the faith the club and supporters had shown in me. When the dam breaks you usually get swept along by it. It's rare to score one and then begin another period of prolonged drought.

My experiences a year earlier had helped me. I'm at Southampton, and I can't get a game. I'm 24 years old and I can't get a game, even though we're in the relegation zone and we've just sold our main striker, James Beattie, to Everton, and the bloke ahead of me is 19-year-old Dexter Blackstock, who is not scoring goals and will end the season out on loan to a team two divisions below us. Neither is it just down to one manager who doesn't like me. We've had two already, Paul Sturrock and Steve Wigley, and neither of them liked me. I had come here having struggled to make any sort of impact at Aston Villa, and now I'm not even playing, and I'm starting to think, 'Is the Premier League actually for me?'

Harry Redknapp arrives, a toxic cloud following him up the coast from Portsmouth where they cannot believe he has left to go to their biggest rivals. The first thing he says to me is, 'You're not playing? What the f*** is going on?' The second thing he says to me: 'Right, you and Kevin Phillips are my strikers. You two are going to score the goals to get us out of this f***ing mess.'

I loved it. He made you feel ten feet tall, which you could argue I was almost used to, certainly more than 5'7" Kevin Phillips, but it was still a joy. I scored 16 goals after Christmas, got picked for England and got that move to Liverpool. From the scrapheap to the Champions League winners in six months, and a large part of it down to Harry, plus his son. Jamie and I used to commute down to the south coast in a shared car, and he was the first to champion me for the national side, at a time when most people took one look at my body shape and laughed. He also told his old mates at Liverpool what he thought I could do.

Strikers need team-mates to create chances for them. If you don't have that you're half a player, and your record starts looking less pretty. You need to be in a team that doesn't mind attacking. If you're in a side that prioritises shape and defensive solidity, your goals-per-game stats will start dropping off rapidly. Tony Pulis has one way of playing, and it can leave the striker isolated. The midfield is sitting so far back that you can barely make out their faces. He used to call his defence and his midfield the Ham And Eggers, the stuff that gave his teams their strength. Forwards were known as Tip-Tap Charlies. He'd send us off to do some shooting practice on our own and then work obsessively with the rest of the team on shape. We might play with two wingers, but they would spend most of their energy back grafting too, auxiliary full-backs as much as attackers. You could end up feeling quite lonely out there in games, shuttle-running along the halfway line in the vain hope of a pass to feet from a team-mate within five yards of you. But it worked.

You have spells when even the idea of a drought seems impossible. I had a period in 2006/07 when scoring seemed like the easiest thing in the world. A hat-trick against Arsenal, one with the right foot, one with the left, a header; 18 for Liverpool, 10 for England. Every time I played for the national side I seemed to score. I felt like telling the coaching staff: listen, just get me on the pitch. I had players all round me who were top talents playing well – David Beckham on one side, Joe Cole the other, Frank Lampard and Gerrard behind, Wayne Rooney alongside, Gary Neville at right-back, one of the best deliverers of the ball in the game. For Liverpool, Steve Finnan swinging them in from the right, Harry Kewell from the left. I had a brilliant time.

When you ride a wave like that it's a wonderful feeling. It changes your whole mood. You wake up smiling and you spend each day laughing and joking, not a care in the world, pinching the cheeks of babies and helping old ladies across the road. Nothing can bring you down. The team knows what sort of runs you make, they put the right balls in, you make more of those runs, you score more goals. It's a beautiful circle of trust, the opposite of the over-thinking you do when you're mired in a drought. Football should be an instinctive game. The more you try to make something happen, the less likely it is to work out.

There is no hiding-place when you're not scoring. Midfielders can do other things. They can make passes, tackle, track back, go wide, come inside. A striker just has to score.

Only one good thing comes out of the drought: you realise how great it feels to score a goal. Never again do you take it for granted. You celebrate every single one with glee, because who knows when the next one might come along?

CELEBRATIONS

Talking of which ...

I remember watching Eric Cantona celebrate that wondrous chip he scored against Sunderland at Old Trafford in 1996. Two men beaten with a spin and a turn near halfway, a one-two with Brian McClair, a glance up and a lob so sweet it's as if he's played it with a sand-wedge in his back garden. Goalkeeper Lionel Pérez is looking back in disbelief at the ball nestling in his net. The crowd are screaming and clutching their heads in amazement and jumping around in joy. And Cantona just stands there, collar up, chest puffed out, staring round slowly at the bedlam, the gladiator in his arena. Are you not entertained?

Until that moment I had no time for players who failed to celebrate scoring a goal. You see old footage of George Best, jogging back to the halfway line after some ridiculous feat, pausing only to shake an occasional hand. But that was George Best and that was the 1960s. Now we're different. We can show the world how we really feel. We can let our passion run free. And scoring a goal is the most sensational feeling. The non-celebration only brings frustration. It can kill the goal. It ruins it for the fans. Hang on, is he offside or something? Why is he not as happy as me?

Until Cantona. And so I always thought, should I score a worldie, that I would follow suit. I would stand there with my arms by my side and turn to all corners of the ground and let them salute me. The coolest man in the stadium, the coolest kid in town.

Sadly I have never been the coolest kid in town. I never will be the coolest kid in town. And so when I scored my flick-up-and-volley against Manchester City in 2012, I instead lost it. First I started shouting, 'I've scored a worldie! I've scored a worldie!' Then I ran around for a bit with my hand over my mouth. Then I ran around for a bit longer, kissed my hand and waved it at a television camera, jumped in the air and disappeared under a pile of team-mates.

Afterwards, I thought: why didn't I just stand still? I blew it. I was running so long it was almost like the moment had passed. By the time I stopped everyone had sat down. I massively messed up.

And so I have gathered together my golden rules of celebrating goals. Should the moment come for you, wherever it is – Sunday league, park with mates, back garden against four-year-old daughter – don't blow it like me. Do it right. Take them all with you.

BE INSTINCTIVE

Even the Robot was instinctive. I scored for England against Hungary and I just thought, yeah, Robot!

I'd never done it before in a football scenario. I'd only done it drunk a few times, including at a big party David Beckham held in the build-up to that World Cup. The rest of the England lads were roaring off it. 'Crouchie, you've got to do that in a match!' I didn't think I'd be playing, and I thought it was unlikely that I'd be scoring even if I did get on, so I agreed in that dismissive way you do when you don't think something could actually happen. 'Yeah, yeah, course I will.'

And then I played and I scored and it just happened. And pretty soon I tried to swerve it. It was too calculating. It was too much of a trademark.

I'd watched Robbie Keane with his handspring and pretend shooting guns and thought it was wearing a bit thin. Jürgen Klinsmann did his dive celebration in his very first game for Spurs and then moved on. Alan Shearer always raised his arm and ran off, but that was a pure natural reaction. So too was Ryan Giggs's when he dribbled past half the Arsenal team to win the FA Cup semi-final replay in 1999. I loved the fact that he totally lost the plot. I'm running! I'm skipping! Why am I skipping! I've taken my shirt off! I'm waving it round my head!

I feel the same way about Temuri Ketsbaia when he scored for Newcastle against Bolton. The shirt comes off. The shirt goes into the crowd. He tries to take the boot off – the boot that scored the goal. He loses patience and starts kicking the advertising hoarding instead. Phillipe Albert comes over to hold him back. Albert gets shaken off. The hoarding gets booted again. It doesn't matter that there are two photographers behind it, or there were two photographers behind it until they got scared by this shaven-headed, wild-eyed bundle of joy smashing a long piece of wood into their shins.

Imagine Temuri on a night out. Tremendous. Everything off the cuff, everything slightly unhinged, nothing in the slightest bit predictable. You're never forgetting that one.

LEAD FROM THE FRONT

Scoring a goal away from home is often quite a weird experience. Depending who you're playing for, it can be so quiet you think, hold on, was that offside? It takes so long for the noise from the away fans to reach you. They don't know. No one knows. Has that gone in? There is a frozen moment when you can hear a pin drop. You feel like you shouldn't be celebrating, because the consensus in the place is that the goal was a bad thing. Oh no, I've done a bad thing. Wait, I've done a good thing for us, come on, boys!

As the striker away from home, it's you who can silence the home fans. It's you who the away support are looking to for inspiration and then confirmation. Celebrate it properly. Spell it out.

Bolton used to have a bloke at the Reebok Stadium who would run about at the front of the stand waving a giant flag whenever they scored. Fireworks would go off. It really used to wind me up. I wanted to go in two-footed and take him out. If I could have two-footed anyone in the entire game I would have run past all their players and gone straight for him. Now that's not leadership. But the motivation – shut them up, let your celebration be bigger than theirs – was right. It's why I've got no problem with Leicester blasting out Kasabian when they score at the King Power Stadium, and not only because I love the band. It gets everyone fired up. It wins the celebration. Even the Bolton one worked for you if you liked Bolton.

DON'T FORCE IT

Asamoah Gyan scores for Sunderland. He runs to the corner flag and starts a little celebratory dance – great moves, liquid rhythm, everyone loving it. And then Bolo Zenden arrives alongside him and tries to join in.

It's like your dad dancing. It's worse than your dad dancing, because your dad knows enough about his own dancing that he would only do it at occasional family gatherings and only when he was drunk, and he would never seek out the best mover for miles around and stand next to him and try to join in.

I think Bolo just got carried away. You can see it in his eyes. Halfway through it hits him. What am I doing? I look like a puppet being controlled by someone who has never controlled a puppet before. But then it's too late. He's doing it. Thousands of people are watching. Millions more will see it on *Match of the Day* that night. He's gone. He tried too hard.

The season I was voted QPR's player of the season was a good time for me. I was in the first team for the first time, I was scoring goals, and my mates were in the crowd. A game came round, and with it a dare from the lads: if you score, you've got to do a backstroke swimming celebration. I didn't score in that game. I got injured. The season ended. How, I wondered, can I get this celebration in? So I waited until the awards night, went up to collect my trophy, fans clapping me, and as I waved back at them I did the waving like backstroke.

It looked ridiculous. It looked very little like waving and even less like backstroke. All that sustained me was the thought of six lads at the back of the room in stitches.

The Robot was funny because it wasn't even a good one. It was ridiculous. If I'm spotted in a nightclub I get asked to do it every time. I get asked to do it when they're filming the little Sky graphics for the team line-ups, when you walk out three paces and fold your arms while looking into the camera. Unless you're me, when you get a different instruction. Mate, just walk out and do the Robot, yeah?

I'll always do it behind closed doors. When I go to the Donna Louise Children's Hospice in Stoke it's clearly coming out every time it's requested. I've done it for Prince William when he came to meet the England squad. But I didn't want it to be dull. I didn't do it at the 2006 World Cup, and I felt a bit of a twat even doing it against Jamaica. I scored two goals, Roboted, got a penalty for my hat-trick and then missed it. Dinked it. Tried to be flash.

I was livid with myself. What the hell are you doing? How many opportunities do you get to score a hat-trick for England? When I finally did complete my hat-trick the celebration was very different – no Robot, just a frenzied punching of the air and a self-righteous 'F***ing get in!'

Steve McClaren, at that point Sven's assistant manager, came up to me afterwards. What the hell were you doing? Okay, that's never happening again. Except on drunk nights out. And in a few adverts. And for my 100th Premier League goal.

BE TOPICAL

The celebration that mocks a real-life scandal works in two big ways: it shows you can take the mickey out of yourself, and it – usually – kills the original story stone dead.

Think of Wayne Rooney pretending to knock himself out, shortly after footage emerged of team-mate Phil Bardsley actually knocking him out. Think of Gazza and the dentist's chair at Euro 96, of Jimmy Bullard mock-admonishing the other Hull players after manager

Phil Brown had dished out that on-pitch lecture, of Craig Bellamy teeing off in the Camp Nou after a team night out in Portugal had ended with him whacking John Arne Riise with a golf club.

You turn outrage into comedy. You make yourself the subject of the joke. There will be times when you have a celebration planned that would squash a story and you fail to score, and instead the story keeps snowballing, but at least you had a plan.

Just ensure that all are on board. After Robbie Fowler pretended to snort the touchline having been given awful abuse by Everton fans throughout the Merseyside derby, his manager Gérard Houllier tried to claim that he was in fact miming eating the grass, a ritual he had picked up from Cameroonian defender Rigobert Song. It may have been the worst spin of all time.

EMOTION IS GOOD

You can allow a striker the occasional Cantona moment, but it's the uniqueness of it that makes it iconic. All other goals are far better celebrated with everything that's bursting through your mind. Think of Fowler again, this time diving into the back of the net in front of the Kop end, overwhelmed by the joy of it all. Think of Ian Wright leaping around with that huge grin on his face, throwing his head back and roaring at the heavens. Wright looked like he loved scoring goals. That's how it should be. If you don't enjoy scoring goals there's something missing in your internal circuitry.

Thierry Henry took on the Cantona approach and rolled it out too often for my liking. He almost made it cool not to smile. Maybe if you score as many goals as he did you get a bit bored of it. Or you can celebrate some and give it the too-cool-for-school on others; you've got so many spare you can do whatever you like.

Romelu Lukaku has started doing it. I'll be honest: I think it looks a little arsey. It's fine for a manager to stand there straight-faced and arms folded. It makes him look good, as if he's such a great manager he knew the goal was coming because he planned it that way. But there's no way there's a single supporter in the crowd with their arms across their chest, just nodding their head. Reflect the fans' happiness. Don't squash it.

It doesn't matter how many times I score. It gives me the same surprise every time: stone me, this is amazing! That explosion of emotion has made me do some pretty daft things. Aged 20, playing for Portsmouth against Manchester City at Fratton Park, I was so ecstatic at scoring the winner that I sprinted away to look for my relatives – all City fans – in the main stand. I'd been mulling over the spectacular front-flip celebrations that City's one-time winger Peter Beagrie used to do, and in that moment I decided my gymnastics career should begin. I could find none of the family except my dad, jumping up and down going bananas, initiated the flip and collapsed instead into some weird, unathletic roly-poly. As I came out of the dismount, desperately trying to find my feet but failing, I had to use my hands to push myself back up. Even then I stumbled and almost fell over again. Luckily the clip of it is lost in the Setanta years. The collapse of a lucrative television deal is not always a bad thing.

BE NATURAL

I tried to be cool once. Up front for Southampton, away at Crystal Palace, both of us in the relegation zone. Penalty to us, me to take it. As I walked back to the start of my run-up, Andrew Johnson jogged over and whispered in my ear. You're going to miss this. We know which way you're going.

I stuck it away. Beautiful. And as the lads ran over to celebrate with me, the television cameras zoomed in tight on my face at the exact moment I was shouting back to Johnson. 'No! You're wrong! I don't miss those! Unlucky son!'

Sadly, all everyone at home saw was me slow-motion mouthing the words, 'I don't miss those!' As if I thought I was a hero for scoring from 12 yards against a stationary goalkeeper. As if everyone else routinely missed those but I was somehow stronger and better. 'I don't miss from the penalty spot when the keeper's gone the other way!'

It looked so smug. I looked a fool. When I joined Liverpool a few months later it was one of the first things Jamie Carragher said to me. 'What the hell was all that about? That won't wash here. Don't ever do it again.' All that from me trying to be cool. I realised it wasn't me, and followed Carra's advice.

MESSAGES MAY NEVER BE SEEN

I have no problem with players taking their shirts off in celebration. You can do it at full-time, so why not after a goal? If you're on holiday and you do it round the swimming pool no one minds. If you're down the local leisure centre getting ready for a swim not an eyelid is batted. We're no longer in the Victorian era when a flash of adult flesh was enough to trigger fainting. Time-wasting? It's only two arms into sleeves and head through an easily identified hole. No one's painting a picture of it.

In other words, it's never a booking as far as I'm concerned. However. If you're planning to remove your shirt to display a message on the vest or T-shirt underneath, have a think how likely you are to score. Thierry Henry could walk out with 'Bang goes the 0–0 draw' under his shirt because there was every chance he could make his own prediction come true. Mario Balotelli could ask, 'Why always me?' because he was never not going to be in some sort of scrape and always likely to be on the end of a David Silva or Sergio Agüero pass.

But it doesn't always work out so well. I had a team-mate who popped on a vest with a message, got through the game in question and had to pop it back into his kitbag again. He wore it once more in the next match. No goal. And then the next. Four games in he was having to stick it on discreetly so that none of his team-mates could see it. Six games in he was throwing it to the kitman with the rest of his dirty stuff.

It never did see the light of day. And it makes you wonder: how many political protests, how many touching messages to loved ones, will we never know about, because the wearer hit the post from five yards out or shinned a sitter over the bar?

Other players do it for less creative reasons. John Arne Riise first did his knee-slide top-up celebration after scoring for Liverpool against Manchester United, which you can understand. But when he kept doing it, and leaning back, and really tensing, almost pointing at his abs as he did so, I did begin to wonder who it was designed to please. Then there's Gareth Bale's heart-shape that he makes with his hands. I understand it's for his partner at home. Why not just give her a call afterwards? Not for me.

THINK IT THROUGH

Spontaneity is great. So too is posterity.

David Beckham, 21 years old, scores from the halfway line for Manchester United at Wimbledon, at a time in football history where no one is scoring from the halfway line and Pelé gets massive props for even having tried once. Selhurst Park is in uproar. Beckham raises his arms out wide to bask in it all – and then does a massive spit.

Now you might not know about the spit. Becks got lucky; the television companies realised that (a) they would be showing that goal an awful lot, and that (b) an awful lot of spitting would not be a nice thing to watch. So they re-edited the celebration so that we cut from Neil Sullivan clutching the back of his net in despair to Beckham with a big grin on his face and McClair about to climb on his back. But it illustrates the point perfectly: Will this work? Will it stand repeat viewings?

I score my 100th league goal. Perfect, I think. I'll make a '100' with my face. I'll use my index finger for the 1, my curled fingers for the second 0 and my open mouth for the middle 0.

Already you can see the flaws in this. And then of course because I didn't think it through I butchered it even more. I did the 100 from my perspective. As far as the watching world was concerned I was 001. Like a mate of James Bond's but not as good and definitely not as clever.

Also, because of the juxtaposition of my open mouth and my curled fingers approaching it from the side, it looked like I was making an offensive gesture to my own face. I blew it completely. So to speak.

Thank goodness it was my 100th league goal, not my 100th Premier League one. Because of the dominance of the Premier League it's got lost a little. I'm not even sure that many people at the ground spotted it. But the warning is there. I thought it would look amazing, it looked appalling. And all because I failed to give it the proper attention.

ACCESSORIES ARE OKAY

Do it right and it works for everyone. I think of former Fulham striker Facundo Sava pulling that mask from his sock, Newcastle's Jonás Gutiérrez and his Spiderman mask. It brought a smile, it gave us memories.

It would be too much for me to concentrate on. I've scored, my mind's all over the shop, have I got something stashed down my sock, is it this one, no it was the left one, have I got this thing the right way round, oh balls now I've dropped it.

I did once consider hiding upon my person a small pair of glasses. The seed was planted when I scored a goal for Stoke, ran to the crowd, had a programme thrown at me and turned back to see Jon Walters casually flicking through it. I thought I could score, whip out the glasses, grab a punter's programme and make like a professor reading it. Except I knew it would go wrong. I'd be running at the crowd, fumbling in my socks, hopping towards them, shouting, 'PROGRAMME!' and none of them can understand, partly because they're all shouting and cheering and partly because I'm looking down my own sock, and no one actually has a programme to hand anyway, and I end up shouting at some poor old pensioner on the front row – 'YOU'VE F***ING RUINED IT NOW, YOU IDIOT ...'

YOU CAN MAKE A GOAL WITH A BRILLIANT CELEBRATION

There are good somersaults – Nani's one-legged spin, Victor Moses – and there are the bad. A great goal needs a great celebration; a fine strike can be ruined by one that fails to touch the same heights.

Fabrizio Ravanelli smashed a hat-trick on his debut for Middlesbrough against Liverpool. What garnished it was the sight of him running around with his shirt over his head, even if at the time I was amazed that he never ran into the post. I think back to footage of Marco Tardelli, scoring for Italy in the 1982 World Cup final against Germany and running away with fists clenched and eyeballs on stalks, or Alan Sunderland volleying in the winner in the 1979 FA Cup final, white man's Afro waving in the May breeze as he legged away roaring at the blue sky above. Great goals, but remembered long after for the reaction they triggered too.

And then we have Stuart Pearce for England against Spain at Euro 96. The only penalty shoot-out we've won for 22 years, all that emotion and fear and baggage and relief wrapped up in his scream. You have to love how raw it is. He has no idea what he's doing. It's just all pouring out of him. Beautiful.

THINK OF THE AUDIENCE

In my younger days when my dad would come to every match I played I would routinely celebrate goals by running towards the main stand and looking for him. Trouble was, only rarely did I actually spot him. He's a big man, but in a stand full of cheering people one particular face is hard to find. Once or twice I suddenly saw him, and my subsequent pointing finger and arm of delight appeared as a legitimate celebration in its own right.

And then QPR played Luton in the FA Cup, Dad three rows up behind the goal, a big step down and gap in front of those three rows. Wallop – I score. Right away I spot him. I run towards him. He runs towards me. And then he just disappears – down those three rows and off the big drop. I'm still celebrating but now there's no sign of him. I run back to the halfway line for the restart thinking, is he dead? This could be serious.

I didn't see him again all game. It was hard not to blame myself for his spectacular exit. You want to share that wonderful moment with all around you but you need to do it the right way. Many years later, Francesco Totti pulled it off with the Roma ultras, grabbing a phone and doing a selfie with the fans all screaming and going wild behind him. He even does the selfie face – eyes wide, 'ooh check this!' expression. Absolute textbook.

THINK OF THE AFTERMATH

All the way through West Ham's march to the 2006 FA Cup final, their players would do a little victory dance at the end of full-time. Anton Ferdinand would do it, Nigel Reo-Coker would do it. Even manager Alan Pardew would do it. At half-time in the final, Liverpool 2–1 down, it was mentioned in the dressing-room: we have to beat this lot, we can't see them dancing round with the Cup in an hour's time. That dance may have delighted the West Ham players. But it was inspiration for us, and arguably they should have realised that. Pardew was at it again in the 2016 final, grooving on the touchline when Jason Puncheon put Crystal Palace 1–0 up over Man United. He ended up regretting that one too.

Then there is Andreas Möller, before the Euro 96 semi-final just another German striker to England supporters. Then he scores the winning penalty in the shoot-out, and celebrates by standing on the Wembley turf with his fists on his hips and his chest puffed out and a look on his face that is half-taunt and half-outrage. It's the same pose and expression he would be doing in his speedos and flip-flops if his kid was messing around in the pool in his back garden. In the context of the match it was too. In every England fan's favourite tournament he had broken everyone's hearts. He had ruined everything. And his celebration made it all so, so much worse.

THERE IS A FINE LINE BETWEEN BRAVERY AND FOOLISHNESS

I understand that celebrating in front of the opposition fans is frowned upon. I was playing in the match when Gary Neville ran to the Liverpool fans after Rio Ferdinand's late winner at Old Trafford in 2005. None of us will forget Emanuel Adebayor scoring for Manchester City against his old club Arsenal and going the length of the Etihad to knee-slide in front of the furious away support.

I understand it. But I understand too the feeling of having taken so much stick from those same supporters all day long that you just want to shove it back. You've been called horrific things. Your parents have been called horrific things. When you've gone down the wing or stood near the post on a corner you have heard things about your partner that no one should have to hear.

So sometimes we react. Beckham, getting hammered at Stamford Bridge, copping all sorts about his wife, scoring and then giving the Chelsea fans the old shush. The cupping of one hand to the ear, the curving of the celebratory run so it takes you past the noses of the same people who've been screaming that you lack the skill to score just the sort of goal you've lashed in.

Sometimes players get it horribly wrong. I'm not sure Paul Gascoigne really understood the significance of what he was doing when he pretended to play a flute in the Old Firm match of 1998, although the death-threat he says he received from the IRA afterwards may have focused the mind a little. And sometimes supporters get it wrong too. You should probably be able to absorb the pain of an opposition goal without needing to wave two fingers in the scorer's face. Or a single finger, as has become increasingly popular. We all like goals. And if it's a goal you personally do not like, you can be certain that someone with the same primary leisure interest as you will be absolutely loving it.

MANAGE YOUR REACTION

Look, managers should be able to celebrate. They have as much invested in a team as anyone. David Pleat in his tan suit skipping across the turf at Maine Road in 1983 as Luton stayed in the top flight? For me, watching that clip is amazing. You try moving like that, like a man who has never skipped before, like a man who has never run around before with both arms in the air at the same time. It's impossible. I have the same feelings towards Alex Ferguson's run onto the pitch at Old Trafford as United came from behind to beat Sheffield Wednesday in May 1993, Brian Kidd leaping onto the turf beside him and pummelling the air with delight and relief. They've completely lost it, and why not? United have been waiting 26 years to win back the league title. They've just got within a sniff of it.

But you can't milk it. You can't force it. There is a fine line between genuinely buzzing off a goal and making it all about you. You can't take a goal off a player. You shouldn't try to attract the cameras to you when they should be on the scorer and his team-mates.

Antonio Conte jumping into the Chelsea fans worked because it seemed authentic. José Mourinho's knee-slide down the touchline at Old Trafford when winning there with Porto in 2004 goes in the same category. Those who turn to the opposition bench and give it large? Unpleasant. Pardew dancing? Unnecessary. Sven-Göran Eriksson's little clap was fine. Bobby Robson's jig after David Platt's volley against Belgium at Italia 90? Delightful. Sam Allardyce's attempted duet with Jay-Jay Okocha at Bolton? Less so.

DON'T BROWN-NOSE

There is only one condition under which you should celebrate with your manager on the touchline on scoring a goal: when you have celebrated with your team-mates first. Running straight to the bench rather than to your fellow players or to the fans will get you massive abuse in the dressing-room. Rightly so; it makes the skin crawl.

What is nice is the sight of a manager shoving a player back onto the field, buzzing their head off about the goal but trying not to show it. Jürgen Klopp works that move, and it looks good because it reflects what he's like as a character. Just don't aim for your boss first. You are on the shop floor, not with management.

INTERVIEWS

One moment even your own team-mates aren't that bothered talking to you after games. The next you score a few first-team goals and you've suddenly got a television camera in your face and a microphone up your snout and a bloke asking you something no one's ever asked before and you're looking back at him with absolutely no idea of what you're supposed to say.

In the distant days before social media allowed you to talk straight to the supporters, television and the newspapers carried so much weight. If they asked you to do something you did it. If you were a 19-year-old kid and your manager Gerry Francis told you to do it you didn't even consider saying no, even if it was literally going to make you look like a plonker.

I was at QPR. Gerry took me aside after training: a paper is sending a reporter over to do a piece with you for their 'Goals' football supplement. I turned up at Loftus Road to see a full camera crew, a yellow Robin Reliant and a pile of clothes usually seen on Rodney Trotter. This is strange, I thought. Stand by the car with those tower blocks on Shepherd's Bush Green in the background, they said. This will look great, they said.

If anyone tried that now I would tell them where to go. Back then I had no idea I could. I certainly saw none of the fee for it, only the big double-page spread a few days later with 'EXCLUSIVE' smeared across the top and me as a gormless idiot, Uncle Albert and Del Boy in a little box off to the side. I used to get Rodney songs from away fans after that. Triffic.

It couldn't happen now. Kids coming through club academies are given practice sessions in front of cameras. They're warned that what seems a funny tweet sent to a mate aged 16 will reappear as back-page headlines should they make it to the top. We shouldn't see what you might call a Micah, where a young player buzzing after scoring a big goal uses language live on air that was okay 30 seconds ago in the dressing-room but will now turn him into a meme and generate a torrent of complaints to the BBC.

Maybe all this media training has killed the classic footballer's cliché. Once a camera's light comes on you can feel like you have to keep talking. And so you keep going, except the point you wanted to make has been and gone, and so you fall back on words that allow you to desperately think of another, or phrases that mean nothing while you try to come up with some that hold sense.

Twenty years ago you couldn't move on *Match of the Day* for over the moons. Now you'll be lucky to hear one a year. It's as if we're no longer impressed with mere lunar travel. In a post-*Interstellar* world it's all about travel through time or the fourth dimension. We're officially over over the moon. Gone with it too is 'at the end of the day'. I never worked out why the end of the day was more important than the start. Now, in a global game, in an era of 24-hour news and a sleepless interconnected world, there is no end of the day. It's all just non-stop hours rolling by. It's gone.

Each man has their own subconscious favourite. Mine are 'obviously' and 'you know'. It's obviously like a holding-pattern for my thoughts, like a pause, you know, while you work out what you want to say, obviously, in the interview. As a kid I loved Peter Beardsley; he played like the coolest man on the planet. My mates and I used to walk up from Ealing to Wembley just to watch him play for England, running through all those subways under the A40 and North Circular to get there on time for kick-off. His cliché will never leave me: every sentence would start with 'But, er ...' said as if he was thinking longingly about his favourite toast topping. He also favoured an 'unbelievable', another of the great interview losses. We've seen so many extraordinary things now that maybe we just accept everything that happens. In a world where you can talk to your stereo speakers and get an answer in return or grow human ears on the back of mice there is now nothing left beyond our imagination.

Sick as a parrot? Dead as a doornail. In its place has come the new breed: 'We go again'; 'The fans were terrific, on to the next one.' It is the era of the technical cliché – 'We were compact as a team', 'We executed well today', 'Our shape was good'. No one talks merely about a team's formation. Instead it's how they set themselves up. When I was a kid not once did I make reference to 'the final third', and with good reason; a football pitch has been split into halves since 1897.

A new breed, and a new medium in which to spout them. Twitter and Instagram have their own specific clichés. 'Work hard get stronger', accompanied by a gif of a player doing sit-ups in his kitchen. '#nodaysoff', from a player you know from personal experience has loads of days off. 'BetterNeverStops', when you've seen in training that better never starts.

Some clichés hang around for good reason. It makes sense to take each game as it comes, at least until the point where fixture congestion forces you to play two concurrently. If you and each of your team-mates do 'win your battles', as a captain will often instruct you, you're likely to win the match, unless one of you loses his battle in such spectacular fashion that it overwhelms everything else.

Other clichés just don't make sense. There are no easy games, except there are. Take nothing for granted, except you can: three teams will be relegated from the Premier League each season; England won't win the World Cup; the sun will come up each morning, even if in the north-west of England you might not know until at least midday. 'We have to earn the right to play.' You literally have. You're a professional footballer.

'Let's win the first tackle.' Why? What if it's at the other end of the pitch and nothing comes from it? Why not win the tackles that would otherwise lead to the conceding of a goal? 'Who wants this more, us or them?' I honestly can't be sure, I haven't spoken to them. 'Let's win the 50-50s.' Why not be a little more ambitious? Why not win the 40-60s?

Players who begin a personal opinion by saying, 'For me ...' Who else is it for? Pundits who talk about who won the mind games. It's the physical game that counts. You don't get a battling draw in the mind games and pick up a crucial point away from home.

Looking back, despite the *Only Fools and Horses* stitch-up, I had it easy at QPR and Portsmouth. Even in the Premier League with Aston Villa I didn't have to do much. Then I got called up by England and it blew my mind. I went from doing the *Southampton Echo* and Solent Radio, one chat with one chap from each, all wrapped up in 20 minutes, to walking into a media centre like a barn and seeing 30 TV crews, 15 radio stations, 50 or 60 print journalists and reporters from every major European nation. Suddenly the local paper is the *Daily Mail*, the *Mirror* and the *Telegraph*. TV was daunting because of the lights and the heat, but at least your meaning could not be misinterpreted. If you said Wayne Rooney had been a disgrace in training, your grin made it clear you were joking. Say the same thing in a huddle with the tabloids and it could be a back-page storm. I would look out at that vast sea of faces and think, right, don't be the one who makes the headlines here. 'Yeah, obviously, you know …'

When you play for England, everything you do is out there. If you play for a while, a switch goes and the transformation becomes permanent. You never come out of it, even when your playing days come to an end. That team I joined was as high-profile an England XI as there has been, not just for their football (and most of them finished as Champions League winners) but for their partners and what they did away from the pitch. Rooney, David Beckham, Steven Gerrard. Frank Lampard, Michael Owen, Rio Ferdinand. My mum can still name 15 of that 2006 World Cup squad. The players in the 2018 squad were arguably just as good, but before the tournament began the same public profile was not there. My mum was down to five.

The build-up to the World Cup in Germany was insane. As Sven-Gören Eriksson became bogged down in tabloid scandals, some players would refuse to do any media. Ashley Cole, even before the reaction to that famous line in his autobiography, wouldn't go near a journalist. Instead I would be rolled out again and again, seen as a good-news story because I had gone from being booed at the start of my England career to scoring a hat-trick in the build-up, the Robot briefly distracting reporters from Fake Sheikh stings and the manager's bedroom adventures. You would be taken in a car after training to the media centre, press officers on either side of you, telling you to talk about this but not that, to make sure you got these two points across, to repeat this dull sentence when you were asked about Sven's morals. It wasn't me. I'd be honest with the handlers: stop trying to steer me, you're making things worse. Just let them ask me questions. It'll be fine, you know. I'm just going to talk, obviously.

Sven didn't really need any help from me. I've never seen a man less affected by having his private life detonated by the national media. He used to laugh at the tabloid journalists doing it. He was almost intellectually intrigued by their fascination with his private life. His successor Steve McClaren took the criticism he received too much to heart. It's one of the unbreakable rules of the job that an England manager's tenure never ends well, but encouraging the team coach driver to run over the *Daily Star*'s chief football writer is unlikely to help.

Even when Sven was caught out by the *News of the World*, talking about taking the Villa job and bringing Beckham with him, he carried on like nothing had happened. When he finally mentioned it, it was with bemusement. 'I have heard a few people talking about this nonsense. You are crazy in the country, you are all mad.' That worked for us players. We thought, actually, it is a load of rubbish. Who gives a monkey's?

At one point a television channel put together a dramatic reconstruction of his affair with Ulrika Jonsson. Someone brought along a copy to the England camp, and a crowd gathered to watch it in the physios' room, lots of jokes and laughter flying round at how bad the acting was and how little the actors actually looked like the lead couple. And then, when it ended, a Swedish voice sighing from the back of the room: 'It was not like this …'

Out in Germany the relationship between news reporters and the team disintegrated. The team was up a hill above Baden-Baden, the press down in the town in the same hotel as the families. By now the press included not just football writers and newshounds who had nothing to do with sport but gossip mags like *OK*, *Hello* and *Grazia*. Each time Victoria Beckham, Colleen Rooney or Cheryl Cole flicked an eyelash it would be a story. Paparazzi took photos of the wives and girlfriends round the swimming pool. Shop assistants would be interviewed about which WAG had bought which pair of shoes and paid how much.

When we went down the hill to see our partners and families we would be sucked into it. You would go out for a meal, see a middle-aged married couple sit down at a nearby table speaking German, and get a few things quietly off your chest. The next day everything you had said was in the paper. The nice German couple would turn out to be English reporters who had recorded your entire evening on hidden microphones. My mum and dad were out one night with some of the other parents when Dad saw a photographer lurking near the door of the bar with another man. As Colleen walked towards the exit the photographer muttered, 'Go, go, go,' and his accomplice deliberately bumped into Colleen so she stumbled and lost her footing. Hey presto – a big photo splash in the paper, the headline all about Colleen being so drunk she couldn't stand up.

It was madness. The girls were going out, the families were going out, the press were following them like hyenas. Meanwhile we would go back to our hotel on the hill after games and find our entertainment was Sven's 68-year-old assistant Tord Grip playing his accordion in the bar.

That was maybe the peak of it all. It's less aggressive than that now, not least because declining circulations mean the tabloids have lost some of their power. Fans will go straight to a player's social media accounts or those of the club they support. That's not all good news. It used to be that you had to speak to the papers because you didn't want to piss them off. Now some players think it doesn't matter. They will walk past reporters after games with their headphones on, pretending they can't hear the questions, even though their music isn't turned on. The phone trick is pulled – putting your smartphone to your ear and pretending to be deep in conversation. Always tricky when someone calls you in the middle of that ruse and the ringtone blares out for all to hear. Then there's the Thomas Müller approach, realising in a panic that your phone's in the bottom of your bag and so holding your passport to your ear instead and trying to style it out with a grin and a wink.

The higher wages have become for players, the less they want to talk to the press. The egos are bigger. The necessity seems less. Actually it's almost more. We get paid those wages in part because of the amount of media coverage the game gets. As the scrap for television rights gets more intense, each company will want their guaranteed access to players. If Facebook come in, they'll want it like the NFL: cameras inside dressing-rooms, reporters waiting for you by your peg. You can't enjoy the money if you don't acknowledge its source.

And you can enjoy it. Be a robot after scoring goals but not in interviews. Be yourself, not someone else's idea of who you should be. You don't want players to trip up but you want them to be honest and you don't want them to be scared to say something. Roy Keane was iconic in part because he spoke his mind. Look at the passion that Jürgen Klopp speaks with. His bond with Liverpool supporters is more intense because they can see that he cares. They can see who he really is.

If you don't like the way you are being written or talked about, steer clear of it. If you've lost 5–0, you know that Gary Neville and Jamie Carragher are going to be dissecting your failings on *Monday Night Football*. You're already aware of your failings. You lost 5–0. Swerve it. In the same way I'll only watch *Match of the Day* if I played well. If you've had a shocker the last thing you want on a Saturday night is an old mate telling everyone to watch your ghastly miss again. If you've had a great game you might watch it to discover that your best three moments haven't made the final edit. Your drag-back, that rasping shot from distance and the time you tracked back to rob the centre-half in possession are all lost to the mainstream audience. You know they happened. Be content with that.

I understand not all are naturals. Carlton Cole is a lovely bloke but could occasionally have that brain-freeze we all experience when you look like a man trying to remember the alphabet in Japanese. Nigel Reo-Coker decided to complain about the way he had been treated by West Ham fans after a badly timed transfer request by being interviewed in a barber's shop, surrounded by his entourage, having his hair minutely adjusted. As vibes go it was a stinker. It's harder still when you've just arrived in England and you're struggling to make sense in a new language, even more so when your new English team-mates have been teaching you rude words when you've asked them instead for simple phrases. Sorry, boys.

I once tried learning Spanish myself, to prepare myself for the inevitable call from Barcelona or Real Madrid. Key phrases like '*Buen toque para un hombre grande*', should you not already know the translation for 'Good touch for a big man'. I couldn't stick it; the nice woman who was teaching me said she would start with the difficult stuff, the verb endings, so the rest of it would be easy, but she got it the wrong way round. I couldn't get through the hard bit. I told her – if only you'd got me thinking it was a breeze you'd have had me hooked.

Like most failed linguists I did regret my lack of perseverance. Jonathan Woodgate threw himself into it when he went to Real, and got a lot of respect in Madrid as a result of busting the stereotype of the lazy Englishman abroad. When he got back to Spurs he was involved in the group banter with the native Spanish speakers like Wilson Palacios and Giovani dos Santos. Watching them laughing and joking, looking like they were having a great time, I felt like I was missing out on half the fun. When Fabio Capello took over with England he told everyone he would have the language nailed within six months. He said that in Italian, obviously, and he continued in the same tongue. I was never really convinced he was genuinely trying. With Fabio it was always his way that was right, and others who had to bend to him. I contrast that with what Mauricio Pochettino has done since he arrived in England, unable to speak except through an interpreter. As a young, hungry manager he made the effort, and has become a much more effective coach as a result. We all know how it ended with Capello.

The post-match interview is never easy. I always look half-dead after a game, and it's hard to keep your composure when your most childish team-mate is making obscene gestures in your eye-line. We're not all Bolo Zenden, making sure you've brushed your hair before the lens swings your way. But be creative. Work in a strange word that your partner has bet you can't: whale, redemption, garlic. Quote a song lyric and see if you can get away with it. Be yourself, no matter what they say.

HOUSES

There used to be a generic footballer's house. Mock Tudor, detached, out beyond the orbital motorway but never into the sticks. Bit of land, swimming pool with concrete paving-stone surrounds, snooker room with corner bar. A large and aggressive dog, a large and aggressive sports car. Far from the sort of streets and bars that other twenty-something men of the same background would be enjoying, possibly a subsequent sense of alienation, softened a little by spending all those spare afternoons potting long reds while wearing flip-flops and a free tracksuit.

That was then. That was the 1980s and first half of the 1990s. Now it's bigger. The Tudor beam has been replaced by the glass wall. The snooker table has gone, superseded by pool table, arcade games, huge flatscreen and PlayStation. The standard of cars on the drive has improved.

Walk up that drive, should the large security gates have been opened internally to let you in. There may be some distance to travel to the front door. Step through the double doors. Take off your shoes to enjoy the feel of cool stone underfoot.

There may well be a fish tank ahead of you. I had one team-mate who spent more on his than most people would on a small apartment. It had sharks in it. Genuine actual sharks. It was like walking into the lair of a Bond villain.

The kitchen will be vast and open-plan. There will be cupboards that have never been opened and utensils that have only rarely been located. Walk through the fold-away patio doors and out into the garden, a pool to one side of you, a five-a-side pitch to the other. The pitch is clearly for the kid in the dad rather than the dad's kid. I have hosted barbecues and spent the entire afternoon playing five-a-side with the other dads, none of our kids in the slightest bit interested. Spot the basketball hoop above the garden trampoline, and spend even more time trying to clip a football into the basket from 30 yards. Make sure that your mate films it on his phone just as you float one straight in. I'm sure you've seen the evidence on my Twitter.

There may be an orangery. You may wonder what an orangery is. It's not a word that impacted on my youth, but Wayne Rooney is now among those to build one at his house. I first became aware of them when Gareth Barry got married in one. It was basically a conservatory. An ornate one. I didn't see any actual oranges to pluck from a tree and enjoy as a half-time snack. Perhaps they were out of season.

To think that during my first season playing second-tier football I was still in the bedroom at my mum and dad's in Ealing that I had grown up in. Trophies on the shelves, classics of the genre, a square black plastic base, a silver-painted footballer on top, possibly caught in the act of volleying, the ball sat beautifully on his laces. It was only a ten-minute walk to QPR's training ground but my mum still used to drop me off. On one bedroom wall was a photo of me playing against Arsenal, running alongside Patrick Vieira, looking like I was bossing him. Mum had stuck it up.

My first actual property, two bedrooms on the marina in Portsmouth. It would have taken you about 20 seconds to work out it was the abode of a man just out of his teens, living on his own. There were no pictures on the wall. There was one large couch and one larger television. The couch was too big to get through the door, and was only there because Kev the Kitman (the former boxer) managed to carry it on his back up a ladder and heave it onto the balcony.

There was very little going on in the kitchen. One cupboard contained some stir-in sauce and some dried pasta. Every now and then I'd throw a bit of chicken from the fridge into a saucepan with them to make Fusilli alla Crouchi.

There were three of us Portsmouth players living close by – me, Shaun Derry and Courtney Pitt. Realising our culinary skills were lacking, that we were falling back on too many takeaways too often, we decided to begin a prototype version of *Come Dine with Me*, where we would all shop together and then take it in turns hosting an evening meal. There was no great leap forward. My meals were still pasta-based; my best nights were when I actually got as far as chopping something up, whether that was a piece of meat or a solitary tomato. Dezza was usually voted the winner, but it was more that he was third worst rather than the new Heston.

The players with kids tended to live in Fareham, and when you went to their houses it was like entering an entirely different form of habitation. There would be a vase of flowers in the hall, walls that had actual pictures in frames hanging on them, a fridge with things within their sell-by date on every shelf. At my place I had no idea where the saucepans were. Instead I had an inflatable goal with a little ball. We used to have penalty competitions after we'd washed up. Three men, having already played football all day, eating pasta with a small amount of chopped tomato and then playing football some more. In a child's inflatable goal.

I was miles off it. I didn't have a clue. At least I sort of realised, and got a cleaner in twice a week for the bathroom. And the overall vibe was great. When the sun was out down there, standing on the balcony looking out over the yachts in the marina, stir-in sauce drying on your chin, you almost felt like you could be in Monaco rather than Portsmouth.

As the money coming into the game grew, so did the size of the houses young footballers could live in. I went round to the house of one young lad who was playing for Manchester City. From the outside it looked like a family home. It was big enough for three families, yet inside there was just him and his mates. In two rooms it was total carnage: the bedroom, where the bed clearly never got made; and the games room, where it looked like an amusement arcade in a seaside town – racing games, fighting games, air hockey, American pool, half-eaten packets of crisps, half-drunk cans of Coke. He really needed a two-bed apartment. That was all he was using. The other rooms were like unexplored parts of some vast jungle. Here be dragons, here be a guest suite with underfloor heating.

There is no real need for footballers to grow up. You can wear shorts all day. Someone else takes care of all your logistics. Most of your meals are made for you. The ones that aren't feel like an enjoyable novelty.

That whole vibe is summed up in the games room. I've now grown out of computer games, being almost 40. But even the players with kids can still be found spending their evenings playing *FIFA* on the PlayStation, beating themselves at pool and winning on fruit machines that can never pay out.

Back in the day I was a huge fan of *Championship Manager*. I felt like a pioneer; I got into it before any of my mates. The strange thing was when I started to play in real life against people I had managed on the computer. Then I started picking myself in my own teams. When my mates did get on board they would forward me the emails the game sends you: 'Peter Crouch hands in transfer request'. With it would come the outrage – who the hell do you think you are, messing up my team with your diva behaviour?

You can walk into another player's house these days and get a slight sense of déjà vu. Don't I recognise those curtains? Haven't I seen that wallpaper before? Then you realise it's because the same interior designers tend to do everyone's houses. Because of the money sloshing round the Premier League, you shortly after realise it might be one of the many who have tried to mug you off over the past 15 years. Most of the spiel begins with a simple, 'This is my fee up front, all the furniture and fittings I'll get at cost for you.' It ends with a nagging sense that 'cost price' is a concept subject to massive hyperinflation. The only certainties are that it will cost a lot and that you will be the one paying the price. And it works, since lots of footballers have no idea whether a couch costs £100 or £5,000. They have no idea what it costs to move an interior wall or to install a chandelier in a room that, because it has a golf simulator and table-tennis table in, probably doesn't need one.

As with many aspects of the game, the influence of the foreign stars has improved us. A few years back I lived in Hampstead, and you would always be bumping into current and former Arsenal players – Santi Cazorla, Olivier Giroud and Nacho Monreal, Robert Pirès and Thierry Henry. All the English boys were out in Hertfordshire – which is lovely, but not really where a young man usually wants to end up. You grow up there and you might go back there when you settle down, but in between you more normally want the big city. It's all about temptation: French players pop out for cappuccino at 10pm, we go and get out of our minds at 6pm. The cosmopolitan continental player can handle the buzz and sin of the Smoke. The English player has to get out beyond the suburbs to avoid all possible excitement.

There are exceptions. At Spurs our Brazilian midfielder Sandro enjoyed the good things in life, and the unusual: during his time in England he became obsessed with darts, had boards shipped back to his mum's in Brazil and began an unlikely friendship with oche legend Bobby George. His parties were treble 20 all the way. He'd show you videos on his phone of what looked like a full-on club rave – DJs waving records in the air, fireworks going off, girls in bikinis, him dancing on a podium with his top off. You'd ask him which club he'd been in. He'd look surprised and tell you it was his lounge. Then he'd fall asleep – on the team bus, in the changing-room, at whichever point his body stopped moving. I often wondered how the house sale went when he moved on to play in Turkey. 'This charming six-bed property has three bathrooms, a large kitchen-diner, a swimming pool and a number of strange stains on the living-room ceiling. And full sound-proofing, so if you scream when you find something under the carpets no one will ever be able to hear you.'

I had the chance, when at Southampton at the age of 24, to buy a double-fronted house bang on the green in Richmond upon Thames. It was in a bit of a state – it was an old nursing home – and needed a fair amount of work doing, but I loved the idea of it. A kid from Ealing, moving up in the world, the green in summer all games of cricket and Frisbee, great pubs across the way, the river to stroll down. Instead everyone around me advised me to move out to Surrey. You'll get more for your money out there, Peter, it'll be nice and quiet. And so that's what I did, against all my instincts, even with Richard Ashcroft from the Verve in the house next door, me heading out to the stockbroker belt like John Lennon moving out to Weybridge in 1964 for his Fat Elvis period while Macca stayed in town digging all the avant-garde scene.

I was guilty of it again years later, when I joined Stoke and got a massive house in the village of Prestbury. It was just me and Abbey. We didn't need a massive house. Why didn't I just get a small one? Some players go all-in on buying when they really should just rent too. I knew one lad who had a lovely place off the King's Road in Chelsea, moved to a club in the north and bought a Spanish-style villa. He only made a few appearances for the club but he still can't sell the villa.

Us footballers flock together. People tell us where to live and we live there. We see a team-mate in an area and think, I'm with him every morning and every Saturday afternoon, why not man-mark him at all other times too? There must be more footballers per square mile in Alderley Edge and Prestbury in Cheshire than anywhere else in the world. Manchester United players, City players, Liverpool and Everton players, Stoke, Burnley. There are these weird communities in little pockets across the country, radiating out from training grounds and stadiums: Liverpool legends in Southport and Formby, Tottenham old-boys in Broxbourne, West Ham in Brentwood, Arsenal in Cockfosters, Villa in Solihull or Sutton Coldfield. There used to be a little gated cul-de-sac in Liverpool where every one of the Spanish players ended up living – Pepe Reina, Luis García, Fernando Torres. It was like a version of Earl's Court for Iberian millionaires.

Yarm is an otherwise unexciting village on the River Tees. But because it's pleasant, and within driving distance to Middlesbrough's training ground at Rockliffe Park and the Riverside Stadium, almost all of the glamourpuss players signed by the club ended up living there. Juninho, Emerson, Gaizka Mendieta, Neil Cox – they all became Yarmites, and thus a sleepy place of 8,000 inhabitants now has three designer clothes boutiques as well as the more predictable staples like a small post office and village stores. Egyptian striker Mido bought a huge farm just outside, with 50 acres of land, a lake and a fishing river running through it. He already had a place in Knightsbridge, but being a footballer, decided he needed a farm too despite having no experience of animal husbandry and a nagging sense that he would soon be sent on loan to Wigan.

I did a coaching course with him years later. He's still got the farm, mainly because no one wants to buy it, at least at the price he paid for it. He's now a manager back in Egypt, which makes hands-on farming even more difficult, but apparently his family love it. For two weeks every summer he brings his kids over to the north-east of England and they run wild in his pastures and paddocks. They love it so much they pester him for the other 50 weeks of the year. 'Daddy, can we leave the beaches and guaranteed sunshine of the Med and go back to Middlesbrough, please, please ...'

You have to be careful. There are a few player liaison officers at clubs who will work a little margin into their roles when a young foreign player arrives in town. The kid doesn't have a clue where he should live. He doesn't know any estate agents or understand how the British property market works. So the unscrupulous liaison officer will point them towards a particular company or property and skim a little cream off the top of the deal. I've had it myself, years ago – being taken to a house, thinking, they seem very keen on showing me this one and very few others, looking at the particulars and wondering, why are all these properties being marketed by the same man?

In some areas the only person who can afford to buy a house a footballer is selling is another footballer, which doesn't necessarily make the process easier. During the first few years of my time at Stoke, Abbey and I rented a house in Alderley Edge. The previous occupant had been single, and the place still felt like a bachelor's pad. The master bedroom had a bed the size of a six-yard box and a shag-pile carpet so deep it was like walking through thick grass. Abbey took one look and refused to sleep in there. She was too freaked out by the thought of what might have taken place within those walls. We had to sleep in the second bedroom and use the main one as a guest room.

Then there was former Chelsea and Spurs midfielder Scott Parker, who spent ages building and kitting out the house of his dreams in Weybridge. I knew how much effort he had put into it and I knew how much he loved it, so I was surprised to be driving through the town shortly after he had finished it to see him and his three kids coming out of a flat.

'Scotty, is that you? What's happened to the house?'

'Yeah, Torres has bought it.'

'You what?'

Torres, signed from Liverpool by Chelsea, had apparently taken one look at the place on moving south and said, yep, I want that one. Scott hadn't put it on the market. Torres had just offered such a crazy amount he was unable to turn it down. That's what a £50m move can do for you.

Scotty had no choice but to shrug. 'Okay, I'll just start all over again ...'

TRANSFERS

This book is called *How to Be a Footballer* for a reason. I've tried to take you inside this crazy world of ridiculous houses, cars and bizarre tattoos, a world where nothing may make sense to the non-footballing person.

But there is one part of our world so weird, so cloak and dagger, that even those of us at the centre of it all aren't really sure what's happening. The only thing you can say with any certainty about transfers is that there will always be someone, somewhere, who is having the wool pulled over their eyes. It might be the selling club. It might be the buying club. It could be the manager. It's often the player, and it's the agent more often than you might think. Frequently it's the fans.

Who gets what? Where does all the money go? It's like watching a match with a telescope. You can see some bits perfectly, but never the whole thing at the same time, and by the time you've worked out what's going on in one part, the scene where your eye fell earlier may have completely changed again.

Who makes them happen? Same answer. Sometimes the club you're at. Sometimes the club that fancies you. Sometimes an agent, who may never tell the player involved that it was his work all along.

When a salesman works on commission it can be the commission that makes him work. If they're pushing you to one particular club, can you be sure that you're hearing about all the offers on the table, or only the one offering them the juiciest slice? Is that the right club for you or him? Should you actually be moving at all, when you're perfectly happy where you are, in a side that works for your specific skill-set, with a manager who understands what you do?

My first transfer was from Spurs to QPR for £60,000. I still have no idea how that figure was arrived at. I certainly had no control over it. I think the sale happened because Tottenham's director of football David Pleat didn't fancy me. I was a teenager, I'd never played for the first team. QPR manager Gerry Francis told me things were better sorted without agents, which he would, so I went down and signed the first contract they put in front of me. My dad read through it once. 'Go on, just sign it.' I would be on slightly more than I was at Spurs, but it was still only a couple of hundred pounds a week. I was the lowest paid player at the club by a long way. I wasn't complaining, because I had achieved nothing in the game.

Eight months later I was put up for sale at £1.2m. An increase made sense. I'd scored goals for QPR in the Championship. But why £1.2m? Why not £1.1m, or £1.3m? I'm asking you like you might know the answer. I certainly don't. You're selling me? Right.

This time my agent was involved, although I was once again perfectly happy with the salaries being offered. More intriguing was how I should choose between the three clubs who were interested. They were all Championship clubs: Portsmouth, Burnley, Preston. Burnley manager Stan Ternent arranged to meet me halfway between Turf Moor and Loftus Road, which turned out to be a service station on the M6. Being sold the club, being told how big their ambitions were while sitting in a Little Chef seemed a touch ironic, although I did love Stan.

There was no all-day breakfast and pot of tea from David Moyes at Preston. He settled for a phone call, and we talked for about an hour. It's like a courtship. You want to be made to feel special. And the most effort came from Graham Rix at Pompey, freshly arrived from working impressively with young players at Chelsea. He had worked out what my strengths were and he had a tangible plan. I'm going to buy Mark Burchill and Courtney Pitt, I'm going to have two fast runners up on either side of you. You'll be the tip of my diamond.

I knew that was the best way to use me. It still is. I knew too that Portsmouth was only an hour and a half from west London, where I'd spent all my life. I was still living at my mum and dad's, still sleeping in the same bedroom I'd had as a kid. So the stuff that all teenagers think about came into play. Right, if I go to Pompey I can still get my mum to do my washing.

The move came with a dose of reality. There is still the urban myth that players personally receive 10 per cent of any transfer fee they're involved in. Maybe before big wages came in that was true. You went for £150,000, you got £15,000 spread over four years. Not any more, although I didn't mind. I had enough to put a deposit down on my first house, a two-bed place on the marina for £217,000. Lovely job, I thought – a great place to live, goals flying in, super weather, a manager who rates me.

Which is where football intervened. Nothing is forever in football. Nothing is immune to the power of the transfer. Rix was sacked. Harry Redknapp moved into his seat. And pretty much the first thing he said to me was, you're off to Aston Villa.

No say in it once again, just a fresh start in a new place with people I'd never met before. What will Birmingham be like, I wondered? Where should I live? Am I ready for the Premier League?

Villa wanted to persuade me. As negotiations went on over the contract I was put up at the Belfry Hotel. My room was incredible. The Brabazon Suite, overlooking the 18th green, the Ryder Cup due to come to a thrilling crescendo there in just a few months. I walked in with my dad and thought, this is unreal. My dad winked at me. Oh yes, son. We've arrived now ...

I signed. I drove back to the hotel. I walked past reception. Hello, sir, the club have asked us to move you to a different room. Oh, okay. Key in the door. Walking in. Almost banging my nose on the opposite wall, the only thing stopping me tripping over the single bed being the ironing board that took up the remaining floorspace.

It was smaller than the bathroom in the Brabazon Suite. It was only slightly larger than the wardrobe. It was half the size of the bedroom I'd had at mum and dad's.

I ended up staying in that room for three months, except when the Ryder Cup was on, when I had to move out even of that. No spectacular view of Paul McGinley's winning putt, no strolling around with the players, no celebrating an epic victory over the US or jumping in the lake. It got so lonely that I would just go out driving by myself, not aiming to get to anywhere in particular, simply aiming to get away from the single bed and my reflection looking back sadly from the mirror on the wall. Sometimes I'd look for places on the map that had weird names. Sometimes I'd just head off and make random turns. I'd end up at a fast-food drive-thru, get a burger and drive back to the Belfry, sitting there on the bed with my quarter-pounder and fries and try to avoid any glimpse of the mirror at all.

It got grim fast. I was going loopy even faster. I wasn't scoring goals. I felt like a sailor in the old days of the navy, wanting to sing shanties about the sweet salty air of old Portsmouth harbour and how much I missed it.

To the rescue came Lee Hendrie and Gareth Barry. Slightly older than me, already veterans of the Brummie social scene. They lived in the Solihull/Knowle/Dorridge golden corridor. I moved out of the Belfry's broom closet, bought a nice flat by the cricket ground in Dorridge and began to explore a series of pleasant rural pubs rather than the takeaway menus of roadside burger franchises. My only regret was that I couldn't score more goals for Graham Taylor, a lovely man and the first manager who believed I was Premier League quality. He'd taken a chance on me early. He gave me my top-flight debut, he was in charge when I scored my first Premier League goal. He took genuine pleasure out of seeing me play for England. I remember him jogging down the steps of the stand when I went back to Villa with Liverpool as an established England international. 'I always knew you'd do it, Peter.'

The football chaos theory intervened once more. Villa chairman Doug Ellis flapped his wings. David O'Leary took over from Graham. David O'Leary didn't rate me. David O'Leary sent me to Norwich on loan.

This time my hotel for three months was Dunston Manor. It was a big old country house in the countryside, which is to say every bit of Norfolk except Norwich itself. I had no girlfriend. I became institutionalised. I expected my towels to be folded each morning and to return each afternoon after training to a chocolate on my pillow. At my own house I would never cook a hash brown for breakfast. I wouldn't own a hash brown. At a hotel buffet breakfast you can't ignore them. They possess some magical allure. You have a bowl of cereal, like normal. You have some fruit, to be healthy. And then you walk past a tureen of bacon, of eggs, of hash browns winking at you, and you think, why not?

On the pitch all was wonderful. Norwich manager Nigel Worthington had signed me, Darren Huckerby and Kevin Harper, all on loan. I was scoring goals again. We were winning every week. We won the Championship to get promotion up to the Premier League.

And on it went, never seemingly in one place for long enough to settle in, always on the move, continuing my own personal tour of English football's geographical outposts. David O'Leary still didn't fancy me at Villa, and sold me to Southampton. I couldn't keep buying houses every time I arrived at a new club. It was getting ridiculous. Right, I thought. I'll stick all my cash in a place in Surrey, use that as my base and rent everywhere else.

I thought there would be animosity at Southampton. I'd been at Portsmouth only two years before. Harry Redknapp took care of that by making the same move without a stop in between. I scored goals but we were relegated on the final day of the season, although none of that was Harry's fault. Three managers in one season seldom ends well. Chairman Rupert Lowe was trying to sell the club; he brought former England rugby coach Clive Woodward in as a performance director, and when Clive was going around telling people who had actually worked in football before that we should be scoring off at least eight in ten set-pieces, quite a few were telling him that corners weren't conversions and Clive, haven't you noticed that there are defenders; and a few more, quite possibly

Harry among them, were telling him they wanted him nowhere near any ball that wasn't egg-shaped.

Those goals had got me noticed again. Liverpool – newly crowned champions of Europe – came in for me. I went to see Harry, who a few years before had sold me from Portsmouth to Villa for £5m, rebuilding the Pompey team and getting them promoted as a result.

'Harry, this is an amazing opportunity, I'm really rather keen to go.'

'I'm not f***ing surprised, son, that's superb.'

I went to see Rupert Lowe. 'Hi, Rupert, about the Liverpool offer ...'

'You're not going anywhere.'

'Yeah, but ...'

'We need you to get us back up to the Premier League.'

'But I spoke to Harry, and he says I can go.'

'Well, I've spoken to Harry too, and he says you're staying.'

Head full of confusion, I phoned Redknapp. 'Harry, I've just spoken to the chairman. He says you've told him I'm staying. I thought you understood. I thought you'd cleared it.'

'Yeah, of course I understand, Crouchie, but that doesn't mean I want you to actually go ...'

Harry wasn't planning to stay much longer himself, although I didn't know that at the time and neither did the Portsmouth fans, who still thought he was Satan in a Saints-badged padded jacket. But suddenly I'm having to do pre-season training with Southampton, and much as I love the place, and the fans have been wonderful, it's the Championship versus the Champions League. My head is in turmoil. It's not every day the best team in Europe come calling. If this falls through, I'm thinking, it's going to kill me.

Rupert Lowe wasn't at the training ground. Neither was he answering his phone, at least to me. So I decided to go to see him. At his house. In the Cotswolds.

It was a big old farm with a big old drive, but the gate was open. I drove in and rang the doorbell. No answer. So I went round the side, through another gate and into the back garden, where I found Rupert in his easy chair reading the paper. He almost spat his gin and tonic all over me.

He claimed he had no reception on his phone, which I took with equanimity. We had a chat. We saw eye-to-eye. A £7m bid for a player you paid £2.5m for just 12 months earlier tends to do that. And so I was on my way, thanks to Harry but no thanks to Harry.

Six changes of club by the age of 25. You're flotsam on the tide, and I was washing up on the banks of the Mersey. I had a couple of mates in Liverpool, and I'd had some fun nights out there. One of them lived in Huyton. It was 15 minutes from the training ground. While I was back in another hotel, I could pop over to his for a cup of tea. If he cooked dinner I'd often stay over. All these little connections make the landing softer. I felt at home within days.

Since Sky Sports News turned Deadline Day into a cross between a soap opera, a flash sale and a Hollywood thriller, transfers have become more hyped than ever before. It's now no longer simply about a young man moving employers. It's a power struggle, it's a gossip factory, it's a mass collective panic. Helicopters are put on stand-by. Reporters stand outside training ground gates and shout questions at passing cars. Stooges are born. I genuinely felt sorry for Peter Odemwingie, told by someone – club, agent, manager – to get himself into a nearby hotel so the deal could be done, inadvertently going to the ground, caught by the cameras and ending up signing autographs with a guilty look on his face for the supporters of a club now frantically trying to reverse at pace.

It's all done at such pace, broadcast around the world, fuelled by rumour and rubbish on social media. And yet clubs still use fax machines to get the paperwork done.

Why is there even paperwork when everything is now electronic? If paperwork, why fax machines, when even the most backward company had theirs mothballed around the same time mobile phones stopped being clam-shaped?

The devices used by football clubs may well be the last working fax machines in the world. I'm certain that Gareth Bale's world record transfer involved a fax machine, because we share an accountant. The chap involved still has the gold pen he was given by Ramón Calderón, which is apparently always the Real Madrid president's gift when he signs off a *galáctico* deal. I would love to have seen the fax for Neymar's move from Barcelona to Paris Saint-Germain when that came through. Imagine the relentless beeping. 'Hang on, there are even more noughts coming through here ...' 'There can't be.' 'Oh my God, there's another page!'

You can experience sliding doors moments. You are moments away from signing for one club and something happens to derail that particular train. An hour or so later you're on another one heading in an entirely different direction. There was a time at Liverpool when Villareal seemed a real option. I asked Pepe Reina about it. He was unequivocal. If you get the chance, go. And then as quickly as the doors had opened they slammed shut. I would have loved Spain. I was ready.

After my second spell at Portsmouth, Steve Bruce wanted to take me to Sunderland. I fancied it. The training ground and stadium were fantastic. The fans are amazing. I looked around the place and thought, what a great place to play football. At the same time Roy Hodgson was keen to sign me for Fulham. It looked like a straight choice between the side of the Thames or the Wear.

And then from nowhere Spurs came in. They had been struggling under Juande Ramos. Redknapp had taken over, turned them round and was now looking to push on for Europe. Straight away it just made sense to me. I had unfinished business there, having been flogged by Pleat a decade before. I knew Harry would play me the right way. Suddenly the fact that Sunderland and Fulham were offering more money made no difference.

I was with Abbey by this point. In any normal relationship you would discuss such a significant move with your fiancée. You'd take into account her feelings – whether she knew anyone in that part of the world, whether she thought she could settle, which of the options would work best for the two of you.

Not in football. Not with Abbey. She had no say in it, and she didn't want one. She understood that a footballer has a short career and needs to make the most of it. She also has her own, very successful, career. Sunderland would have been just fine. Stoke has been great.

And she knew that none of it was my fault. When the time came for me to leave Spurs, I first heard about it from our chairman, Daniel Levy. I hadn't given a moment's thought to moving on, but Levy had. He was to the point: We're getting Emmanuel Adebayor in, you've got to go, and you're going to Stoke.

I went straight to Harry's office. 'Hang on, I've got two years left on my contract. I love it here.'

Harry made a sympathetic face. 'I love having you here, you're a great option to have. But I got to let you leave. Levy will only let me have one or the other. And as part of that I've got to say that I'm letting you go.'

I wasn't happy, so I asked Harry to phone Levy. He gets through. 'Yeah. I know. Yeah. I've told him.'

He puts me on speakerphone. 'Hello, Mr Levy. I'm not leaving. I'm mid-contract. We're in the Champions League. I'm doing well.'

'Yes, but we're bringing Adebayor in.'

'I'm more than happy where I am, thanks. I'll see you at training tomorrow.'

'We'll make it worth your while. But you're done.'

'I know you're getting a decent deal. Me and Palacios for £20m, you said. So unless you give me this and this, I won't leave.'

Levy, outraged: 'What? No player has ever had this!'

Me, politely, watching Redknapp crying with laughter: 'Okay, see you in the morning.'

The line cut out. Harry was trying desperately not to burst out laughing.

Certain managers are forever associated with signing certain players. You think of Sam Allardyce with Kevin Nolan, José Mourinho with Nemanja Matić. For Harry it was always supposedly me, Jermain Defoe, Niko Kranjkar and Sandro. I was with Harry at four different points in my career. But he didn't always sign me; he inherited me twice, and he also sold me twice. Maybe this is why he is still a little hazy on the details. He remembers signing me for Portsmouth from QPR, except it was Rix who signed me for Portsmouth the first time, although Harry then built a whole team from selling me on to Villa. I loved him as a manager. He was sensational at man-management. But I was never his teacher's pet, and I was never immune to being moved on if he felt he could do better without me.

Those are strange times in a team dressing-room, when rumours appear in the newspapers that a certain player might be on his way out, or stories swirl of a big-name new arrival. Your mates will wind you up. If so-and-so comes in, you're finished, son. No one wants to slag off a potential new team-mate, in case it gets back to them when they do arrive. In your private moments that gossip can make you feel anxious. If that rumoured deal involves someone who plays in your position, you can find yourself wishing it falls through. It's your livelihood. Why would you want someone joining your company who does your exact job but better? You hear on the grapevine that you're being touted round as the makeweight in another deal. Oh, you think. My employers rate me so highly that I'm not even worth a whole player. Great.

There are transfers when you think, whoa, he must have a good agent. Tal Ben Haim always got great moves. From Bolton to Chelsea, and then West Ham. You're watching Milan one evening and Philippe Senderos pops up. Hang on, are there two Philippe Senderoses? He's failed at Arsenal, now he's with the multiple European champions? Julien Faubert going from West Ham to Real Madrid, making a grand total of two appearances, once falling asleep on the subs' bench. Tyrone Mears moving from Derby to Marseille. There are transfers that don't appear to make sense: Nicklas Bendtner going from Arsenal to Juventus on loan, and in all the time he was there Juve failing to sell a single shirt with Bendtner on the back; Robbie Savage going from Birmingham to Blackburn, saying it was because he wanted to be closer to his home in North Wales, when actually it was further away. David Unsworth playing a solitary season for West Ham before realising he was homesick for his old club Everton, moving halfway home with Aston Villa and then finding that was still too far away and moving back to

Everton without playing a game, and then later in his career playing for Portsmouth, Ipswich and then Sheffield United, as if he were looking at a map and trying to work out how far he could go around the country to make up for his previous lack of adventure.

There are transfers you regret. When I left Liverpool it was because Fernando Torres looked undroppable. I was only very seldom going to start ahead of him. So I moved on, and very soon so did he, and pretty soon the Liverpool attack comprised Andy Carroll, who you might describe as something of a Crouch-type player. When he wasn't playing it was David N'Gog and Andriy Voronin. The sight of those two haunts me to this day. I wanted to be at a place I was valued, and I loved it at Portsmouth, but who wants to leave Liverpool?

Then there is the nitty-gritty, the negotiations once a deal is in place, the inducements and the special clauses. Usually this is where an agent impresses his player. Sometimes the player even does it himself. Gary Neville certainly did, mainly because Gaz could talk anyone to pieces. If there was a committee, Gary would be on it. I could have done it by my last contract negotiation with Stoke. At my age you either get one or you don't. I was happy with what I was on, and I wasn't going to break the Bank of Stoke.

The more a club wants you, the more you can demand. That doesn't necessarily mean money. Sometimes a certain shirt number matters more than another grand a week. I always remember Alan Shearer moving to Newcastle from Blackburn and taking the famous number nine shirt from Sir Les of Ferdinand. It must have been heartbreaking for Les, who had done brilliantly since moving from QPR. Les, we like you, but we like Wor Alan more. It was a mark of Shearer's confidence and how good he was that he got away with it; 283 top-flight goals will do that.

He wasn't alone. Mesut Özil insisted on the number 11 when he went to Arsenal. Thierry Henry wasn't happy when he went back to the Gunners and Theo Walcott had his number 14. I could never do it. Nine is what I should be, but I made 14 my own at Southampton, 15 at Liverpool and 15 at Spurs; 25 at Stoke. Taking anyone else's number would feel too rude to my new team-mate. I'm better than you, hand it over. You're literally taking the shirt off his back. In any case, it can't be that lucky; every now and then I'll stick one of my shirt numbers on roulette, and it's never yet come in.

I've heard of players actually paying a team-mate to get their shirt number. Darius Vassell wanted to be ten. Renato Sanches initially insisted on number 85 when he joined Swansea, as he'd had that at Lisbon. The Premier League wouldn't let him; squad numbers have to be consecutive. The highest they could offer him was 35. Perhaps that's why he had such a diabolical season. He'd lost half his power.

There is the buy-out clause, which was always thought of as a joke, so ridiculously high was it, until Paris Saint-Germain happily paid the £198m that Barcelona had placed in Neymar's contract. There is a figure, no matter how high, that will always get a deal done, going back to Chris Waddle's move from Spurs to Marseille in 1989. Tottenham chairman Irving Scholar has no interest in selling. Marseille bigwig Bernard Tapie puts £4m on the table, almost double the British transfer record. Scholar gulps and changes his mind.

Then there are the other clauses. The sensible ones: the rumour that Roy Keane's Manchester United deal automatically made him the best-paid player at the club, no matter who was signed for how much. The head-shaking ones: Giuseppe Reina signing for Arminia

Bielefeld and stipulating he wanted the club to build him a house for every year of his contract, failing to specify the size of the property and receiving a house made of Lego for three years instead.

There are bonuses. At the start of each season every player will get a sheet from the club laying out what each win in each competition might bring. How far you get in the FA Cup, where you might finish in the league, with nothing below 17th; a certain amount for a certain number of points. Most are negotiated by the club and are the same for everyone, some will be specific to your contract. There are triggers – a certain amount of games played will lead automatically to another year's contract. Sometimes a club will refuse to play a player to avoid having to give them that extra year.

It's all a pat on the back rather than an incentive. There's no way I've ever thought about a bonus in the middle of a match. You're playing to win anyway, to score goals. When Liverpool reached the Champions League final in 2007 we got a good bonus, but it only reflected what the club had received. Had we won we would have doubled our money, but it was the trophy and the glory that motivated us, never the thought of cash.

It can all be horribly cut-throat. Some agents will drop stories into the tabloids about a move that was never on the cards, just to kick-start interest or to bump up their player's wage demands at the club they're already perfectly happy with. Clubs will tout players around without their knowledge. Players trying to force a move might not try so hard on the pitch. Sell me or get nothing from me in games. As a team-mate you can understand why a player sometimes wants to leave but you'll never accept that sort of behaviour. The best way to play it was demonstrated by Cristiano Ronaldo before he went from Manchester United to Real Madrid, and by Philippe Coutinho before his move to Barcelona: you're not moving yet, but you will next year; great, I'll run myself into the ground until then.

Yet you can never strip it of emotion. A great player leaves your club and as a fan you feel devastated. I still remember the pain when Sir Les left QPR, even though they were a club who always sold in the end – Andy Sinton, Darren Peacock, Andy Impey. I was devastated when Roy Wegerle moved to Blackburn. In an era of hard work rather than outrageous skill, he stood out in a kid's mind.

And then it happens to you. Jamie Carragher grew up as an obsessive Everton fan, yet spent his entire career with their greatest rivals. Michael Owen started at Liverpool and took in Manchester United. Luís Figo swapped sides in *El Clasico*. I grew up as a Chelsea fan like my dad, but when I started as a youngster at QPR my allegiance began to change. Swapping the club you support is rightly considered the lowest of the low, but as a player you experience pressures that don't touch the supporters in the stands. Every time I played at Stamford Bridge I copped the most unpleasant abuse. It was horrible, and I gradually lost love for the club. The pleasure came instead in scoring against them.

Should you celebrate when scoring a goal against a previous club? There should be an element of respect, but your job is to score goals. Inside you will still be getting that sweet release of adrenaline and emotion, so why not let a little show? I've usually left clubs in good circumstances, and so I've got a good reception when I've gone back. There is affection there on both sides when I've returned to Anfield and White Hart Lane. The real football fan understands that. Don't rub it in, but don't pull the whole 'I'm gutted' act. It doesn't wash.

And never ever kiss the badge, unless you're a one-club man, unless you're Francesco Totti or Steven Gerrard or Andrés Iniesta. I would have been perfectly happy being a one-club man, but since I've played for so many I could never do it. I'd need a whole range of badges to kiss, and if you're kissing one, can you really cosy up to another too? If you kiss a badge you have to rule out transfers. If you have been offered a million a week to play for Bognor Regis and you don't move, you can kiss to your heart's content. But to kiss the badge when you've been there five minutes is despicable. It's disrespectful to players who have been at the club longer, it's disrespectful to the fans, who genuinely will love the club forever. In fact, I would bring in a rule: if you are ever caught kissing the badge, you have to get a tattoo of that same club badge. When I played with Gary Holt at Norwich he still had his Kilmarnock tattoo, and he was quite happy.

Let us remind ourselves too that transfers, no matter how insane some fees might seem or how opaque the whole business remains, can also be things of wonder. United paid £500,000 for Peter Schmeichel. They paid £1.2m for Eric Cantona, and £1.5m for Ole Gunnar Solskjær. Between them those three took them from glamorous also-rans to multiple league champions and eventually the Champions League. Raúl went on a free from Atlético Madrid to Real when Atlético closed their youth academy to save a little money when he was 15. Some 741 appearances and 323 goals later, that looks like a slightly better deal for one side of the city than the other. Leicester City signed Riyad Mahrez for £400,000, won an impossible Premier League title and then had Manchester City bid £60m for him. Some of it might not make any sense. But some deals do.

MUSIC

To all those who would mock the musical tastes of footballers, who would say that it used to be wall-to-wall Phil Collins and now it's wall-to-wall Drake, that footballers should never be allowed near a mic, I have two words: John and Barnes.

Ah, Italia 90. The perfect World Cup, apart from the ending. Ah, 'World in Motion', probably the greatest ever World Cup song. And John Barnes at the centre of it all, his rap the crowning glory of a tune that can never be forgotten.

He's still got it, too. I saw him a few years ago in Dubai, up onstage at an event in a hotel. Everyone else was sitting down. I was staring around in amazement. 'This is a disgrace! You've got John Barnes up there doing his rap from "World in Motion"!' There was no way I was going to accept a reaction like that to John Barnes, even if he had been rubbish, and he wasn't. Take it from me, John Barnes is good live.

So I marched to the front and stood right underneath the lip of the stage, singing along with him, and then he spots me and invites me up onto the stage, and then suddenly the two of us are doing it together, only the very occasional 'ner ner mmm' from me towards the very end, the bit that only John Barnes can remember.

It was a special moment. Since then we've holidayed together. That's what John Barnes and his rap can do.

It used to be that every player's initiation when they made their debut for a new club was to sing a song in front of the rest of the team. It's dying out a little now, which saddens me, but I will always try to instigate it. The choice of tune is one issue, the performance another. You're not expected to bring your own microphone, but you are expected to use a bottle or serving-spoon as a pretend one and act as if it's real. Do badly and you can expect to be booed off; if you're at the pre-match meal you'll be accompanied by a hail of bread rolls too.

As a teenager at QPR I went safe and chose 'Wonderwall'. I just shouted it. Job done. When I moved to Portsmouth I was a little more confident and a little more ambitious, and I did 'Informer' by Snow, because I've got the rap in my locker. It went down well, so much so that I used it again at Aston Villa. I'd do it again if the opportunity arose. I only do the John Barnes rap in the company of John Barnes.

It's widely accepted that you're allowed to use the same song at more than one club. The critical thing is that you make an effort and you bring something new to your cover. At Southampton our Belgian defender Jelle Van Damme was dying on his backside during his rendition, boos ringing out around the dining-room of the hotel we were staying in, the first roll just bouncing off his head, when he saw the opportunity to make amends. Jumping off the table he was using as a makeshift stage, dropping the fork that he had been crooning into, he seized the hand of one of the waitresses cleaning away the dirty plates, brought her into the correct *Strictly* starting position and began waltzing her round the room. He totally turned the audience around: cheers, rhythmic clapping, the waitress all

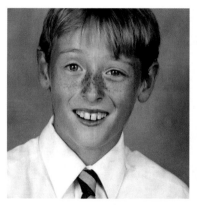

The face of innocence. The face of a boy whose ideal day consists of football before school, football during school and football after school.

In my youth team days at Spurs, my hair weighed almost as much as I did. I'd like to say the curtains look is timeless, but I'm unable to.

My mum found this photo of me appearing to dominate the great Patrick Vieira and stuck it on my bedroom wall. These are the perks you get when you're still living at home aged 19

At Portsmouth we inaugurated a tradition: whoever took the Robin Reliant home had to add a new feature. The spoiler made more sense before the car became the world's first stretch Reliant.

Why am I looking so smug? I'm driving a courtesy Hyundai that comes complete with a concierge dashboard button. I mainly used it to ask where the nearest McDonald's was.

Oh, Stephen Ireland. Where is your mind?

I like to think I was ahead of the game – not only taking a selfie on a disposable camera, but doing so at the wheel of a Renault Mégane. Don't tell me I don't know how to party.

Carra stitched me up by asking Prince William if he wanted to see the Robot. He did and I couldn't disappoint the future king!

My champagne bottle often looks smaller compared to that of men beside me.

Classic Robert Huth-style defending — try to pull your arm off. I loved Huth. He once cycled the 40 miles from home to training because that's the kind of thing he does.

My first goal for England, at Anfield. When a cross comes over like that the poor defender is like an injured gazelle about to be attacked by a lion. Okay, a giraffe. But a fierce giraffe.

I loved playing with Steven Gerrard, a perfect example of how to be a footballer.

Top boot from the 2006 FA Cup final, bottom from the Champions League final in Athens. Both with my name on the side in case I lose them and they're handed in to lost property.

Djibril Cissé launches his own clothing range. Stevie G and I have made an effort for his big night and come as two 16-year-olds off to the snooker hall. The fella on the far right was one of Rafa's less inspired signings.

Djibril once wore a skirt on a night out. What sort of real man does that?

One minute you're missing a
simple volley for England, the next
you're an internet meme called
Peter Crouch Can Do Anything.
I see genuine commercial
possibilities in the second of these.

That said, social media really isn't hard to get right . . .

Peter Crouch ✓
@petercrouch

Perhaps I shouldn't stand next to jockeys 😔

11:29 AM - 22 Jan 2015

16,435 Retweets 19,553 Likes

♡ 814   ⟲ 16K   ♡ 20K

---

55 is coming 🏴󠁧󠁢󠁳󠁣󠁴󠁿
@PenmanDeclan

Can't believe Sterling is getting all this stick for getting a tattoo of his big pal Peter on his leg 😂

12:24 PM - 29 May 2018 from Troon, Scotland

44,498 Retweets 140,176 Likes

♡ 1.1K   ⟲ 44K   ♡ 140K

Peter Crouch ✓
@petercrouch

ImPECcable 🏠

10:32 AM - 6 Dec 2014

11,718 Retweets 9,146 Likes

♡ 648   ⟲ 12K   ♡ 9.1K

Peter Crouch ✓
@petercrouch

Summer for me is about time with family .

9:58 AM - 19 Jun 2017

148,432 Retweets 327,126 Likes

♡ 3.2K   ⟲ 148K   ♡ 327K

Peter Crouch ✓
@petercrouch

King of the go kart podium . 🏁 Only wish I didn't have to take the ceiling tile off to enjoy it 🏠

11:45 PM - 3 Feb 2015

784 Retweets 1,165 Likes

♡ 34   ⟲ 784   ♡ 1.2K

The plaintive sound of former England assistant manager Tord Grip and his accordion. Nothing soothes the pain of a World Cup quarter-final defeat to Portugal on penalties like an ageing Swede playing a basic melody on a bellows-driven squeezebox.

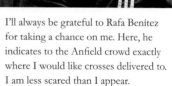

I'll always be grateful to Rafa Benítez for taking a chance on me. Here, he indicates to the Anfield crowd exactly where I would like crosses delivered to. I am less scared than I appear.

Harry Redknapp is a vastly underappreciated manager. Equally, he frequently comes out with things that make you look at him with this expression smiles, him spinning her round and finishing by leaning her back over one gentlemanly arm.

You will get the occasional player who refuses, usually out of fear. At Stoke our Senegalese midfielder Badou Ndiaye asked if he could do a dance instead. Surely that's worse, we thought, but his moves, accompanying the singing of his fellow new-boy Kostas Stafylidis, were majestic. He absolutely won us over. Several of us actually wanted him to carry on.

The rule applies too to staff. Our club doctor at Stoke was on sick leave for a period last season, which meant the academy doctor had to step up to the vacated first-team role. Word first began to spread that we might see something special when a video circulated on the players' WhatsApp group of the outside of his closed hotel room door, and a high-pitched noise coming from behind it that you could just about identify as the chorus from 'Wonderwall'. I could have told him: shout it, you'll be fine. Instead he got cold feet and switched direction entirely until he ended up at Big Shaq and 'Man's Not Hot'.

Bear in mind this is a man who has been through many years of university, who has multiple degrees, who at least has reached his goal of working with a Premier League team. And here he is, standing on a chair, headphones in, trying to read the lyrics off his phone as the video plays on YouTube, bread rolls raining down upon him, words coming from him that you should never hear from a doctor's mouth. 'Da ting go SKRRRAHH ...'

Some of those old clichés held truth. As I came through the Spurs youth team in the mid-1990s every player used to worship the holy trinity of Collins, Stewart and Springsteen. Much as some might knock it, I had a few leanings that way myself. 'In the Air Tonight' is right up there. I love the robot-voice bit '... well I remember ...', I love the big build-up that follows, I love the drum solo. As for Springsteen, I grew up with him. My mum's in love with Bruce. She spotted him once in Mallorca, where he has a holiday home, and she went to pieces. My dad is actually christened James Bruce Crouch, but my mum swapped it round so she can call him Bruce. All his mates have now followed suit.

But those days of domination have gone. I haven't heard any Collins in a football dressing-room since the year 2000. I was told when I got to Aston Villa in 2002 that recently departed manager John Gregory had been a massive Bruce fan, which made sense; you see what era he lived through as a player, you see the hair. The insider shout was that on a Saturday night, if Villa won a game, he would drive down Broad Street in Birmingham with the top down on his convertible. It may be an old wives' tale, but that was the rumour, and what a Bruce move it would be.

What swept Phil and Rod and Bruce away was garage. It was everywhere at the turn of the century. You couldn't avoid it. You couldn't resist it.

It wasn't for me. It was never going to be. But when you're a kid in a team, whether at school or at your club, you're still finding yourself. You're still trying to fit in, and the youth teams at QPR and Spurs could be unforgiving places; a lot of working-class lads from the tougher parts of London, the banter harsh, the atmosphere sink or swim. And the soundtrack was all garage.

I had two mix-tapes that Ledley King gave me, one featuring DJ EZ, from north London, the other MC Creed and PSG. All the Ayia Napa crew. I used to play them in the car as I drove the lads to and from training in the green VW Polo, hating every second but too scared to say so in case everyone called me a square. I kept trying my best to fit in, kept pretending I loved it, even tried dancing to it. Some of the lads actually had good moves. Their dancing genuinely used to bring ladies over. I thought, I'll have a go at this. And my shimmering brought me nothing.

Me, Ledley, Alton Thelwell, a lad called Millsy from the Isle of Dogs, Ross Fitzsimon. We all went down to Club Colosseum in Vauxhall, off Nine Elms Road, me sober as a judge, listening to this terrible music, looking out over the sea of heads all bang into it. And it suddenly dawned on me: it's not for me, this. I hate every element of it. Plus I'm going to go outside and get mugged. This was a time where punters were getting shot and stabbed in there every week. I should be in a school disco, not a hardcore south London club. What am I doing here?

Sadly that wasn't the end of it. The entire Spurs youth team went to Ayia Napa that summer. Unable yet to break away, I paid £300 for ten days all-inclusive, walked into the apartment, saw its two single beds and trod in a weird yellow-coloured puddle on the floor.

It was the worst week of my life. I hated the music, I had no luck with the girls. Every night you would see half the youth teams of the Premier League out in the clubs, all having a great time, and me feeling sad and lonely. It got to the point where I hired a moped and drove out into the countryside, just for a break. I found a little bay, a cove, and climbed down on the rocks all by myself and had a little swim. That's how much I was trying to get away from it.

On the final night, at the end of my tether, I slipped away and stumbled into Carwash. What a night! Tunes you could dance to, girls who would talk to you, minimal chance of getting shot. I left there on a high: that was the best night ever. Then I remembered. Oh – we're going home tomorrow.

But I came back to London a changed man. I realised I had to be strong. 'Do you know what, I'm going have to make a conscious decision to throw these mix-tapes in the bin. Sorry, Ledley.'

I've never gone back. Now there are a few of us loud and proud with our love of guitar bands: me, Joe Allen, Leighton Baines, Joey Barton. I go to gigs with Joe, I saw Leighton at the Arctic Monkeys. I try to educate the rest of the Stoke lads. There is always a Bluetooth speaker in the changing-rooms, and as the senior player I've put myself in charge of it. A playlist with some Ian Brown, The Enemy, Oasis, Kasabian, The Smiths, late-sixties Rolling Stones. The staff like it. No one else does. Saido Berahino came up to me with a straight face and asked me if it was a movie soundtrack. It was a genuine question. That's what I'm dealing with.

There are those who get on the speaker, cop a load of abuse for their music and crumble. They'll start flicking through their tracks looking for a winner. When that happens you're done. I've seen it affect a player's performance on the pitch, because they're still trying to work out where they went wrong when they run out. You might get away with Kasabian's 'Club Foot', because it stirs even a garage heart. Jean-Eric Maxim Choupo-Moting tapped his foot to The Enemy's 'We'll Live and Die in These Towns'. But you have to stick to your guns. When your team-mates realise that you'll carry on no matter how much stick you get, they give up.

We had a more collaborative approach with England at the 2006 World Cup. Each of the squad was asked to select a favourite song, and they were assembled onto an iPod playlist. It was an eclectic mix – a burst of Jay-Z followed by Johnny Cash and 'Ring of Fire', courtesy of Jamie Carragher. The most popular choice was Michael Carrick's selection of Byron Stingily's 'Get Up (Everybody)', the most hated Paul Robinson and '500 miles' by The Proclaimers. Sven? Sven just wanted Tord back on the accordion.

Footballers, of course, often fancy themselves as singers. Plenty have released singles. Rio Ferdinand briefly had his own record label. Shane Long, Sandro and Andy Reid can all play guitar to a high standard, and not just Phil Collins standards. I can't sing, but I would genuinely love to get up and give it a go. I see myself as a lead singer and lead guitarist rolled into one. The voice of Mick but the licks of Keith. Basically Bruce. My wife's brother is in a band, and he's tried to teach me a few bits and pieces, but the magic wasn't there. Disappointing.

I've come close. In my time at Liverpool, Didi Hamann had some mates from back home in Germany in a band called Die Toten Hosen, which translates as The Dead Trousers. The lead singer, a bloke called Campino, used to come over to watch us at Anfield; he was such a hard-core Red that he once broke his foot kicking a dustbin with disgust after a bad defeat. Didi lived in the flat above me, so the three of us used to enjoy a few beers when Campino was in town. I happened to mention to him one weekend that my mate was having his stag-do in Munich the following summer. Oh, we're playing in the city around that time, you'll have to come along.

I assumed he meant in a bar somewhere. It turned out to be a stadium holding 40,000 people. Die Toten Hosen are huge in Germany. Campino is as big as Bono. We watched the entire gig from the wings, marvelling at the noise, blown away by the size of the crowd.

Towards the end, Campino turned to me in the wings. 'Peter! This one is for you!' And he launched into 'You'll Never Walk Alone'. A verse in, I was beckoned onto stage. He gave me the mic. I virtually shoved him out of the way. Singing as loudly as I could, waving my arms around, giving it everything. 'You'll NEEE-VERRRR WAAALK ...' There was a point when I realised I was on stage by myself. Just me, my terrible shouting-singing and 40,000 swaying Bavarians. I don't even think I was a Liverpool player by then. I think I'd moved to Portsmouth.

It was a strange and wonderful night. The stag was marrying an Irish girl, so spent the day dressed as a leprechaun. Green top hat, ginger hair, ginger beard, baggy green felt suit. Campino had got him involved earlier in the gig. 'I want to introduce you to a friend of mine – Greg!' Greg walked onto the stage, in no way ready to be introduced to 40,000 drunken new friends. I'm not sure the leprechaun even has any cultural weight in the south of Germany. They may well have thought he was just a strange ginger man in a very gaudy, ill-fitting suit. In the event Greg hardly rose to the occasion. He stood there, clearly overwhelmed, gave a small embarrassed wave and trudged off. That was Greg's big moment and in some ways it went perfectly and that was exactly the unassuming way I know he would react to 40,000 Germans – the coy wave.

Musicians and footballers do have a great deal in common. Footballers often want to be musicians. Musicians want to be footballers. The two careers have the same character: people doing their passion, never growing up; the chance to earn a great deal of money, an insane kind of celebrity; doing what you want and no one telling you to stop. You have to be dedicated to the practising but you can dress however you like. You can go from being unknown to a household name in a matter of weeks; you can fall away just as fast, should you get a bad injury or your second album doesn't sell. And you're constantly chasing the high of performing: the adoration of the crowd, the noise and the fear, the endorphins and the adrenaline, the inability to sleep afterwards.

I've become good friends with Serge from Kasabian, and he has a theory that footballers are the rock and roll stars of this century. Musicians and bands don't have the power and influence they once did. It's all about the labels. Footballers, meanwhile, have more power than the clubs. If you want to leave, you will. If you're in demand you can make obscene amounts of money. It's the escape for working-class kids from tough backgrounds, the meal ticket out of there for them and their families. With it comes the same snobbery from those with better educations in less lucrative professions: these kids don't deserve this, look at how they spend it, look how they live.

And so we're interested in each other. I hang out with Serge, I've enjoyed the company of Paul Weller and Carl Barât and Jarvis Cocker, who is a Sheffield Wednesday supporter. I met Paul McCartney at the *NME* awards. I say I met him – I walked past him and said hello. He didn't say hello back. But I was definitely in the same room as him. And in the *NME* there was a snapshot of me and Macca in the same frame, me in the background but looking his way and because of my height appearing significantly closer to him than I actually was, and the photo had a speech bubble coming out of Macca's mouth saying, 'F***ing hell, Peter Crouch is here!' I got it blown up and stuck it on the wall at home.

Footballers date musicians. In the 1950s it was England captain Billy Wright and Joy Beverley of the Beverley Sisters. In the 1990s it was Jamie Redknapp and Louise Nurding and Posh 'n' Becks, in the 2000s Ashely Cole and Cheryl Tweedy. Now we have Liverpool's Alex Oxlade-Chamberlain and Watford's Andre Gray both dating members of Little Mix. Nothing in the 1980s, probably because the pop stars were massively cool and the footballers were not, unless you had a thing for the moustache/perm combo.

I'm a little jealous that Alessandro Del Piero got to appear with Oasis in the video for 'Lord Don't Slow Me Down'. I'm delighted that I'm in one for a band called Peace. I'd been to see them a couple of times, exchanged mobile numbers, and then got a call after training one day with Stoke – we're filming 20 minutes down the road, fancy coming along? As a young player I'd been hugely impressed by the recording debut of Manchester United striker Andy Cole, when he covered the Gap Band's 'Outstanding' in harness with Pied Piper. I still remember where I was when I first heard it: driving round Hanover Square in my mum's car. Landmark tunes have that effect on you. Cole fascinated me, not just for the goals he scored – and he scored a lot of goals, the number he scored at Newcastle alone is a sweet, sweet joke – but for his attitude. He always struck me as headstrong, insisting halfway through his career that he wanted to be known as Andrew rather than Andy. I think I saw the single as part of the same mentality, the video where's he's driving round Manchester in the dark both ridiculous and beautiful. And so when my own chance came, and Peace's video also requiring me to sit in a car and look moody, I could never turn it down.

The link-ups continue. Gary Neville, who likes his Stone Roses and Charlatans, has a Union flag guitar which he asked Noel Gallagher to sign. Noel wrote 'MCFC' all over the front and a touching personal message on the back. 'Dear Gary. How many caps have you got for England? How many do you think you deserved? I'll tell you – F***IN' NONE. Lots of love, Noel Gallagher.'

Back in the day, Dion Dublin and Nolberto Solano would jam together at Aston Villa's training ground, Dion on sax, Nobby on trumpet. Dion even sorted out the music for my wedding: Beverley Knight on vocals, Dion on his sax, one brother on guitar, another brother DJing. Mehmet Scholl, formerly of Bayern Munich and Germany, released two mix albums of weirdish indie. David De Gea was spotted at a Slipknot gig in Manchester, his love of metal shared by Robert Huth, who used to put extreme heavy stuff on in the dressing-room just to see the horror on his team-mates' faces. Petr Čech is a decent drummer, and enjoys doing so in the classic drummer's look of a sleeveless white vest. At Liverpool Ryan Babel used to rap, albeit not to the same standard as John Barnes.

None can match the efforts of former Real Madrid and one-time Stoke striker Jesé, who released a single called 'Yo Sabía' under his stage name Jey M. It's got a reggaeton vibe, plus a video that ticks off every hip-hop cliché you could round up: sports cars, girls wearing bikinis two sizes too small for them, caps worn on top of the head rather than pulled on, gold chains, gratuitous bottom shots, US sportswear, unnecessary sunglasses and meaningless hand gestures. We made him perform it live for his Stoke initiation. To be fair to him he did know all the words and as a result drew a generous reception from his audience.

Of all the changes I've seen in professional football over the two decades, the one I perhaps regret the most is the death of the FA Cup final song. Why did it stop? When did it stop? The last one I can remember is Status Quo and Manchester United's 'Come On You Reds' from 1994. I had no interest in United but I still bought the single. You think of Spurs in Cup finals and you think of Chas 'n' Dave. Neither was I ever given the chance to do an England World Cup song. The fact that they no longer do one is to me a scandal. I would have been all over it.

There is a tremendous clip on YouTube of violinist Nigel Kennedy playing a punk version of Vivaldi's *Four Seasons* to the 1990 World Cup squad. I'm not sure how many of them had heard

HOW TO BE A FOOTBALLER

of Nigel. I'm not sure some of them had heard of the violin. The expressions on their faces are extraordinary. Trevor Steven looks as if he has just spotted Hitler walking in. Peter Beardsley looks like he's just foreseen his own death. But they had already made their contribution to music history with 'World in Motion', a tune that can perhaps only be approached in impact by 'Three Lions'.

Personally I'm a 'World in Motion' man. A million per cent. But I've often wondered what that must have felt like for David Baddiel, Frank Skinner and Ian Broudie, looking out from the heaving stands at Wembley before the semi-final against Germany, Scotland, Holland and Spain all beaten, your song sung after every win, bellowed in every pub, by people dancing in the street. Looking around the stadium that summer night and everyone is singing this little thing you came up with for fun. Even the Germans took it home with them along with the trophy. Sigh.

When you score a goal at a big club, you look around as you run away in celebration and you see the whole stadium on its feet. And you think: I did that.

It's an intoxicating feeling, something most people will never know. I think about that when I see musicians playing live. They've got that goal feeling for an hour and a half.

I can't sleep after games. Too much adrenaline, too much endorphin. Night games? No chance. Even if I've played rubbish and we've drawn 0–0 and I've only played ten minutes, I still need a few beers to come down; if I went straight home and got into bed I'd just lie there twitching for five hours. How musicians manage blows my mind. But I can understand, a little.

ABUSE

I like being tall. I wouldn't change it for the world. It's me. I was born tall and I carried on tall. There was never a sudden growth spurt, just a consistent growth vibe.

And yet … If you have a big nose, you don't get strangers coming up to you in the street shouting, 'Bloody hell, look how big your nose is!' If your ears stick out a little you can sit safely in a pub without a succession of strangers telling you that your ears stick out. It's not considered socially acceptable to point out a lack of height. 'Whoa, you're small! What's it like down there? Eh? Eh?'

Maybe being tall is seen as a good thing. Maybe that's why, four or five times a day, I still get people I have never met before looking at me with amazement and feeling the need to tell me quite how tall I am.

I have noticed. When I was on trial with QPR from Spurs, just a kid, a total unknown, I could hear it coming down at me from the Loftus Road stands, tight up to the pitch. Standing on the touchline, waiting to come on, and laughter all around. A voice yelling out. 'What the f*** is this?'

I had some business cards made a while ago. On nights out I could see people approaching. You get to know how it works – the pointing across the bar, the nudging of mates, the craning of necks. Usually one false start, a stiffening of resolve, the wander over with a look of comedic delight on their face.

If I'd had a few beverages I would wait until they were in front of me, mouths open to speak, then put my finger to my lips to make a shushing sound and hand over the card. It had five bullet-points on it.

- Yes I am tall
- Yes I am 6'7"
- No the weather isn't different up here
- No I don't play basketball
- I'm so glad we had this conversation

It was amazing to watch. You'd see their mouths opening and closing as they began to ask each question and then spotted the exact answer.

As a kid without business cards or confidence it was so much harder. I went to a nice primary school and then a much rougher secondary school, and the abuse from day one was awful. In Year Seven I was as tall as the sixth-formers. They took one look at me and piled in – 'Who the hell is this kid?' It was ruthless.

My way of dealing with it was humour. I wasn't hard. I couldn't beat anyone up. But I was good at football, and those two things got me through school fine. The bullies would say something to me, I would say something funny. I would either take the mickey out of them or myself. It depended how hard they were. If the answer ranged from quite to very, I'd make myself the target. When they saw me play football, it brought more swear-words, but more benign ones this time. 'F***ing hell, look at this kid!' I'd be put in the teams two years above my age. When I was winning trophies for them they no longer wanted to abuse me.

It would begin again when we played other schools. It wasn't just the kids. It was the mums and dads on the touchline. 'Who the f*** is this!' 'Oi, ref! This kid's too old!' 'Get this lanky joke off!'

My first game after signing a permanent deal with QPR was away at West Brom. When I missed an early chance I could hear the crowd at the Hawthorns laughing at me. I walked back to the halfway line thinking, is this game for me? Do I want to put myself through this every week? I could get a different job. I could be a painter and decorator. I could have the quiet life.

A few games on, home to Gillingham, us 2–0 down. Gerry Francis signalled for me to take my tracksuit off and get ready to come on as a sub. You couldn't miss the groans coming down from the stands. Another voice coming through the background hum as clear as a bell: 'What the f*** is he bringing him on for?'

I'll always remember the exact instance I scored my first goal. A corner came in. I chested down, pulled back my foot … and slipped. In that tiny moment, no more than half a second, I could hear the groans. I can hear them now. Eighteen years ago and it still feels like yesterday. And then I lashed it into the top corner, and suddenly it was all cheers, and adrenaline, and a wonderful buzz inside. From the depths to feeling a hero in the time it takes to strike a ball. A few minutes later, jumping high to nod a cross down for Chris Kiwomya to bury the equaliser. Now it was worth it. Now it was, I do want to do this. It's worth the shit I'm going to get. I can get through it.

We lost the following game, away at Barnsley, but I played really well. Okay. I've got the Rangers fans on my side. And it went on – voted player of the year that season, a move to Portsmouth and the goals coming straight away. To Aston Villa, and it began all over again.

The worst away ground was Gillingham's Priestfield Stadium. The abuse began when I ran out and it never let off. 'Freak! Freak! Freak!' The songs – 'Does the circus know you're here?' It was bad for me on the pitch and it was worse for my dad in the stands. As we walked towards the tunnel at half-time on our way to the dressing-rooms I could see some trouble kicking off in the grandstand just to one side. That's strange, I thought. That's the posh seats. I looked a little more closely. My dad on the floor, holding some bloke down, the bloke's mate laying into my old man. Me trotting down the tunnel. 'Oh. It's my dad ...'

He just couldn't handle it at the start. He was in fights every week. Standing on the terraces, and fans all around him abusing his son, calling him a freak, mocking him. It was more unpleasant still in the little area set aside for players' families, where every parent was biased and vocal about it. 'How the hell is that lanky strip of piss playing ahead of my boy?' Clapping with delight when you messed up, because it made their son look better. 'Johnny's never missing that chance, this kid's pants.'

You make your debut for England. It's an incredibly proud day. You've been dreaming about it since you first fell in love with football. And all the talk around it in the media and on phone-ins was still, 'Who's *this*?' and 'How can *he* be playing for England?' In one of my first games, a World Cup qualifier at Old Trafford in October 2005, I was booed as I came on. Maybe a little of it was the Liverpool connection and rivalry, although Jamie Carragher wasn't getting the same treatment, and I was replacing Shaun Wright-Phillips, who had spent most of his career at that stage at Manchester City. We were 1–1 in a game we needed to win, I was the striker being sent on to change things, and that was the reception I got. If you've never heard what it feels like having 70,000 people booing you, it's not great. You can't hide from it. You can't pretend it's not happening. In a moment, on that touchline, you can feel yourself changing. From a lifetime of thinking, all I want to do is to play for England, to instead, why would I want this? I was 23. I was just a kid.

We came back to win the game. Then when I came off the bench again, against Uruguay at Anfield, I scored the equaliser, my first goal for England. Picked again against Hungary, another goal, this time with a turn and angled shot from the edge of the box, followed by the first sight of my Robot celebration. I had felt like I needed to score in every match to get picked. Thankfully I was – a hat-trick against Jamaica, into the World Cup and the opening goal in our second match, and at last it felt like it had turned round.

It almost went full circle. Now it was all 'good touch for a big man', as if it was somehow impossible that someone my size could control their feet when they were four inches further away from my brain than another striker's might be. I didn't mind it, even the implication that taller players could only be in the team to head the ball. It was better than 'bad touch for a big man'. And Sven wanted me in the England team for both my goals and the celebrations. At a time when there was lots of negative press around the national side, he thought it brought back the fun, the smiles. 'Keep doing the Robot, it takes the heat off me!'

A decade on, it has all settled down. Maybe I haven't wound too many people up. I resisted joining social media for a long time, reasoning that there could be little fun in opening a new avenue for fans to abuse me. Happily, there don't seem to be as many idiots as I feared there might be. When it does come, it's almost water off a duck's back. People want a reply from you, so they say something unpleasant, the Twitter equivalent of throwing stones at a sleeping dog. Don't let them win. Put your phone down and do something pleasant instead.

Abuse that's amusing I don't mind. When it's nasty and it's in your face it's much harder to ignore than on social media. Abbey and I were once catching a late flight from Manchester to Ibiza for a little holiday. Sitting in the departure lounge, everyone else drunk, we got spotted by a group of lads off on a stag-do. Thirty of them, jumping up and down in our faces, jabbing fingers – 'You Scouse bastards! You Scouse bastards!' Abbey was scared. I felt helpless. I couldn't take on all of them. We had a three-hour flight ahead of us.

Worse stuff still. Chants about Liverpudlians that no one there should have had to listen to, let alone the subject of it all. We had to leave. Sack off the flight, walk back out through passport control and security, ask for our bags to be unloaded. We drove to London and caught a British Airways flight from Heathrow the following day instead. To hear those chants in a football ground is one thing. To hear it at an airport with your partner is quite another.

Grounds have changed too. Twenty years ago, playing as a winger at away grounds, you could be hit by the spray as fans spat abuse at you. Playing in front of the old Chicken Run at Upton Park could break players. It could be worse for home players if they were struggling. To play at West Ham required a strong character, because if it wasn't going well then you would hear about it.

Quite a few couldn't handle it. I have seen great players freeze. You can hide in plain sight on a football pitch. Don't go looking for the ball. Don't show for it. It's easy. There are certain players that you'll see on the ball all the time if you're winning and then never at all if you're behind. If you're invisible no one can see you. If you don't have the ball you can't make mistakes, and if you don't make mistakes no one can abuse you for making them. It takes a brave player to say, having given one or two passes away, yup, give me the ball, I want to go through this again.

The support from some sections of the crowd is not as it was. It used to be that everyone would get behind the team no matter what, even if individual players copped it. They saw it as their duty and as part of the fun. Sing your hearts out for the lads, no matter what. Sing from the first minute. Sing even louder if you go a goal behind. Now some of the fans, the more corporate ones, expect to be entertained. It's like going to a show, or watching *Britain's Got Talent*: entertain me, or I will boo you. The bigger the expectations, the more difficult it can be, as Arsenal have found out, as West Ham have experienced since moving to the London Stadium. At Spurs, if we weren't winning at half-time we'd often get jeered off. Football's a hard game. You're not always going to be ahead, but it doesn't mean you're not trying. It's why some big teams play better away from home. Away supporters are different. You don't travel all that way to boo your own team.

For specific players, the drop-off in noise and anger has meant an easier ride. Now there are more families and kids, many more women. The cost of tickets has priced out groups of smashed-up young lads. It gets self-policed. If one fan starts off with something deeply unpleasant he'll often be told to shut up by those around him.

Unless, that is, the player starts abusing the crowd instead. Matty Etherington, our winger at Stoke, was a terrible hothead. Once, heading down the left wing at pace, the crowd urging him to cross it, he decided to cut back instead onto his right foot. One side of the Bet 365 Stadium all shouting at him: 'Gerrit in the box!' Matty gesturing at them even as he held on to the ball, getting ready to lay if off into midfield. 'F*** off! F*** OFF!'

The stuff that goes on between players has dropped away too. It used to be that a centre-half and a forward would be in each other's ears for the whole game. You'd be told you were useless, except in rather more direct terms. You'd point out that they were a trifle slow, that they were perhaps fortunate to share the same pitch that you were jogging around. Again in slightly spicier fashion.

I tried it once against John Paintsil, the former Fulham defender. God, you're crap. What's your name again? None of us have heard of you. Do me a favour, turn round so I can see what it says on the back of your shirt. Hold on, what? Pants? Pants seal?

All this going on as the game progressed, as he followed me round the pitch marking me. 'Do me a favour, Pants-Man. Wow, you're bad. How are you even in this team? How are you on this pitch?'

It was his eyes that first told me. He'd gone. He'd lost it, and he wasn't getting it back. Getting up into my face. 'I don't care. I am going to break your legs. I am going to end your career.'

Uh-oh. Chasing me round the pitch, all the Fulham players trying to calm him down except he's not having it. 'I will kill you ...' I can't have a word with the ref, because the crime has not yet been committed. Sprinting around, trying to keep my legs and career intact, thinking, 'Oh, Crouchie, what have you done?'

Playing for Villa against Newcastle, still young, keen to impress as an expensive new signing, I was as keen as mustard. I was chasing everything, closing everyone down. Including Craig Bellamy, the Newcastle striker, quite possibly the mouthiest man in football. Him having to drop deeper and deeper to get the ball, trying to escape my eager embrace. Suddenly losing his temper, and turning to his team-mate Jonathan Woodgate while waving his finger at me. 'Who's this f***ing character? He thinks he's a forward, but he's only interested in defending. No wonder he's not scoring any goals.' All for my benefit, all to make me stop it or to wind me up so much I went after him and got myself in trouble.

Jamie Carragher once asked Bellamy why he was such a little horror on the pitch. He explained that it was his way of getting fired up. He had to shout his mouth off and abuse anyone he saw – opponents, the referee, team-mates – to play at his best. Most of the time he couldn't even remember what he'd said, which may have had something to do with the fact he never stopped. Playing for Newcastle against Liverpool, he saw Carragher play a pass into space ahead of Robbie Fowler and turn away in disgust when the striker failed to chase it down. 'Come on, Robbie!' yelled Carra. 'Get in there!'

That was enough for Bellamy. No matter that he wasn't on their team. 'Oi, Carra! What d'you think you're doing? You can't say that to Robbie Fowler. You're Jamie Carragher. You're not fit to lace his boots!' Carragher standing there in stunned disbelief, Fowler laughing his red socks off.

He'd slag his own team-mates off in the middle of a match. 'You're crap! How are you on same team as me, Craig Bellamy?' No worries or guilt about referring to himself in the third person, just on to the next unfortunate target. It might be one of the young lads, driving out of the training ground car-park ahead of him and stopping to sign autographs for a few kids. Bellamy out of his own car in a flash, arms going. 'What the f***? Craig Bellamy is behind you! No one even knows who you are!'

That Newcastle team had a lot of chat. Bellamy, Woodgate, Lee Bowyer, Kieron Dyer. Neither did they seem to mellow as the years went by and their careers started drifting to a close. Woody came to Stoke towards the end. Against Wolves, Tony Pulis decided to pick him at right-back. He was a never a right-back, and Matt Jarvis tore him to shreds. In the first 19 minutes, Woodgate was booked, gave away a penalty for a foul on Jarvis that put Wolves one up, and somehow escaped a second booking for that offence that would have seen him sent off.

Not that he would stay on the pitch any longer in any case. Pulis pulled him off less than a minute later. Woodgate didn't even make it a quarter of the way into the game.

You'd expect him to be crestfallen, to trudge off the pitch humiliated as the Wolves fans poured happy abuse and scorn upon him. Instead he sprinted to the touchline and gave Pulis a big thumbs-up. 'Best decision you ever made,' he said, and sat down with a grin.

HEADERS

I love headers. I know, I would say that; I've scored móre headed goals than anyone else in Premier League history. I've got a certificate from the *Guinness Book of Records* should I ever get into a very specific pub argument as an old man and need documentary evidence. Headers aren't cool, and they should be. Headed goals can be fantastic. Headers should be cherished.

But they can get you in trouble too. The World Cup, Germany, 15 June 2006. England are playing Trinidad and Tobago in a group match that will put us into the knockout stage if we win, except it's not going well, unless you're a supporter of the smallest nation ever to qualify for a World Cup finals, in which case it's going very well indeed. Eighty-two minutes gone and it's still 0–0, and the crowd are all over us and even Sven, who gets stressed as often as I go pot-holing, is starting to look a little damp under the collar.

David Beckham finds space down the right. A cross bent towards the back post, me jumping over the Trini defender Brent Sancho, getting my head on it and sending the ball crashing past Shaka Hislop's right hand and into the net. Bedlam in the Nuremberg stands, Stevie Gerrard adding another in stoppage time and England on their way, at least until Portugal and Cristiano Ronaldo and that

Rooney red card in the quarter-finals, but that's another story. It's the absolute pinnacle of my career, scoring for my country at a World Cup, the whole nation watching, me buzzing and so full of happiness that there is no chance whatsoever of me sleeping that night.

Except afterwards photos emerge of my hands doing something to Sancho's dreadlocks that I don't even remember. It looks like I've grabbed his hair and used it either to hold him down or to lever myself up. These things happen when you go up for headers. It's all arms and legs and grappling. All is fair in love and the opposition penalty box. But suddenly I'm a cheat, even though I had no idea I'd done anything, and it's only when Ronaldo is described by the British press as even more of a cheat after the mock outrage before Rooney's sending-off and the wink that follows that the heat comes off a little.

Five years later I'm playing with Trinidadian striker Kenwyne Jones at Stoke. The incident is one of the first things he brings up. Crouchie, don't ever go on holiday to Trinidad. Or Tobago. Even now. People remember what you did. People won't forget.

Another four years on, and a story on the BBC Sport website catches my eye. It's an interview with Brent Sancho. His dreads have gone, and he's now in a suit. You can understand why the headline grabs me: 'Peter Crouch is probably the most hated Englishman in our history.' Sancho is in a suit because he's now the government's sports minister. He's a man with power. My name is almost certainly in the national crime database in capital letters with alarms attached. The moment my passport comes up at immigration is probably the point that a decade and more of hurt comes crashing down upon me. All because of that jump. All because of a single header.

Headers get you in trouble. Every game a nudge or a knock. Elbows in the face. My nose broken twice, now so bad I have polyps too, and I struggle to breathe unless I use the Neanderthal technique and use my mouth as the primary suction device instead.

Against Manchester United I went up for a header against Nemanja Vidić and wore his forehead on my face. I needed staples to put me back together. Playing for Liverpool against Sheffield United, I went down for a diving header and got booted in the chops by Rob Hulse, splattering my nose and lips all over the place. At half-time I was lying on the physios' bench in the dressing-room, two black eyes, most of my set-piece teeth missing, blood all over the place. The club doctor had the right sort of bedside manner: you'll be fine, Crouchie, we just need to get you cleaned up, and you might need a little op on that nose, but you'll be fine. My dad came down from the stands to see how I was. You okay, son? Doc says I'll be fine, Dad. He's right, you'll be fine.

Then in come the rest of the team, led by Jamie Carragher. A double-take and a look of total horror. 'What the f*** has happened to your face?' Carra bursting out laughing, turning to the lads and beckoning them over. 'Boys! You have to get on Crouchie!' Gerrard, Reina, Finnan, all coming over, taking one look and laughing their heads off. 'Look at the state of him!' It blew me out of the water. 'He looks like the Elephant Man!' Eh? What? But the doctor said … DAD!

The doc was right. An op did follow, and I was obviously worried how it would turn out. Needlessly, as the new nose was a spectacular improvement on a pretty shoddy original. My nose growing up, I could now appreciate, was terrible. It went sideways when it should have been going forwards and forwards when it should have stopped. In retrospect it was clear that Hulse had done me a massive favour. I'd never had a better nose.

It got to me for a while. I was going into headers with an attitude that was more about preservation than ambition, 'Oi, I've got a smashing new nose here, leave me alone …' But I felt I'd earned my new feature. The operation had been like something from a Japanese horror film. They hung small bags under my nostrils in the aftermath, just to catch all the blood and weird bits constantly coming out. Each bag would have to be changed four times a day, so quickly were they filling up. The blood I could handle. It was the unidentifiable jelly that got to me. All I could do was hope that it wasn't small yet critical parts of my frontal lobe. My dad picked me up from the hospital and immediately made it worse by making me laugh. My nose was bouncing on my face with each giggle, and as it did more jelly-lumps would drop out.

I considered myself lucky that I hadn't ended up with a Steve Bruce, the most incredible nose in British football, or that of former Coventry goalkeeper Steve Ogrizovic. And then, in November 2012, going up for another header, Newcastle United's defender Fabricio Coloccini did me with an elbow. It was a bit of a sly one and a mighty effective one too: my front two teeth knocked clean out, another jammed back into my gums. On the bright side I caught at least one of the pair that fell out. On the downside I then took that one and the one the doctor had found in the grass and tried to put them back in, as if I could defy gravity as well as established dental practice and balance them upside down on a broken mouth.

Forget Bruce and Oggy. Now it was Joe Jordan I was worried about. I was only 32. I wasn't ready to be walking around with a mouth that looked like a garden fence after a gale.

The surgeon advised me against implants. 'If these ones get knocked out, there'll be nothing left for the next set to hang on to. You could ruin your mouth forever.'

I was more worried about ruining my relationship instantly. 'Mate, I can't play without any teeth. Have you taken a step back? I'm bad enough as it is. Get 'em in, let's crack on.'

So far so good. The implants have been so successful that I can take on a crisp apple with significant confidence. Players could once make a virtue of going out on the pitch without teeth, but not in this day and age. The game has moved on.

I still like heading the ball. You might assume that all professional players feel the same way, but alas that's not true. I know established Premier League stars who would rather not. Wingers. Central midfielders. Goalkeepers are far from the worst, to be fair to them. Forget this idea that it hurts to head a football even at times when Rob Hulse's foot or Fabricio Coloccini's elbow are not accelerating towards your passport picture. It's like catching a cricket ball; if you do it properly, if you welcome the act, it doesn't hurt at all. It's when you go in half-arsed that it goes wrong, when you get three-quarters of the way through with it and then pull out. Think about the stakes. Making that header could be the difference between winning and losing a game. You don't want to risk all that because you think, incorrectly, that it'll hurt. But you wouldn't believe how many don't want to do it.

I had to be persuaded myself, in the early days. It had nothing to do with pain and everything to do with style. As a kid I wanted to be Paul Gascoigne. It was all about touch. I wanted to dribble and score beautiful goals. If a ball came in off the ground I volleyed it. If it came in high I would overhead-kick it.

It was only as I joined the youth ranks of professional teams that I realised that idealistic, artistic attitude wasn't going to cut it. You want to show the coaches what you're good at but they want you to work at all of it. They took one look at my dad, who was 6'5", and they realised I wasn't going to fall short of that. And so Des Bulpin, the youth team manager at Spurs, told me he wanted me to be a goal-scoring target man. I could still try to score goals like Gazza's for Lazio against Pescara, but my heading would have to be world-class too.

No one wants to head a ball for hours. Playing with your mates, staying out late past tea-time as it gets dark, you find happiness in thrashing volleys against the fence you're using as a makeshift goal, not popping headers away. But aged 14 I was already 6'4", and I was losing headers to kids who were the same age but with ears level with my nipples. Des embarrassed me into competing more, and with that impetus came my own desire. With desire came success. When you start bullying centre-halves, heading suddenly becomes a lot more enjoyable. I could be good at this, I realised. I could add this to the rest of my game without losing anything of the pretty stuff.

I quickly became accustomed to the assumptions from the sidelines and stands. You're that tall, why else are you in there? When they saw I could also use my feet there came another assumption in its place: it must have been the stuff with his feet that he had to work on. That was the way it had always been with tall players. You called them donkeys and you laughed at their attempts to do anything with their feet except kick out. That I could do both was the reason I played for England. It's rare enough to make you stand out.

From being forced to doing it to scoring some of my most important goals that way. My first goal for England, a header against Uruguay at Anfield. Nodding in a rebound for Spurs against Manchester City at the Etihad to put us into the Champions League at their expense. Banging one in from distance as part of a hat-trick for Liverpool against Arsenal; heading the winner for Liverpool against Manchester United in the FA Cup fifth round in 2006, Edwin van der Sar touching it onto the post, the ball taking an age to cross the line, the place erupting. The first time they had beaten United in the Cup in 85 years, another step on the way to Cardiff and eventual Cup final triumph. Even now Liverpool fans talk to me about that one.

Heading wasn't always so unfashionable. Back in the day the great practitioners were hailed across the land. Andy Gray at Wolves, Villa and Everton. Mark Hateley for Pompey, Milan, Monaco and Rangers. With my mum's roots in Manchester and half the family City fans, I used to get taken to Maine Road on Boxing Day or New Year when we stayed at my gran's for Christmas. My dad, his affections 200 miles south with Chelsea, would tell me to focus my attention less on the final score and more on City's striker Niall Quinn. Quinn's heading was so good it was like he had a mallet on his forehead one minute and a cushion the next, so able was he to batter one in or lay the ball off delicately to a team-mate. He could use his chest like other men use their insteps. His awareness of where his team-mates were and where they might end up was so good it was as if he had eyes on every side of his large square head.

Neither were all the great headers of the ball tall men. Think of Jürgen Klinsmann's movement and the power he generated as he scored on his debut for Spurs away at Sheffield Wednesday, or Nick Barmby's long-ranger for Spurs against Wimbledon in the FA Cup of 1993. Ian Rush, with that cute little glancer in the FA Cup final against Everton in 1989, leaning back and just caressing in

John Barnes's curling cross. The glancing header is the forgotten masterpiece of the genre. We all love a power header, but the glancer is a scalpel to its sword.

I was lucky to learn from one of the greats. As a kid at QPR I watched Les Ferdinand ruling the airwaves. As a youth team player at Spurs I got to train with him. At the age of 17 I was 6'6". Sir Les was only 5'11" but he had the leap of a spawning salmon and the strength of a mature grizzly. When we went up for a header he bullied me. I didn't get close to it. I was miles off.

It was a huge wake-up call, and Les let the education continue in more benign fashion. He showed me where to run and how to time my jump. He showed me the importance of staying strong through the chest and abs, of how to target the weakest defender and leave the big ones looking over their shoulders wondering where I'd gone.

It's the movement that wins you headers. Hang at the back post, because if the cross goes short you can still attack it at pace and get in front of the more static defender, and if it goes long you're waiting to pounce. Give yourself a few yards on the full-back so you have the run on him, and when your winger gets to the byline and hangs the ball up, your eyes light up and the full-back looks suddenly like an injured wildebeest to your stalking leopard. Don't worry about what happens to him. Take the whole lot out when you go. The goalkeeper will be covering his near post and be scrambling back. The centre-back is going backwards as you come forwards. When a cross comes in like that and the defence are laid out in front of me in that fashion I don't ever feel that I'm going to lose.

It can be so beautifully simple. The winger doesn't need to cut back inside, when all that movement and advantage is tossed away. He doesn't need to slide his cross into the corridor of uncertainty between the defence and goalkeeper, because while it looks good and works sometimes there are usually too many legs in the way and too much luck required. You don't need to beat two men before getting the cross in. You don't even need to beat one. Get half a yard, like Aaron Lennon used to at Spurs, and stand the ball up. If I can't score I can knock it down for someone else. The odds are with us.

As a striker you rely on those outside and behind you. You break records for headed goals because you get the sort of crosses that allow you too. At Spurs I had Lennon – one of the most underrated players in the Premier League, and Gareth Bale – one of its great superstars. Lennon knew exactly where to put the defender. Bale could just burn them with his pace. As long as I could keep up with them I knew I'd get chances. As long as I got in the box at the right time I knew I'd get goals.

The best crossers are often full-backs rather than out-and-out wingers. Glen Johnson when I was at Portsmouth, Steve Finnan at Liverpool. They don't over-think it. Run the overlap, get it in first time – absolutely perfect for me. Graeme Le Saux at Southampton got me so many goals by giving himself half a yard of space and whipping the ball in. Danny Higginbottom at Stoke didn't even hit crosses; he just loved to hit long passes from full-back with his clever-clogs left foot. Gary Neville for England, always putting a good ball in, either overlapping David Beckham and taking the pass or dragging the cover with him so Becks could swing one over. And that was almost the dream scenario: Beckham, understanding what my strengths were, driving the ball at me from deeper positions, a lovely pace on them, right over the first centre-back, dropping in between the second centre-back and the full-back for me to run on to.

Charlie Adam at Stoke can deliver balls like a cross from a central position. Robert Prosinečki couldn't move but he didn't have to. He would just roll his foot over the ball and pass it straight onto your forehead. I look at Marc Albrighton now at Leicester and the simplicity of his crossing, or that of Kieran Trippier at Spurs. They understand what works for a good header of the ball. I hate this fashion now of wingers thinking they always have to cut inside, as if the run to the byline and the deep cross have gone out of fashion. Beckham and his United precursors in the earlier days used to do it to perfection. Ryan Giggs, Lee Sharpe, Andrei Kanchelskis. All bombing down the wings, strikers waiting, defenders panicking.

Those partnerships become instinctive. You can tell those team-mates what you want but they understand you and you understand them. If a winger is struggling to get past the full-back, if his feet aren't quite right, you make your run to the near post because you know that they won't be able to get enough on the ball to get it beyond there. There is nothing better than reading that little scenario, gambling on the near post, looking at the centre-back, knowing you're coming and they don't know, and powering in front of them to nod the ball home. If the ball falls behind your run? Volley it.

You have to do the work to cash in those chips. I pride myself on being in the box for every single cross. If I'm not there for even one then I get furious with myself, no matter if it would have gone over my head. You can get six or seven goals a season just from doing that and nothing else; you either score directly or it breaks off someone else and you're in there to put it away. I've scored some horrible goals like that – horrible goals that mattered in beautiful games. I see forwards now lurking outside the box looking for something prettier and sweeter to come along. To get your numbers up, get up in the box.

I'm glad I've played in the era of light, laceless balls. Heading the cannonballs that Tommy Lawton and Nat Lofthouse used to deal with would not have done my good looks any further favours. I understand the fears about concussion and the damage my chosen art might be doing to me, although had I never headed a single ball in my life I'm not convinced I would now be working for NASA as Professor Crouch, in charge of interplanetary probes. Abbey tells me I forget things, but as with many of us it depends on which precise things are being discussed. I'm yet to forget about a golf trip. Picking up semi-skimmed milk tends to slip by a little more. Sometimes there's so much info coming at you that it can be hard to retain it all. Or remember to maybe write it down next time.

If movement wins you headers then technique scores you goals from them. Right on the forehead, an inch above the eyes. Never take it on top of the head. It hurts far more and makes you feel dizzy. Get your neck up and keep your eyes open. The last thing you want is to jump and then pull the old turtleneck, where your head disappears back into your shoulders. It's one of the worst insults a footballer can receive: 'You f***ing turtle!'

Calculate where the cross is going. Line up the target and then go. Time it sweetly. If you run too early, if you jump too early, if you move your neck too early, it will go wrong. If you stand still and jump you aren't utilising either your height or your advantage over the centre-half. Get a run on it, keep your eyes open right until the very end and watch it onto your forehead. There is no better feeling than when you open your eyes again and see the ball sliding down the back of the net. Timing and desire, the weapons that make even smaller players great headers of the ball: Dwight Yorke, Paul Scholes, Tim Cahill.

Even now, when everything you do on a football pitch is logged and analysed, when every tiny marginal gain is seized upon and exploited, headed goals are still seen as a strange British virtue in European football, a Plan B if scoring goals the nice way isn't working. I found playing in the Champions League almost easier than playing in the Championship. In my second and third seasons at Liverpool I averaged a goal every two games in Europe; at Portsmouth it was four goals in six games, and with Spurs seven in ten. You could bully centre-backs in Europe in a way you could not in England simply because they were not used to that way of playing. If your full-back or winger got a good cross in, some defenders didn't really want to head it. Neither had many come up against a player as tall as me. It's a cliché, but a fabulous, World Cup-winning central defender like Fabio Cannavaro could bring the ball out of defence beautifully all day long and intercept pretty much everything on the deck, but he's not even 5'10". Put the right cross in and I'd nail him. I know I would. It was the same reason why I could score more than a goal every two games for England; all that encouragement from Des Bulpin, all those lessons from Sir Les, had given me something I hadn't even wanted but which brought my greatest success. In 2007, the year Liverpool made it back to the Champions League final again, I was second only to Kaka for goals scored in the competition. The majority of those came from centre-backs not knowing how to handle me. I came as rather a shock.

And so I love and appreciate headers like few others. The diving ones, like Keith Houchen for Coventry City in the 1987 FA Cup final. The hanging ones, like Pelé in the World Cup final of 1970, when he stayed up in the air for so long at the top of his leap that it was as if someone had pressed pause on the video. The neckers, like Gerrard's first to kick-start the Miracle of Istanbul in 2005, the creative, like Javier Hernández's back-header for Manchester United against Stoke in 2010, when you couldn't work out how he'd done it even when you watched it back. The ones that look better because the goal-scorer's hair adds emphasis to the power of the header, like Ruud Gullit's in the European Championship final of 1988; the ones that look better because the scorer has no hair at all, like Yordan Letchkov's for Bulgaria to knock Germany out of the 1994 World Cup.

The best defenders lay traps to bring you back to earth. When you played against Neville rather than with him he would give you a little nudge just as you jumped. It didn't need to be a big one. When you're in the air you have nothing to brace yourself against. You would have the ball in your sights and the goal in your peripheral vision and then suddenly you're two inches from where you want to be, and the ball hits your head but not where you want it and everyone in the crowd thinks you've messed it up. Oh, I had that … It should have been a penalty every time, but because I'm so big and the nudge was so subtle and low, the referee would read it the same way as the crowd. You would land awkwardly, Neville would trot off and pick up the loose ball.

The big boys would take you on shoulder to shoulder. Martin Keown and Tony Adams, when I was starting out, Sol Campbell. All over you, never giving you a yard. John Terry at Chelsea, except Terry was partnered by Ricardo Carvalho, who was a good defender but absolutely perfect for me. I would leave Terry to it and pull on to Carvalho every single time. José Mourinho wasn't stupid. He would try to get his two centre-backs to switch round.

I'd switch back myself. Always pick the weak spot. Always look for the wildebeest that's limping.

There are other tricks. It used to be defenders standing on your toes as the ball came in to stop you jumping. That mutated into shirt-pulling, the crime that so seldom gets punished. John Carew marked me at a corner once when he was playing for Villa. I was wrestling with him as the cross came in, my eyes lighting up at the trajectory, but I couldn't seem to get off the ground. Why aren't I moving? It was his raw strength. He was just holding me exactly where he wanted me with no apparent effort. Carew, the strongest man I've ever touched.

As a striker you lay plans to upset their traps to bring you down. On corners I put one of my team-mates between me and the best defender. Now he can't stand on my toes. Now he can't hold me down with a little finger like Carew. Instead I can get a run on him, and he can't see enough to know which way I'm going. Even if he sees me start one way I can fake it and go back the other. I don't need the six-yard box to myself. All I need is a few yards and the momentum and the timing. The best blocker I've had? Ryan Shawcross. He's clever enough to know exactly where to stand and when to move where. Also he's incapable of scoring himself, so you may as well use him to get in the way.

All headed goals feel good. Flicks, dives, glancers, powered. Even tap-ins bring their own joy. I scored one against West Brom in August 2017 when their 'keeper Ben Foster and defender Ahmed Hegazi smashed into each other to leave me three yards out with an open goal in front of me. With those you're celebrating before you've scored. Everyone loves a free gift.

I'm not sure my Premier League record will ever be beaten. I say that not to blow my own remodelled nose but because the header and the scoring of great headers is not cherished by others as I have loved it. Andy Carroll might have had the chance but sadly he can't stay fit for long enough. I'm the only active player in the top five.

But it is an art that should live on. Because if you've never done it, you'll never know how beautiful it feels: the cross coming in, not too fast, not too short, the excitement thumping in your chest, the defender back-pedalling, your eyes widening, the instant algorithms run and timings calculated, you charging in and flying over the top of him and flying through the air and BANG ...

HAIRCUTS

I'll be honest. I'm used to paying a tenner for my haircuts. I know, you'd never tell. So when my wife Abbey told me she'd met a hairdresser at a modelling shoot she had done, and that he was really good, and that he could come to our house, I said why not, let's have him over.

He looked the part. Tattoos, funky hair. His chat was average, and my hair, once he'd stepped away from it, looked exactly as it does after my £10 director's cut. I thanked him. 'How much is that, please?' Thinking it would be one of those scenarios where you pay what you feel is appropriate, probably with a little tip on top for his troubles.

He looked at me with a straight face. 'Yeah, that's two hundred and fifty pounds.'

Two hundred and fifty quid? I couldn't even hide it. I burst into laughter.

'What are you talking about?'

'Oh no, that's my rate.'

'When were you going to tell me? I haven't even got £250 in the house!'

I called Abbey downstairs, still laughing. 'Abbey! This bloke's asked for two hundred and fifty quid!'

She started crying with laughter too. 'You what?'

Then came the apologies, not from the hairdresser, or from Abbey to the hairdresser, but from Abbey to me.

'I'm so sorry Pete, I got it wrong. I had no idea! Two hundred and fifty quid?'

I had another look in the mirror, just to check. It was just a trim round the back and sides. Not even a scalp massage.

I ended up paying him. I gave him £200. It was all I could find. And then I gave him my tough face, my angry one, as I showed him the door. 'You. I never want to see your face again. Got it?'

I have no idea what he was thinking. People must have been paying him £250 on a regular basis, unless he just assumed that because he was in a footballer's house that money no longer held any real meaning, and that because I was a footballer I probably couldn't count as high as 250 because there were insufficient digits on my body.

On the bright side, I haven't seen the hairdresser's face again. I like to think he's still blushing. I fear he's still working, quite possibly in the employment of former team-mates of mine. Footballers and haircuts have always been an uneasy marriage. When it works it's beautiful. When it goes wrong it's either a comedy or a tragedy.

Things are acceptable now that when I was starting out would have led to fist-fights and disgrace. It's considered perfectly normal for players to bring their own personal hairdryers into the team dressing-room, often in bespoke hairdryer-shaped bags. Forget blow-drying your hair. It blows my mind. Even Jack Butland brings his own, and he's a goalkeeper. Of all the positions in a team, you wouldn't expect it from a goalkeeper. The way things are evolving it can only be a matter of time until we see a rough, crook-nosed central defender towelling himself off after a match and then plugging in his own set of straighteners.

I grew up on the sporting mullet. The best of the genre for me was Chris Waddle's, not only for the hair itself but for the player it sat on top of. I loved him at Spurs and I loved him even more at Marseille. I had a VHS tape of his best moves, including that goal he scored where he flicked it over the goalkeeper before backheeling it into the net. It was a beautiful goal scored in a lovely kit but it looked even better because of the mullet flopping about as he nudged the ball home. They used to call him Magic Chris, and I could understand it. I bought the white Marseille home shirt as a result, the one with the pale blue hoops around the top of the arms. To make it match I asked my dad if I could have a mullet too. Bored of whacking out tenners on my hair, innocent of a world where it would one day be socially acceptable to ask 250 quid for the privilege, he did it himself.

There was more to Waddle than merely the mullet. When he had it cut he didn't suddenly become Samson after his row with Delilah. Somehow he seemed underrated, named Football Writers' Player of the Year in 1993 but unable to get in the England team. There was 'Diamond Lights', the single with Glenn Hoddle, and there was 'We've Got a Feeling', the record he put out with his Marseille team-mate Basile Boli, which was accompanied by a video almost as impressive as Chris's hair. But the mullet defined him: spiky, always moving, defiantly at odds with a more boring world.

Like many young men who first sported a mullet in the 1980s I came back to it in the early 2000s, rescuing it from the wilderness where it had been kept alive only by eastern Europeans and Australians in vests. I didn't go the whole hog. It was mainly shaved at the sides and floppy on top, with a little length left at the back. But it felt reassuringly familiar, and it looked better than the curtains I had at QPR, which when my hair went lighter in the sun each summer made me look like I was rocking a highlighted bob, or something a little girl might have in Year Two. That itself was preferable to the times I've taken it really short all over, when the lack of hair has accentuated the shape of my physique and made me look like an awkward teenager. Or a very long baby.

I've never bleached. I'm aware it's a rite of passage for many footballers, and I for one was in full support when the entire Romania team decided to bleach their hair at the 1998 World Cup. It spoke to me of team unity when it spoke to others only of custard. It's a risky game, bleaching. The first time you do it you're never sure if it's going to be white like a ghost's or get stuck in that weird dark-yellow halfway, as Ryan Giggs's did when he had his done in 2002. When Marko Arnautović had his done at Stoke he looked exactly like one of the women who works in the kitchen at the training ground, only with smaller biceps.

We live in a footballing world where players are more open about artificial enhancements than ever before. Find yourself ageing too fast and you can go down the Just For Men route, like one of my former Stoke team-mates. The trick, I'm told, is not to go too dark too rapidly. It's hair-dye, not a time-travel machine. Then there are the laser implants for those whose issue is less the colour grey than a lack of hair to change colour. They're easy to mock but they're not as easy to spot as you might think. Just ask a certain creative midfielder at Spurs. Fillers, plugs, weaves, all now rife in the Premier League. When Wayne Rooney had his implants done he initially told us all he was going to choose really long hair. He was deadly serious. 'If it works, I want it to work properly.'

And they do work, most of the time. Look at Antonio Conte and his jet-black floppy fringe. He literally looks 20 years younger than he did as a patchy, balding man of 24 at the 1994 World Cup in the USA. We all know it's down to the wizardry of a surgeon, but we forget. When I see him getting interviewed now I don't remember the old days. I just see a handsome Italian man with magnificent hair.

It's fine for footballers to be bald now. Shave it back, stay lean around the cheekbones and in many cases you can actually look better, certainly more youthful than the footballers of the distant past who stuck it out with bushy side pieces and the stringy combover. Some of those young men of 26 looked double that. Bobby Charlton barely seems to have aged since lifting the World Cup.

The awkward stage is the in-between period where it's too long to shave but too sporadic to fool anyone. Gradually you see the emergence of a patch of hair towards the front of the head that we might refer to as Shearer's Island, which begins as a peninsula but is inexorably swamped by rising sea levels. There is a point where you just have to accept that climate change has won, but I can understand that it's hard. It's not a nice time for a man. One day a mullet, the king of the scene, the next a shininess in the bathroom mirror and a chill around the ears whenever the wind blows. It's why I will never criticise Marouane Chamakh for the strange gelled-down flaps and weird spikes he has had. He was stuck in the transition, trying to make the best of what he had left in the brief period before it finally waved goodbye.

Sometimes you have to make a few mistakes to find out what works for you. Aged 14, as a youngster at Spurs, I travelled to Northern Ireland with our under-16s to play in a tournament called the Milk Cup. Someone decided that we should all shave our heads. You could either get it done yourself or be held down and have it done to you. There is a video of me scoring in one of the matches, and I look like a refugee running scared from some barbaric regime. My mum was furious when I returned home, but like those Romanians a few years later we found a little time on our collective barnets made a significant difference to the camaraderie of the squad.

It is to David Beckham's great credit that in all the many styles he had down the years there was only one genuine misstep, the braids. He had the right type of hair to try so much – floppy but with body, a very solid covering all over – but he had the courage too, and in doing so changed the whole attitude of British men to their hair. Admittedly there is a greater safety net if you are a greater player. Roberto Baggio could get away with his beaver's tail at the 1994 World Cup because he was Roberto Baggio. It's much harder if you're Steve from Kent, or Phil Stamp.

I think too of Ronaldo, the original Brazilian one rather than the Portuguese Cristiano, and when he shaved all but a strange wedge at the front during the 2002 World Cup. He could pull it off because he was banging in the goals that decided the tournament. Many years later I met him in Ibiza, the only former player I have ever asked for a picture. I used to love him. During his time at Inter Milan I would watch an entire game just to see him take a single shot; even when he was getting fat at Real Madrid he was still scoring 30 goals a season.

When I hailed him in Ibiza I was hoping he knew who I was. He didn't. I was gutted. He was lying there with an ashtray on his belly, a fag between the fingers of one hand and a beer hanging out of the other. He didn't move. His lady friend was ferrying him beers and changing his ashtray when it got full, which was quite often. It was amazing to watch.

A good footballer's haircut can add to their mystique. Carlos Valderrama was a fine player, but would we still instantly be able to summon a memory of him bossing the midfield in his yellow Colombia kit if it wasn't for that enormous gingery Afro up above? You could argue it's the same for Marouane Fellaini, in both good and bad ways. David Ginola's long, flowing locks would exaggerate his moves. When he sent a defender the wrong way his hair was often still going the right way, and the poor full-back couldn't help but follow it. I used to watch him at Spurs when I was in the youth team. He would drop a shoulder, his hair would swish past a second later and you suddenly realised you were in some sort of a trance. He was a great player but his hair made him look better still. When he cut it short and it went grey, something was forever lost to the game.

These are haircuts that help a career. Would Paul Pogba be spoken about as much if you didn't notice him as often because of the hair? No matter that if you shave 'POG-BOOM' into the side of your hair it grows over within a few days, leaving merely a hairy outline. You see it during a match from the corner of your eye and it sticks. Ivan Perišić does a solid job on the wing for Inter and Croatia. When he dyed his hair red and white in a diamond pattern he became impossible to ignore.

An interesting philosophical question: if David Beckham looked like Paul Scholes and Paul Scholes looked like David Beckham, which one would be the more famous footballer? As a keen observer of the game you like to think you can see through mere appearances, but looks matter, and looks spread. Haircuts that Beckham was rocking in 2002 would slowly percolate down through the footballing pyramid, so that by 2004 strikers in League One were wearing a bleach-topped fauxhican with pride. By 2005 every lad outside every suburban pub had the same.

An adventurous haircut requires commitment. If you want a pony-tail, do it properly. These tiny little stubs, the ones that stick out like the tail of a shy mouse, are simply not enough. I'm not averse to having a go myself – work through the latter part of a season with my QPR-era curtains, get it to a decent length come May and then crack on over the summer until, come the August and a fresh season, I would have the full Emmanuel Petit. Sadly, I can't handle having hair that hangs over my eyes when I'm playing. I feel like it's hindering my football, and a scrunchie or Alice band is too much for me. If I still have enough hair at the age of 50 I'll give it a go, like a longer, wrinkly version of Orlando Bloom in *Lord of the Rings*.

I have no issue with those who push their hair into styles that others might fear. Joe Allen was born in Carmarthen and started playing football in the west Wales coastal town of Tenby. Despite that, he now looks like a guitarist in a hard rock band from 1969, long hair held back by a thin elastic band, beard to complement it. Shaun Derry was a hard-as-nails defensive midfielder. For most of his career you could no more imagine him with a hairband than you could a tutu. And then suddenly for 18 months at Leeds he looked like an Italian playboy, at least in his own head.

Gareth Bale, in his early days at Spurs when he was being played out of position at left-back – which was like playing Ronaldo in goal – would have a little clip in his hair to hold it back. As he matured as a footballer, as he was released to go rampant down the left wing, no one batted an eyelid. But when he was struggling, when he was getting exposed, that clip used to wind Harry Redknapp up no end. He saw it as a weakness, in the same way he thought Gareth would go down injured too easily in training and refused to let the physios on to see him. It's the hair equivalent of the gold football boots. You have to be able to back a haircut up, or you leave yourself exposed to all manner of criticism.

There are of course those players who have no doubts about their hair, who are convinced of their peerless style even as others doubt them. David James scrolled through a few – blond corn-rows, a small 'fro, a bigger 'fro. Even saying the name 'Bolo Zenden' makes me think of my old Liverpool team-mate standing in his Y-fronts in front of the mirror in the dressing-room, combing his long locks like Rapunzel, Jamie Carragher shaking his head in disbelief. I bumped into Bolo on the beach in Ibiza one summer. He was wearing budgie-smugglers. All I could think was, aren't you worried about getting your arse-cheeks burned?

Dirk Kuyt was particular about his own stylings. He would leave a series of large tubs of hair gel in various places around the training ground so that he could dip in whenever he wanted. It was weird stuff, bright yellow, with a jelly-like consistency to it. He would smear it all over his curls to give him something of a wet look. I had a little finger-dip once, just to see what it was like. The aroma was relatively mild, the hold quite weak. He had it specially imported from the Netherlands. My sample made me wonder why.

Equally fussy is my Stoke team-mate Jean-Eric Maxim Choupo-Moting. Each week brings a fresh look. Our defender Marc Wilson, a white Irish lad, had his head turned. He went from a normal haircut to thinking his hair was Afro-Caribbean. He used to get his barber Jamal to come up from London once a week to trim his beard and shave some lines into his scalp. The return train fare to Stoke alone will have set him back a couple of hundred quid. Suddenly he's past the magic £250 stage and he's not even flinched.

It all comes down to self-belief. Rio Ferdinand would tell us stories about Cristiano Ronaldo when we were on England duty, about how when they were at Manchester United Ronaldo would stand in front of the mirror naked, running his hand through his hair, and say, 'Wow. I'm so beautiful!'

The other United players would try to wind him up. 'Whatever. Leo Messi is a better player than you.' And he would shrug his shoulders and smile again. 'Ah yes. But Messi does not look like this ...'

GOALKEEPERS

They're different. It's a footballing stereotype. But there is a reason why stereotypes exist, a set of core truths that created the idea in the first place. So it is with goalkeepers. Can you be normal and be a goalkeeper? I don't think so, and I say that from personal experience rather than laziness. Even one of the very few you believe is normal will suddenly do something really strange. Lulled into a false sense of security, you'll think, what the hell? And then it comes to you. Of course. He's a 'keeper.

Peter Shilton, wanting to get taller as a teenager and so hanging from the bannisters at his parents' grocery shop and asking his mum to tied heavy bundles of house bricks to his ankles. John Burridge, doing handstands around his penalty area and then climbing up the posts to sit on the crossbar during a game. Asmir Begović, who I played with at Portsmouth and Stoke, pushing a shot round the post and then jumping to his feet to scream, 'This is my house!' Even us lot, on the same team as him and semi-prepared for this sort of madness, were taken aback. Standing there as the referee signalled for a corner, looking at each other with wonder in our eyes. 'What the hell is he on about?'

They're not just slightly different. Everything about them is abnormal to an outfield player. They train miles away from the rest of us. I've been a professional footballer for two decades, and I still have absolutely no idea what they're doing. It's like a separate sport, and one that isn't as good. It's like witchcraft.

David James, a classic of the genre. I had the pleasure of his company during the 2006 World Cup in Germany. On a day off, sitting on the terrace of our extremely nice hotel, Baden-Baden and the countryside of the Black Forest laid out in front of us, a discussion among the squad as we enjoyed a bite to eat as to how we might spend the afternoon. A couple decided to play golf, a few to go for a swim. A group opted to go shopping down in the town. What do you fancy, Jamo?

A pause. 'I've just seen that chimney.'

'Eh?'

A stare into middle-distance. 'That chimney over there.'

'What?'

'I'm going to go over there and draw it.'

He was true to his word. A taxi summoned, a taxi taken out into the distant countryside. David gone until dinner, when he returned with a sketch of the chimney that drew amazement and applause from the various golfers, swimmers and consumers. Suddenly it made sense. Of course he had driven ten miles to be near a chimney. Of course he had the talent to draw it, as well as the equipment on hand to pull it off. You don't get full-backs producing art. Strikers can't draw. Our talent is in our feet and foreheads.

I think of Rob Green and his special mug, kept behind the bar of his favourite pub, pulling a chair up to the fire and spending the evening on his own, drinking tea and reading a book. Quintessential goalkeeper, both in the concept and the execution, not worrying for a moment what anyone else in the team might think. I hope I'm not painting too unflattering a picture of footballers when I say that no outfield player would ever do that, unless they were foreign. But then goalkeepers often seem to be more educated, or to be able to give the impression that they're more educated. Maybe David James bought the sketch off a local street artist. Maybe Rob Green just took a book to the pub to throw it on the fire. But I doubt it. You can trust goalkeepers. You can trust them to do things that you wouldn't trust any other footballer to even think of.

Another common trait. Almost all of them believe themselves to be better with their feet than they actually are. Two points to make on that: If they're so hot with the ball at their feet, why are they goalkeepers? Secondly, why does every club make them do relentless footwork drills, practising receiving the ball, giving it simply, if they are already masters?

Heurelho Gomes at Spurs wasn't the best with his feet. It was as if he had a curly foot. He simply couldn't strike a ball cleanly through the middle. You shouldn't be curling goal kicks; you're too far away to be trying to bend them into the opposition's top corner. But if his feet were wrong his hands were perfect, large and glue-like. He had the longest fingers I'd ever seen on a human. If you were going to design arms in a laboratory that would be absolutely ideal for catching and punching and palming away a ball, you couldn't come up with better than his.

Heurelho knew his limits. He had no desire to play up front, or in the little hole behind the front two. David James actually did it. He was playing for Manchester City against Middlesbrough in the last game of the 2005 season. City needed to win to leapfrog Boro into what was then the UEFA Cup places, but with five minutes to go the game was locked at 1–1. Jamo was quite busy enough in goal, yet that didn't stop City manager Stuart Pearce. He took midfielder Claudio Reyna off, stuck reserve 'keeper Nicky Weaver on in his place and in goal, and moved David up front.

He charged about the place like an angry bull. There were air-kicks, fouls and first touches further than Heurelho Gomez can kick it, comedy gold for everyone except City's £5m striker Jon Macken, who was sitting on the bench, coming to the realisation that perhaps Pearce didn't fancy him as a player. 'I wanted to unsettle them and in some ways it did,' Pearce said afterwards. 'It unsettled everyone – them and us.'

James was still playing for England at the age of 39, although not as a lone marauding striker. He was playing club football professionally into his 44th year. It's another aspect of a goalkeeper's existence that sets them apart from us footballers who can actually combine foot and ball successfully. I played with Dave Beasant at Portsmouth when he was 40, which since I was 19 at the time made him older than my dad. It hurt him to find out.

Now I'm closing in on a similar age, with memories of playing professionally when some of my team-mates weren't born. As a kid I thought of anyone over the age of 30 as ancient, but you always put goalkeepers in a separate category because age didn't appear to wither them in the same way. Beasant was still a fine goalkeeper at 40. James was not to blame for our exit from the 2010 World Cup in South Africa. You don't expect goalkeepers to have the same taste in music and clothes as everyone else even when they're in their 20s, so the fact that they're out of sync in their dotage makes no difference. Brad Friedel was rattling past 40 when we played together at Spurs, and he was as weird at that age as he had apparently been at Liverpool almost 15 years before. He was a lovely chap but he could talk a glass eye to sleep. For the same reason you tried never to get into an argument with David James. He'd talk you into submission. He knows everything about everything.

Goalkeepers, of course, can see no flaw in other goalkeepers. There is a refusal to criticise any other member of the union or admit he's done anything wrong. You will be watching a game as a team, and a poor goal will go in; 16 of the 18-man match-day squad will be shouting how you have to save that, shaking their head at the positioning, bemoaning the handling. All except two voices. 'Terrible defending, that.' 'Definitely the centre-half's fault.'

You can wind a goalkeeper up a treat with a simple comment such as, 'Well, that was straight at him.' To a goalkeeper that is an insult. It is to underplay the rapid-fire decision-making that has put him in that position. It's by design and many years of training that he happens to be exactly where the shot has gone, not accident, but an outfield player would never admit to such. Instead we prefer to escalate the wind-up – shouting, 'Catch it, you clown!' when they punch a cross away to the halfway line under enormous pressure, yelling, 'Just catch it, man!' when they somehow fingertip away a shot heading for the top corner.

In response a goalkeeper will always have an instinctive reaction just as illogical and unfair. A goal goes in, they leap to their feet to scream and shout at the nearest unfortunate defender. They make a near-impossible save; they leap to their feet to scream and shout at the nearest unfortunate defender. It's 'keepers Tourette's. Logically a great save should be celebrated as a striker celebrates a goal, with a huge grin, a punch of the air, a sprint over to the home support to soak in the adoration of the fans while team-mates attempt to jump on your shoulders. Instead they mark the moment by roundly abusing those same grateful friends. They try to underline what a great save it was by highlighting how exposed they were left by their defence. Suddenly it's not just a fine save. It's an incredible feat of solo brilliance that has got this useless bunch of outfield players right out of jail.

As a kid, spending Saturday afternoons at Stamford Bridge being a ball-boy, I was a huge fan of Chelsea's Dmitri Kharine and his distinctive combination of curly mullet and tracksuit bottoms. The former made sense for a man who grew up in Moscow in the 1980s. The latter didn't. If you've been raised in Russian winters you don't get to south-west London and think, really like it, but shorts aren't going to be enough in this climate.

As a grown man in the Premier League, the best I have seen was Peter Schmeichel. He totally dominated his penalty area. It was his zone, not the opposition strikers'. He would own the air above it like a great centre-half, and he could make saves so good that you sometimes thought (incorrectly) that there might be something fluky about them, like the jumping star-shape when a cross went behind him to the back post and the striker thought he had an open goal, or how wide he could spread himself in a one-on-one. When he had the ball in hand he could set up attacks like a quarterback, his throw-outs sending those fleet-footed Manchester United wingers away. I played with him at Aston Villa, when he was supposedly coming to the end, one of several veterans in our team, like Ronny Johnsen, David Ginola, Paul Merson, Alan Wright and Steve Stone, one of the reasons that the 21-year-old me was signed. He was pretty arrogant even then, and he had every right to be. You couldn't argue with him, even if you were brave enough to try.

No one's favourite player when they're a kid is a goalkeeper. Jamie Carragher's was – Neville Southall. Graeme Sharp too, but Southall for the saves that made you leap around as much as he did. He's now the size of a mature walrus, and takes on matters on social media that I never thought would concern Neville Southall: homelessness, gay rights, the freedoms of transgender youngsters. It makes me like him even more.

Another cliché for you: English goalkeepers prefer to catch crosses, overseas 'keepers favour the punch. That too has solid evidence behind it. We also used to think that the homegrown talents were sensible and calm where foreigners were eccentric like Jorge Campos or borderline insane like René Higuita. No longer does that hold so true. You'll struggle to find two more unflappable men than Petr Čech and David De Gea. The days of Portsmouth signing Japanese captain Yoshikatsu Kawaguchi and finding their glamorous overseas import utterly incapable of dealing with the challenges of the Premier League are long gone. As is Yoshikatsu. He was a lovely chap, but at just 5'11" tall and with all the bulk of a bulrush he would get smashed all over the place every time a ball went up in the air. It could never last.

De Gea is probably the hardest 'keeper to beat now in the country. You just feel he's going to read you whichever way you choose to go. Even if you go hard and low, which is the great fail-safe for a striker, he can get to it with his feet or legs. It doesn't look as clean to untutored eyes as using your hands, but who cares? Goals are not chalked off for pretty dives. Points are not awarded for artistic merit. Make the save any way that works. Make the poor old striker use his own hands to clutch his face in despair.

It's a strange thing, that one-on-one between centre-forward and goalkeeper. It's a battle of nerves and wits as much as physical skill, of bluff and double-bluff. As a striker clean through, you try to put disguise on what you do. Make them show their hand first.

On penalties, always commit to your decision. As soon as there is any doubt, as soon as you dally, your chances of missing skyrocket.

Before matches, goalkeepers will sit with their specialist coach and watch compilations of the opposition strikers' penalties on an iPad, looking for patterns, looking for little physical tells. Strikers will never do the equivalent and watch clips of the way 'keepers tend to dive, which might seem strange, but it's all about cause and effect. The penalty-taker is the one in control. The 'keeper is reactive. They will have a favoured side, usually diving the way of their stronger hand. Right-handed goalkeepers tend to be better going right than left. But they will make their decision on your penalty-taking history, your body-shape as you run in and then, if they have time, the actual direction of the shot.

They'll try to read your eyes. It's hard for a striker in their run-up not to instinctively glance towards the spot where they want to put the ball. A goalkeeper would look for that little flick from me and then go that way. Then came the first bluff. I would glance at one corner and then stick it in the opposite one. That worked for a while, and then the 'keepers and their coaches and their iPads figured that one out, so when you gave them the eyes they'd instead automatically go hard and fast the other way. Now you have to go with the double-eyes – look left, actually go left – and sometimes even the triple, which is the point where you can no longer remember where you actually wanted to put it and just welly it down the middle instead. You step into the ball with your eyes flicking left and right as if you've lost your mind and are convinced that each post is talking about you behind your back.

Strikers love making 'keepers look stupid. You don't have to be 1970s' Reading and Cardiff maverick Robin Friday, flicking V-signs at goalkeepers left prone by his wonder-goals, but a little embarrassment never does anyone's ego any harm – sticking them on their backsides, leaving them scrabbling in the mud like an old man looking for his glasses. There is an unwritten rule in shooting practice that if you chip the 'keeper successfully then it's total humiliation, which is perfect. The whole place will be laughing at them. But if they stand tall and catch it, they can have their revenge. They're allowed to boot it as far away as they like, and you have to run off to fetch it.

It's a universal law across the British game. If I signed for a new club tomorrow, tried to chip the 'keeper in my first training session and saw him catch it, I'd know exactly what was going to happen next. It's an insult to the goalkeeper's manhood, to their height, to their jumping ability. David James used to react with fury if anyone even tried. 'How f***ing dare you!' It's the same if a young player attempts to nutmeg an established outfield player. 'Oi! Have some respect!' I wouldn't have liked to be in the Denmark dressing-room after Davor Šuker chipped Schmeichel at Euro 96. Karel Poborský's scoop-chip over Portugal's Vítor Baía later in the same tournament might have been even more of a slap around the chops.

A centre-half always loves a 'keeper who dominates his penalty-box more than they will an out-and-out shot-stopper, but there is nothing better for a defender than a certain goal that is somehow clawed away by your number one. For all the mickey-taking, outfield players know that a top goalkeeper makes the difference between a great team and a great team that wins trophies. There were years when Schmeichel was the biggest single factor in Manchester United bagging the Premier League title. Encapsulated in a single game, think of United going to Newcastle in March 1996, six points behind them in the table. Newcastle were all over United in the first half, but Schmeichel kept them alive with a series of ridiculous saves. Eric Cantona's goal might have won it, but Schmeichel made that volley actually mean something.

There's a persuasive argument that great goalkeepers are undervalued in the transfer market. By May 2018 there wasn't a single one in the top 35 most expensive signings of all time. They appear to be a black spot in the vision of some managers. I find it strange that Arsenal needed a good one for years and didn't address it. Liverpool spent £75m on Virgil van Dijk but had three seasons when Jürgen Klopp had to rotate Simon Mignolet and Loris Karius, not to mention a Champions League final where Karius was at fault for two of the three goals Real Madrid scored. A third of van Dijk's fee could have signed him a Jack Butland.

Sir Alex Ferguson didn't always sign great goalkeepers. You could argue that in 27 years he had two world-class ones, Schmeichel and Edwin van der Sar. There were a fair few who fell short, to various degrees: Jim Leighton, Massimo Taibi, Mark Bosnich, Fabien Barthez, Roy Carroll. But he was ruthless in getting rid of them, and he left United with the gift of De Gea, sticking with him when others said he was too skinny and too weak on crosses, watching him develop into the best in the world.

De Gea has confidence. Ferguson believed in him but De Gea believes in himself too. If he makes a mistake it doesn't affect him. It doesn't lead to another. That ability not to overthink things, not to worry about the consequences of an error or dwell on what might happen, is a secret skill of many top players. I look at Mignolet, who is virtually a professor. He speaks eight languages. Maybe he's too bright, ridiculous though that may sound. Sometimes as a footballer you need a naivety. I've conditioned myself to not think too much on the pitch. If you dwell too much on the importance to so many people of what you're about to do then you'd never do it – you'd never take a penalty, or be able to finish a one-on-one. You might not even want to go out on the pitch for a big game, because there is too much to lose. I know very well-educated footballers who are excellent players but can't perform in front of 10 people, let alone 40,000, because they've thought too much about the consequences. Wayne Rooney has no fear. It allowed him to score from long range on his Premier League debut, aged 16; it's why he was England's youngest ever goal-scorer, why he could score four goals at Euro 2004 as an 18-year-old, why he could score a hat-trick on his debut for Manchester United. Don't worry about the what ifs. Just do what your instinct tells you.

No normal person wants to be in goal. If you dedicated yourself to the position from the age of five and grew up to be at least six feet tall, I'm pretty sure you could make it as a professional. You could have a good career. Secretly, however, those of us who have never had to do it do appreciate those who can. Look at what happens when an outfield player has to go in goal, because of a goalie being injured or a sent off after all the subs have been used. It's one of my favourite little plot-lines, so amusing to watch because it looks so wrong. The stand-in can't move properly. They seem to forget about their hands. They try to save everything with their feet, including shots at chest height.

And we appreciate that the goalkeeper lives his professional life under the ultimate jeopardy. Do your job and no one cares. Make one mistake and you kill your team.

You will be remembered not for your best save but for your worst mistake. Think of England's goalkeepers alone: Seaman being lobbed by Ronaldinho in the 2002 World Cup quarter-final, after the horrors of Nayim seven years earlier. Paul Robinson's miskick of Gary Neville's back-pass against Croatia in 2006, Scott Carson's fumble against the side at Wembley a year later. Poor old Rob Green spilling Clint Dempsey's feeble shot at the 2010 World Cup. It happened to Ray Clemence against Kenny Dalglish and Scotland at Hampden Park in 1976, and Peter Shilton in the critical World Cup qualifier against Poland in 1973.

It's like someone saying to me that they can't recall a single one of my goals, only the time I hit the crossbar, unmarked and from two yards out. Frightening, unfair and illogical. A goalkeeper's world summed up in a single sentence.

GOING OUT

I'd like to say professional football players are without exception excellent ambassadors for the game. I'd like to say that, but I can't, because I've walked out of a nightclub with my team-mates to see our star midfielder reclining across the bonnet of a Ferrari, arms folded, waiting for girls to come out so he could wink at them and then progress it from there.

I have no idea how long he'd been waiting. I do know that it wasn't even his Ferrari. He'd hired it solely so he could park it directly opposite the nightclub front door and lie on it. I have no idea if it worked as he planned. I couldn't watch. I was so disgusted that I turned on my heel and walked away with my nose in the air, which was probably pointless because from where he was lying my nose was in the air already.

Neither was this an exceptional display of foolishness. Where once a footballer's night out involved bad lager and worse kebabs, we now have the phenomenon of the Grey Goose Wanker. The Grey Goose Wanker spends his night behind a velvet rope. He wears sunglasses indoors. He wears a cap when the house dress code specifically forbids it but he gets away with it because he is a footballer and he is about to spend an eye-watering amount of money, and through his mere presence is going to attract many other revellers into the same joint to also spend a great deal on drinks that come with sparklers, plastic monkeys and actual flames coming out of the top. I know this because I've been one.

The Grey Goose Wanker goes behind the velvet rope and sits on a banquette. He stares at his phone for a while even though he's in the sort of place people usually go to socialise. When he feels the moment is right, he calls over a lackey and orders his beverage of choice. Moments later it materialises from behind the bar, in a silver bucket of ice, with various mixers on the larger tray that surrounds it and a party number of glasses and things on fire wedged into any spare gaps. As the great display is brought to his table he reclines in his upholstered lair, arms outstretched on the back of the seats to either side of him, and he watches the moths come to his flame: first one or two girls, then a few more, until all the seats are taken and all the glasses are full. At last he may look as if he is enjoying himself, but you can't guarantee it. This is the Grey Goose Wanker. And he stalks the VIP corners of this land.

It happens because footballers are lucky. We are lucky because, no matter what we actually look like, in the eyes of some we are as attractive as young gods. You are charming. You are funny. You still can't dance but no one seems to care. No one seems to notice any more that you have the physique of a runner bean and the nose of someone who walks into walls.

I first experienced the faintest touch of it when I was 15, playing for Spurs under-16s in the international youth tournament I mentioned called the Milk Cup. It was held annually in Northern Ireland, our matches played on Coleraine Sports Ground, my team-mates including Ledley King, and we won it. Our first taste of what we thought was glory, and we wanted to party all night long, which since we were in a sports hall in Portrush should have been an issue. Instead we were somehow allowed to do almost whatever we liked. Girls wanted to talk to me. Girls wanted to carry on talking to me even after they'd talked to me. At school I'd barely been able to pull a hamstring. I returned to London a new man, a spring in my step, hope in my heart for the future.

It took time to work its lucky spell. Two school friends from Ealing and I decided we wanted to go clubbing. We were 16. You could applaud our ambition but not our tactics. We got the tube to Hammersmith and walked up to the Palais. My first mate walked up to the bouncers and breezed in. My second mate did the same. I approached the door almost confident. I was getting on for a foot taller than them. I was taller than the bouncers. Nothing could go wrong.

Unless they checked one critical detail. 'How old are you, son?'

My answer was good. I'm 18. The delivery was not. My voice was yet to break. I barely sounded 12.

A hand across my chest. 'Son. You sound like Michael Jackson. Come back when you've hit puberty. Or you're Michael Jackson.'

To be fair to my mates, when they saw I hadn't made it, they came back out themselves. It wasn't that much of a sacrifice; a discussion on the way home confirmed that none of us had really wanted to go to a nightclub anyway. When the two had got in they had been further put off by the music, the décor and the cost of the drinks. This is horrible. Why would anyone want to come here?

Certain other venues carried more cachet. The QPR youth team of the time had some talent in it – Kevin Gallen, Nigel Quashie, Danny Dichio. Word spread that Dichio, a keen amateur DJ, was doing a few gigs at The Spot in Leicester Square. It seemed impossibly glamorous. Ledley and I would go into town and attempt to catch his efforts on the wheels of steel.

This time we came armed. When you first joined the PFA, the Professional Footballers' Association, you received a membership card. Auspiciously, it was gold. Despite the fact that I was yet to play a single minute of professional football I kept it in my wallet and pulled it out when again denied entry by bouncers. Once or twice it even worked. Better still was a letter we all had made up, purporting to be from an important company, confirming that yes, we were all 18, because of course those are the kinds of letters that important companies send. I kept mine in a green folder. Official-looking. A businessman simply enjoying a little downtime. In clothes his parents had bought for him.

Perhaps the bouncers decided we'd made so much effort they had to let us in. Maybe they just felt sorry for us; another ruse came when we made up fake IDs, saying that we were at Greenhill College in Harrow. My mate, who is dyslexic, had it printed as Greenall Colleg. I know it wasn't a university but I was still pretty sure you'd struggle for admission if you couldn't spell its name.

To the reserves at Spurs, and another tiny shift up the pecking order. After evening away games the team coach would drop us back at White Hart Lane. There was a nightclub right next to the ground called Rudolph's. I believe it later became Valentino's, which makes a certain sense. It's now a car-park, which also makes sense if you ever went in. It had red faux-leather seats, shiny chrome tables and a carpet that was sticky in the patches where there was still carpet. On the wall outside was a large sign: 'RUDOLPH'S: FOR NIGHT PEOPLE'. Nineteen years old, all of us wearing our tracksuits, as glamorous as the venue and determined to be in there as long as it would let us.

The closer you got to the first team the more floor lighting in the nightspot you visited. Going out in Chigwell from the training ground, taking in Epping Forest Country Club or Nu Bar in Loughton. Ledley and I hearing about the generation of London-based players above us like Frank Lampard, Jody Morris, Andy Myers, Michael Duberry and Frank Sinclair in places uptown like Sugar Reef and Emporium. Actually getting in to Café de Paris and being amazed by what proper footballers could do there. We were not yet proper footballers.

But we were learning. One summer's afternoon a few of us had some beers on the river at Richmond. Full of the joys, we decided to push on to Park Avenue, not the one in New York but the one opposite Nando's. You can tell all you want to know about Park Avenue from its most prominent online review: 'Do not go here. Always filled with old men and it is not the place to go in Richmond. I would not recommend this place to anyone. Many other and much better places to go. Not here.'

There may have been many other and much better places but this was the one we wanted to get into. A familiar scenario: my mates breezed straight in, I got stopped by the bouncers. This time there was no issue with my age. The problem was my choice of footwear. Not expecting to push on to the heights of Park Avenue, I'd come casual in white trainers. It was made clear to me that it was smart black shoes or bust.

I didn't really want to buy a new pair of shoes that my meagre wage couldn't handle, but neither did I want to go home. Bowling unhappily along the A307, I then spotted a shop giving away free samples of cheap black socks. It was the work of a moment to take a pair in large, pull them over the outside of my white trainers and march straight back to the club. This time the bouncers couldn't get me in fast enough. I spent the whole evening cruising around in my new trainer-sock combo, the happiest man to ever sample the unique Park Avenue experience.

These were boozy days for young footballers. The wisdom of the continental ways – never beer, occasionally a glass of wine with dinner, early to bed, don't even talk about cigarettes – had yet to soak through to the lower parts of the Championship. At QPR we would follow Gerry Francis's toughest day of training, Terror Tuesday, with an all-dayer that began at Jono's Irish bar on the Uxbridge Road and finished at some heinous tourist trap in the middle of London like the Punch and Judy. One evening we spotted the entire Arsenal first team in a bar close by – Tony Adams, David Seaman, Ray Parlour. I was awestruck.

It's gone full circle now. Players go out today as if they're in hip-hop videos. It's bling rather than booze, posing rather than pool halls. It's all imported from sports in the US, the old English nights out displaced in the same way as the American grey squirrel took over from the indigenous red.

I understand you have to move with the times. You can't live in the past. Even the best agent can't engineer you a move there. But it's difficult not to go a little misty-eyed when I think of the innocent japes I used to enjoy on the town. When I joined Portsmouth from QPR, it was the first time I'd ever lived away from home, in my little flat by the marina at Port Solent. My team-mates Shaun Derry and Courtney Pitt also had flats there, across the water from each other. We each bought a little dinghy with an outboard motor and zipped over to see each other whenever we fancied a few beers on a different balcony. Good times.

There was a pub on the marina where we might while away a quiet post-match Sunday. The three of us were in there one afternoon, only one drink in, behaving perfectly respectably. Until I came back from the toilet, picked my pint off the table, went to sit down and found that one of the lads had kicked my stool away. When you're 6'7" you go down slowly and in style. Beer went all over me, down my chest and over my jeans. That was embarrassing enough as a 21-year-old in a busy pub. It was even worse when I went back to the toilet, spent ten minutes trying to dry myself off under the hand-dryers, came back to a fresh pint and had the same stunt pulled on me all over again.

I was the club's big new signing. The following morning Shaun, Courtney and I were called into the manager's office. Chairman Milan Mandarić was in there too. Somehow they had got the CCTV footage from the pub the day before. In grainy black-and-white all you could make out was an unmistakably tall striker stumbling backwards throwing drinks over himself. No sign of the rogue foot kicking away the stool, no evidence that I was in fact completely sober, on the basis that my T-shirt had drunk more lager than I had. Peter, you're the club's record signing. Dezza, you're club captain. Do you genuinely think this is acceptable behaviour?

To Villa, and great nights out in Birmingham. Sobar, the Arcadian on Hurst Street, Bambu in the Chinese Quarter. Stoodi Bakers on Broad Street, which is also now a car-park. Lee Hendrie and I were once called in to see manager David O'Leary. You've been seen out too much. You need to be more like Gareth Barry. Lee and I looking at each other. Really? Gareth Barry? He was with us ...

Southampton had its own unique charms. I was still a young man, still single too. Our Norwegian defender Claus Lundekvam was 32 at the time, but he would still insist that I join him at the Leisureworld complex on a Tuesday night. 'It's Hotshots, the student night. You can get shots for a pound a go!' Claus had been earning Premier League wages for eight years by this point. He loved that place.

The point where I left student nights behind was the moment I was picked by Sven-Göran Eriksson for England's summer 2005 tour of North America. After our final match in New York, most of the squad headed home to the UK. I was due to join some mates for a summer holiday in Miami. On the final night, David Beckham informed Sol Campbell, Rob Green and me that he would be taking us out. Fun? Glamorous? I'd never experienced anything like it. One night you're in Rudolph's in a free tracksuit, the next you're cruising NYC with DB. Thank you, football.

Inevitably, I missed my flight to Miami the next day. It wasn't even close. I was still asleep at the hotel when it took off. I stumbled down to the airport some hours later and tried my hand at the usual hungover acting. 'Gone? But I was told I was on the evening flight!' 'No, sir.' 'Oh my God! What a mistake!' They let me on. I didn't even need my green folder.

Don't get me wrong. I've been an idiot on nights out many times. The evidence of my silly drunk dancing is all over YouTube via the smartphone footage of strangers. By the time I realise I'm being filmed I feel like I'm in some sort of impenetrable bubble with just me and my mates. They say you should always dance like no one's watching. They haven't seen that footage on YouTube.

Panacea in Alderley Edge was the place where so much of it went on. Alderley Edge is not a big place. It's the poshest village in Cheshire, and all the millionaires from Manchester City and United live there or close by, but the population shouldn't be large enough to support a top-end nightclub. Because of the footballers, because of how much footballers would spend there, because of how many coachloads of girls would arrive from Leeds or Preston or Bolton on account of the footballers, it made a fortune. You would walk in, past Mario Balotelli's camouflage-painted Bentley, step inside the velvet rope and be ushered upstairs to a private table, where the bottle of chilled vodka – Grey Goose or otherwise – would be brought to you with those mixers, glasses and party lights. On every table a footballer, by every footballer five girls, except on the table where Mario Balotelli was sitting, where there would be 20 members of his personal entourage.

Panacea has now gone. Not to be a car-park, not this one, but because it was burned down in suspicious circumstances. Twice. It was never going to end well. But I hold my hand up. It could be good fun in there, at least until your decision-making process started feeling the effect of all that Grey Goose and brown-nosing. I've been stitched up on nights out and I've made errors too. Your judgement at the start of every night is always impeccable. Your judgement at the end is usually terrible. There was a reason pubs used to shut at 11pm and a reason why you got in trouble at 3am if you kept your boozing calibrated to the old opening hours. English players had much to learn from the foreign imports and their tactics of only going out once 10pm had struck and they had enjoyed a good post-dinner snooze. We were booze sprinters to their endurance athletes. We could start earlier and we could rule the all-dayer with its midday start. But when midnight came we were like characters from an upside-down *Cinderella*. Footmen turned into monsters. Ugly sisters became princesses. Grey Goose turned into a good option.

You had to watch yourself with some of the men as well as the girls. In my early days at Portsmouth I made the error of buying a full round in a pub in the wrong part of Southsea, which is already the wrong part of Hampshire. Clearly I convinced someone that I was being unnecessarily flash, because when I turned back from the bar carrying the tray of drinks, one chap just cracked me straight in the face. I went down under the drinks, he legged it under the cover of darkness.

I console myself with the fact that I never sat there staring at my phone, or refusing to talk to anyone. I never saw the point. Why would you go out to do what you can do on your own at home? I never wore a cap when no one else could and I have neither owned a camo Bentley nor left it where it's impossible to miss.

You can't live in the past, but you can appreciate what it has given you. The humble pub has maintained its place in my affections even as the club full of glamour models has slipped away. There is a reason why there is a pub on every street corner in London and one to be found on the most dark and distant moor. You go there not to be seen but to talk about nothing while at the same time talking about anything. You'll spend four hours with your mates and leave with absolutely no idea of any developments in their personal lives or careers but having discussed the worst crisp flavours ever invented and argued about whether it would be better to have a nipple that dispensed sun-cream or an armpit that dispensed talcum powder.

Perhaps understandably, much of this baffles new overseas signings. A team dinner at 7pm, no game for a week, a spontaneous plan to go to the pub at 3pm.

'What are you going to do for four hours? Are you eating?'

'No, that's the restaurant at 7pm.'

'Is there a singer to watch?'

'No.'

'You are just talking?'

'Yes.'

'For four hours?'

Of course you have to judge it. Never midweek, never ever the night before a game, best on a Saturday night after a match when you don't have another one for week and you're so full of adrenaline that you won't be able to sleep without a couple. Summer's fine. You have to enjoy life. But even the size of a pint can leave some imports aghast. The first time Bruno Martins Indi held a full lager it blew his mind. 'We have game on Saturday!' 'Yeah, but tonight's Tuesday. That's ages away. Also, we're only having one beer.' It was as if we were offering him a space-walk.

Foreign players and coaches made us more sensible. There were exceptions; I think of Adrian Mutu, losing himself in the bright lights of Chelsea, or José Dominguez when he slipped into Spurs reserves as I came through, falling asleep in the warm-up because he'd been out so late, falling asleep at half-time if no one stopped him. London swallowed him up. But as a footballer you want to play for as long as you can, so it doesn't take much convincing to make you eat the right things and drink in moderation, even if you do sometimes mourn the passing of the old Christmas parties, like the nights with Liverpool when we would take over John Aldridge's bar by the Sir Thomas Hotel, all turn up in fancy dress and take it from there. At Spurs Harry Redknapp once announced in a press conference that he was banning Christmas parties. Unfortunately for him we'd already had it. Robbie Keane had flown us over to Dublin the previous weekend. There had been pubs and a lot of singing. Two days after Harry's announcement there were photos of it all over the Sunday tabloids. He called a meeting about that one. A serious one.

There were certain team-mates you always loved on a night out. Didi Hamann was wonderful because he was so unlike the Didi

Hamann you imagined. His time in Liverpool had turned him into a curious cross of German and Scouse. He would start the evening with a copy of the *Racing Post* under his arm, as if interrupted on a lunchtime stroll to the bookies, and end it occupying the middle of the dancefloor, throwing shapes with a look of blissful pleasure on his face. Didi would be the first man in my Night Out XI, a line-up that would also have to include Robert Huth (finds it impossible to sit still, random fun inevitably follows), Jonathan Woodgate (master of the deadpan) and Sean Davis (see Robert Huth). The definitely wouldn'ts include Marc Wilson (complete liability – every new signing at Stoke would be handed the job of looking after him), Glen Johnson (jealousy – can enjoy himself all night and wake up the next day like it's never happened) and Ledley, who despite all our attempted forays in our younger days has still not learned to handle a single beverage. You are filled with regret at the memory of those who were once the life and soul and are now never seen again, having met someone who disapproves or having made a radical lifestyle change. A name will come up and a reflective silence will follow. 'He would love this …' someone will say, choked with emotion, and all will look down at their drinks and shake their heads with sorrow.

But I'm bringing the mood down. The nights when you're out dancing, and you look around you and realise as if lightning has struck you that there is a correlation between a footballer's ability to dance and how creative their position is in a team. Strikers can dance, flashy wingers can dance. Goalkeepers cannot. Centre-halves move as well as oak trees. You never saw Jamie Carragher dancing. Another defender I know dances as if, rather than hearing the same tune as the rest of us, he is listening to an entirely contrasting genre on his iPod. Sandro and Wilson

Palacios at Spurs were dreamy movers. Kevin-Prince Boateng, who I played with in my second spell at Pompey, had some extraordinary moves. When he won the Scudetto with Milan he did a full Michael Jackson routine on a stage at the San Siro, lights down, team-mates clapping along, PA booming out 'Billie Jean' – moonwalking, spinning, flipping a trilby around. The damage that would have done at Panacea.

Me? I'm all effort and love. Few things give me as much pleasure as throwing shapes. At the time I think I'm right on it, but the delusion never lasts long. I understand my limitations. I've got one where I try to use my hips like Shakira. My hips don't lie.

And the fun is still there if you put yourself in the right places at the right times. On a trip to Dubai with the Stoke squad, as a senior player, I was put in charge of the whip. All of the players out there gave me money and I bought our rounds with the collective pot. One particular player could understand neither the whip nor how I seemed to be able to afford so many consecutive rounds. 'Bloody Crouchie, being flash, buying all the drinks. I'm not having this …'

And so he tried to go toe-to-toe with me, buying the entire team a round every time I did. I must have told him ten times: 'I've got the whip, it's not my money, WHAT ARE YOU DOING?' He refused to listen. Drinks for the players, drinks for the staff, matching me and then overtaking me, going silly with the choice of beverages, throwing his credit card at the bar staff like it was his last night on earth. 'I'll show that idiot Crouchie …'

What he did show me was the receipt he woke up with on his bedside table. Thousands of pounds. Many thousands of pounds. It still makes me chuckle now. The night that keeps giving. You could have bought the freehold of Rudolph's with that and had change to rebrand it as Valentino's.

CHAMPIONS LEAGUE VS FA CUP

The biggest final in club football awaits. Your club has been building to this all season; you have been thinking about this moment for the whole of your career.

You travel to Spain with the coaching staff and squad for a special training camp. With a few days to go until you fly on to Athens to take on one of the great teams of world football, your manager allows you and your team-mates a precious few hours off, to reward you for all that hard work, to relax body and mind for the great challenge ahead. Instead you almost kill both the club's main striker and yourself.

It wasn't meant to be that way. Us Liverpool lads had gone go-karting aware that we couldn't be messing around. We didn't intend anything to go wrong. But then I came into the pits in my kart, clearly at top speed and showing off, ready to slam the brakes on and get a cheer from the boys for a cheeky skid finale, and I stamped my right foot down hard on the pedal and ... nothing.

Xabi Alonso and Dirk Kuyt straight ahead of me. Kart not slowing at all. Xabi diving one way. Dirk right in the firing line.

Dirk turning round at the last moment, everything slow motion but also absolutely top speed, me shouting, everyone shouting, the newspaper headlines already in my head: CROUCH MAIMS STRIKE RIVAL, LIVERPOOL ACE KARTED OFF, LET'S GO FLY A KUYT.

To give Dirk his due, his reactions were first class. He knew he didn't have time to go sideways. So he went up – an explosive jump right over the kart, splitting his legs in midair, me looking up in one frozen fraction of a second to see a Dutch gusset right over my head and an expression further up that either said 'PEEEE-TEEER!' or 'FUUUUU ...' depending on your lip-reading skills.

God, the relief when I roared through those pits without feeling bumper on footballer. God, the terror when I then realised I was straight back out on the track at top speed and still didn't have any brakes.

You take matters into your own hands in a scenario like that. Your brain just makes decisions for you. In my case it panicked. So it was that I undid the safety harness, climbed onto the seat of the still-racing go-kart and threw myself off over the side.

The car crashed into the wall of safety tyres and burst into flames. I hit the tarmac and rolled about for a bit. Cuts all over my arms and legs, a stagger back to the pits and a host of jabbing fingers and angry expressions and furious questions. What the hell were you doing? Are you trying to kill someone? How scary was it getting that view of Dirk's Dutch gusset?

I kept desperately repeating myself. The brakes failed. The brakes failed. One of the stewards ran out onto the track, put out the fire on my kart and brought it back into the garage. He had a look at what remained of the engine. Yup, the brakes had failed. Sorry, Mr Crouch. Sorry, Liverpool Football Club.

That was my first unforgettable experience of a Champions League final, an occasion that for a modern player is the peak of everything you do. But it wasn't always this way. As a kid it was another cup competition that was the pinnacle of the game you loved. The FA Cup final.

I loved everything about it. The suits. The television cameras in each finalists' breakfast room. The footage of the coaches travelling to Wembley. Your whole family watched it: your gran, your mum, the aunt who would watch no other football for the rest of the year. The whole country stopped. It was Cup final day.

It always seemed to be a sunny day. It never rained. My mate's bedroom when we were kids was at the top of a three-storey house just south of the A40. We used to lean out of his window, look across that little slice of north-west London and see the twin towers, the flags wafting in the warm May air, hear the chants and songs over the top of the traffic roaring round Hanger Lane. We would stare out of the window, run downstairs to the TV and see the stadium on there, run back upstairs and stare at the real thing again. It used to fascinate us. It's a dream. It's real! It's impossible. It's just there!

The Cup final gave you your defining footballing memories as a child. The 1991 final between Spurs and Nottingham Forest, Gazza's injury, Stuart Pearce's classic Stuart Pearce free-kick, poor old Des Walker's own goal, the strange stooping accidental header. I loved the long shorts that Spurs wore. It was the first time I'd seen an alternative to the high thigh-line. It gave me hope for the future. There may yet be a way I can be a professional footballer without looking like I'm wearing Speedos.

I went to the final of 1994, Manchester United thumping Chelsea, my dad heartbroken as a lifelong Chelsea fan. I went with him again in 1997, when Roberto Di Matteo's record-breaking early goal helped Chelsea win it that time, Middlesbrough the teary ones.

It's a beautiful trophy, the FA Cup. So too is the European Cup, all smooth lines and graceful handles, but there is something about the FA Cup that all the other trophies can only aspire to. You can draw it as a kid. It works on banners and home-made flags. And when you actually get to hold it, as I did after Liverpool beat West Ham in that brilliant final of 2006, it's an emotional moment not just because you've won something for the club but for all those reasons on top. You look down and see this wonderful silver pot in your hands, and you can't quite believe it's there. Running from TV to distant bedroom view of Wembley is one thing. Seeing your own fingers cradling the actual trophy is an even sweeter contrast.

I did all the things I'd seen players do when I was a kid and I loved them all. I waved the trophy at my dad in the stands. I put the lid on my head as a makeshift hat. I drank champagne out of it. I held it one-handed down by my side as I strolled along the touchline, which is the coolest way of holding it, as if you've forgotten you've got it, as if you're casually saying, what, this old thing? Yeah, I've just won it. Want a look?

I got a scarf off a supporter on the victory lap. I thought about a red and white quartered cap. I thought about all the great players from history who had held it and I didn't want to let go. I loved the open-top bus tour that we did round Liverpool the following day, all shades to hide the hangovers, waving it at the rammed streets of the city centre.

The only classic I missed out on was a Cup final song. I would have been all over one. We could have used a Scouse band, which at that time would probably have meant The Coral or The Zutons. I feel like I missed out, because the opportunity is unlikely to come again. Imagine the press release: 'Stoke City and Peter Crouch have released an FA Cup third-round exit song.' Imagine the upbeat, singalong lyrics: 'We put out a reserve team / Because the league was considered more of a priority / We played Coventry but picked the kids/ So did Coventry to be fair ...'

So if I had to choose between FA Cup and Champions League, the FA Cup would win nostalgically every time. But if I could play in one more final now, or choose which one to watch, it would be the Champions League that came out on top.

It's sad, but the magic of the Cup has leached away. Managers who would rather target 14th place in the Premier League than 17th place and a glorious Cup run to the semis. Staging those semis at Wembley. Moving the final to 5.15pm rather than three in the afternoon. It used to be that an FA Cup final win was the crowning glory for a manager. Now it doesn't even keep you in a job. Louis van Gaal was sacked 24 hours after he won his with Manchester United. Arsène Wenger found that three FA Cup final wins in four years, rather than a triumph, became a stick for his critics to beat him with. It has become a poor consolation prize for not winning the Premier League. 'Oh, he only won the FA Cup ...'

In its place has come the Champions League final. The best players in the world, playing together in concentrated form rather than spread across national sides of lesser quality. Leo Messi's Barcelona would probably beat Leo Messi's Argentina. Cristiano Ronaldo's Real Madrid would have thumped Ronaldo's European Championship-winning Portugal. If you win it as a manager it confers legendary status upon you, because it's so difficult to achieve. It's a two-year process: one season to qualify, one to work your way through qualifying rounds and group stages, going home and away against the real big boys of European football, no short cuts, no way of fluking it.

It's why Rafa Benítez will forever be a hero at Liverpool and any club that has won the European Cup will forever be known around the world, no matter that before it became the Champions League you needed to win far fewer games. Forest are still thought of as a big club because of the two miracles Brian Clough pulled off. People know about Aston Villa in little faraway corners of the globe because of Peter Withe and Nigel Spink and 1982. You judge a club by the number of European Cups they have won now more than league titles. Certainly if you're a Liverpool fan looking 30 miles east to United and City.

I remember going to the 1992 final at Wembley, walking through the underpasses from Ealing. I was a Sampdoria fan because of Gianluca Vialli, because of Roberto Mancini, Attilio Lombardo. It wasn't a great final, despite that Barcelona team featuring Pep Guardiola, Michael Laudrup and Hristo Stoichkov. And when Ronald Koeman scored that free-kick in extra time to win it for the Catalans I walked back through the underpasses with a lump in my throat. But a seed had been sown, and when I played in the competition for the first time with Liverpool in the autumn of 2005 it brought a thrill that no other competition could match.

A first away game, a qualifier against FBK Kaunas in Lithuania. Going away to Betis and Anderlecht, the biggest atmospheres I'd experienced. The following season, scoring goals all the way through our march to the final, those night-time games under the lights at Anfield, an all-day buzz reaching a beautiful crescendo at kick-off, the banners, the flares and the flags.

And then the final itself, all my family making the trip to Greece to watch, looking around you in the build-up and realising you're part of something so big. Feeling confident, having been the second highest scorer in the competition that season behind Kaka, thinking that Kaka's team were not what they had been, that they were a side who had peaked and were ageing. And then the biggest shock of all: walking into the team meeting the night before to find that Rafa had changed the team, that he was going to play five in midfield and Kuyt on his own up front, and that I would be on the bench rather than starting.

I think he was trying to surprise Milan. He always did like to do something different, to try to outwit the opposition coach. I think too that we should have been more attacking, that we should have gone for it. Dirk was anyway more an attacking midfielder than an out-and-out striker. I thought I would have scored.

So that is the biggest regret of my career, more so than not being picked for England's World Cup quarter-final against Portugal in 2006. At least then I had been on the bench for the previous match against Ecuador. At least then we had Wayne Rooney in the lone role up front. If I had started in Athens and we had still lost I would have felt better. Instead I didn't have an inkling. Seeing the team pinned up on a board and feeling my stomach drop. The lads coming up to me – 'Why aren't you playing?' Having to text my family. It's great you're here, but ...

We all went back to the hotel afterwards for a so-called party, which involved significant amounts of melancholic drinking and asking ourselves where it had gone wrong. It went on late. It became early. As I staggered up the stairs of the hotel, the Greek sun long up, I was passed by Rafa coming back down the other way, off to do his press conference. He gave me a look that seemed to say, 'That's why I didn't pick you, son.'

It could have been worse. On the flight home Rafa told Craig Bellamy that his contract wasn't going to be renewed. No more Liverpool for you, you're gone. Bellers got off the flight fuming. 'That's going to f***ing cost him …' He hadn't even got on as a sub. It almost made me feel better.

ENDORSEMENTS

If you think Premier League footballers are spoiled, being given a free brand-new pair of boots for every single game they play, then wait until you hear this: there is now a machine installed at most clubs, resembling a giant toaster, into which you can insert those new boots to steam them and make them as soft as old slippers.

It takes about five minutes. Put them in a slot, lower them in, wallop. Some lads use it every single day before training. And they say the game's lost its edge.

I got my first free pair of boots at the age of 14. Technically it wasn't an endorsement, as I received no extra cash on top, but when you're 14 and a box arrives at your house with an Adidas tracksuit, a pair of trainers and two pairs of boots, you're already ecstatic. The idea that you might be able to demand payment for receiving free things made no sense. The logic came all from the agent who had arranged the delivery: that box was enough to get me to sign up with him.

As a kid growing up obsessed with football I could name the whole Premier League boot-wearing line-up. Dennis Wise and Paul Merson in their Hi-Tec Kings Cup, with the tongue folded back over the laces. I remember watching Chelsea in a pre-season friendly at Brentford, Wise dinking in corners with those massive fold-overs flapping about. It was as if he barely touched the ball. I thought to myself: those Hi-Tec must come with special dink power. Adidas then topped that by unveiling an elastic strap to keep the tongue from flapping about, in my eyes a greater innovation than the world-famous Predator, which to me felt like playing with a trampoline on your foot. Much harder to trap a ball or control your passing distance with those thick rubber ridges down the toe. I think of Ian Wright and Eric Cantona in their Nike Tiempos, Gazza strutting around in his Puma Kings, Quasar coming into the market and signing up Gary Lineker and Matt Le Tissier.

I've always been fussy about my boots as a pro. I loved Puma Kings, Adidas World Cups and Copas as a kid, and how the boot felt on my feet and what it did for my touch was more important to me than making money out of it. It wasn't until I joined Liverpool at the age of 24 that I actually signed an endorsement deal, and even then I took the lower of the two offers because the Puma boot felt more natural to me than the Umbro one. As a striker your boots are the tools of your trade. Stop scoring and everything else falls away. If they feel even slightly wrong, no amount of money would make me wear them.

Puma were always keen to get me in the latest pair when I was at Liverpool. If you were sponsored by Adidas this was less of a problem; since there would be four or five players in the dressing-room on the same boot deal, they could collectively take the heat when an outrageous new design was forced upon them. Players notice when someone has new boots. The comments will start as soon as you lace them up: 'All I'm saying, mate, is that you'd better be good today …' If your first touch wearing them in training is a touch baggy they'll be all over you. It gets in your head. Paolo Di

Canio had the ego to pull off blue boots before anyone else but few find it as easy. At Stoke one of our young players pulled on a pair of gold boots after less than five first-team appearances. 'Gold boots? At eighteen years old?' 'Good luck with them, son!'

He had a nightmare. Couldn't make a pass, couldn't trap a punctured ball. He ended up changing them after ten minutes. 'Oh yeah, they're just a bit tight.' 'Course they are, Tommy, course they are.'

Puma, either unaware of these dressing-room dynamics or reasoning that the money they were paying me would soften any blow to my ego, sent me a design nightmare. This was around the time that big-name stars were having their children's Christian names sewn into the uppers of their boots. I had no family at that point but they still wanted a gimmick along the same sort of lines. And so I opened a box one day to find a right boot with 'CRO' in giant letters down the outside and a left boot reading 'UCH'.

It made no sense. There was no actual way you could have made the two sets of letters come together to form my name. Even if you tried to stand completely bow-legged, toes of each foot facing in opposite directions, a man standing directly behind you could only have been able to make out a four-letter run, most likely 'ROUC'. The opportunities to stand completely bow-legged in a Premier League match are limited. Also, as an established England international, most people knew who I was without having to look at my feet. Had they been unsure, there was a decent clue in far larger letters across the back of my shirt.

Craig Bellamy, inevitably, was the first to spot them. 'Hang on a minute, what the f*** is this?' Steven Gerrard was next. 'What's a cro?' Jermaine Pennant just started calling me 'Uch', pronouncing it 'Ooch'. Eleven years on, Bellamy still calls me by the same. Pennant started doing it when we were both at Stoke, so now I'm Ooch to Ryan Shawcross and the club physio too. A terrible nickname, all because of an overambitious pair of boots.

Puma did make some excellent boots. They allowed me to stay in black for as long as was fashionably possible, and this at a time when Djibril Cissé was wearing colours so random and intense that they had not yet been given names. We also did one particularly cool ad campaign where I was given robot legs. Perhaps you had to see it. But big tournaments always bring forth big ideas, and by the time of the 2006 World Cup I was in trouble again. This time it was green boots. With photos of grass on them. I think they were being promoted as an unseen boot, some sort of stealth footwear, so that defenders lost track of where your feet were. Perhaps they might have worked it out from the position of my legs, which were not green and covered in photos of grass, and as usual were directly above my feet. As a man of 6'7" the chances of me going stealth felt minimal. Would an apparently footless striker really worry a defender? I had my doubts. But when we played Jamaica in one of our final warm-up matches, half their team were wearing them. I got dreadful stick from the Puma reps for refusing.

Being in that England team opened up a whole new world of endorsements. David Beckham was like some magical magnet, bringing in companies that previously had no interest in footballers. A campaign would be offered to the team, and reasoning that we all have a shelf life, I would often be the one saying, yeah, go on then. My dad worked in advertising and was able to separate the well-written from the dodgy. Most of the time.

There was one for Virgin Media, where I landed at some pub team's pitch in a helicopter to be met by an overexcited manager and a team of fat lads eating crisps. Tagline: pick the right team.

There was Mars, with a grass-roots football campaign, where I opened a new clubhouse, played 15 minutes for the local team and scored with an unopposed stooping header from four yards out. Then there was Pringles, aka Pringoals, Nicolas Anelka doing keepy-ups with a tube, knocking it to me, me flicking it into a bin with the outside of my foot. Cut to us on a balcony overlooking a vaguely European city scene, and – Hello! – Cesc Fàbregas and Dirk Kuyt are on another balcony, all smiles, and below in the street random passers-by and traffic cops and postal workers are all chest-bumping, throwing their hands up and shouting with us. 'Pringoals!'

Of course, I was doing the Robot. In Pringoals™ I had old boys on nearby balconies copying it too. Every company asked for it, the exception being T-Mobile where the whole joke was that I was instead doing a sort of *Saturday Night Fever* routine to Yazz's 'The Only Way Is Up'. The frequency with which I had to perform it in commercials was one of the reasons I sacked it off on the pitch.

Pringoals had its flaws. Empty cylinders are not the easiest or most obvious thing to do keepy-ups with. It's not like thousands of kids in the street were trying it in the aftermath, although I like to think my delivery of the tagline was superior to Steven Gerrard when he appeared in a similar ad with Roberto Carlos and Francesco Totti. 'Hey, Roberto – pass the Pringles!' I've added that exclamation mark to give it more life than the original.

But it was nice having my face on a packet released to the shops, not least for my mum, who sent me a photo from the snacks aisle at her local Tesco's. I was original flavour, if you're interested. Anelka was salt and vinegar, Fàbregas barbecue. And when my first daughter was born, Pringles sent me a personalised tube with

Sophia's name as the flavour. I've kept it so she can enjoy it when she's older. What an heirloom.

Beckham transformed what footballers could do. It was already happening as he broke through; I remember Wimbledon striker Dean Holdsworth modelling for Top Man, only to be trumped by his team-mate Stewart Castledine landing a gig with DKNY. Before you knew it David James was going naked bar his goalkeeping gloves and a football for Armani. But it was Beckham, starting with his Calvin Klein underwear campaign, that drove it all, and it was the Beckham connection that meant Armani became the official suit of the England team for the 2006 World Cup.

I was 25 years old. This was a time when High and Mighty, the clothing chain for the larger gentleman, wanted to have my image in their store windows. Suddenly I'm going along to Armani's flagship store in Knightsbridge, having never dared go there before, and being greeted by a lackey at the door with, 'Ah, Mr Crouch, how lovely to see you ...' Up to the top floor, reserved for VIPs, measured up for a free suit by eight tailors working simultaneously. My God, I thought, this is amazing. I've still got that suit. It still doesn't fit me. Too many cooks and all that.

I had a few glamorous near-misses. In the post-Robot period I was offered the chance to be in a Dannii Minogue video. She was releasing a cover version of Sister Sledge's 'He's the Greatest Dancer'. The script had these handsome guys with amazing moves all trying to impress her, and then right at the end I bang out the Robot and walk off into the sunset with her.

I was all over the idea. A couple of friends pointed out to me that you can never delete a pop video, that it could be my Glenn and Chris 'Diamond Lights'. To me that was a good thing. The more timeless the better. The money was incredible, the script was great. I signed up. Pre-production began. And then the heartbreaker: the record company decided to ditch the song. The world was deprived of an amazing video; I was denied the chance to meet Dannii, who in the period when I was at school and a huge *Home and Away* fan had been my favourite Minogue sister, at least after my first big Kylie period and before my second big Kylie period.

You learn much about a team-mate from his approach with the free stuff he gets from endorsements. Some will share it around the dressing-room. Joe Hart used to hand out bottles of Head and Shoulders to anyone who wanted them. Geoff Cameron at Stoke was good for samples of the US styling products he was signed up to. Djibril Cissé, when he launched his own range of clothing, used to put big piles of it in the middle of the dressing-room floor for you to help yourself to. It was terrible stuff, underwear the same garish colours as his boots. The other French lads in the team couldn't get enough of it. There are lads at every club who appear only to wear clothes they haven't paid for, as if a Premier League salary leaves you a little short for buying your own. Ryan Shawcross is in Nike every day of his life. I suppose the logos all match.

We all get random products sent to us at the training ground. I recently received a batch of Walker's Nonsuch toffee, a Stoke-on-Trent classic. It was extraordinary stuff, and I'm not just saying that because I'm hoping to be signed up as their ambassador. It was a huge box, but when I stuck it in the dressing-room it was cleaned out within half a day. Players were at it, coaches, the manager, club staff.

There are those that pass you by. I would have loved to have done one of the iconic World Cup campaigns: Nike's airport one with Brazil, or the Cantona one where his shot blasted a devil goalkeeper to pieces. I just don't think I was ever cool enough for that. The modelling ones were surely just around the corner.

All good football-specific endorsements come with incentives. With boots your deal will include a retainer, a bonus for playing a certain number of Premier League games, another for goals scored, then Champions League games and goals, and finally England games and goals. In 2007, the year Liverpool reached the Champions League final and I played pretty much every game for England, I doubled the value of my deal.

There can be disputes. If you and a team-mate are both sponsored by the same company, one of you will always get slightly more or slightly better gear. Tension will bubble as looks are exchanged. 'How the hell did you get those trainers?' Phone calls will be made to company reps and agents. 'Oi! Why the hell has he got that? Show me the love!'

When we had goalkeeper Carlo Nash at Stoke he was 40 years old, yet he always had the latest boots. He had his name on them, he had colourways no one else had. With all respect to Carlo, there were better-known players with far worse gear. Questions were being asked round the dressing-room: how has he got that deal, and why don't we have the same one?

Turns out he was going on the Nike ID website, designing his own and paying for them with his own money. He would even make sure they matched his kit: blue boots for a blue goalkeeping jersey, red to bring out the same colour in his gloves. Being footballers we reacted with maturity and taste: Jon Walters drew cocks all over them. Carlo was genuinely devastated. 'What, I'll have to buy them again now!' A young lad at Stoke had an incredible pair of boots that we'd only otherwise seen on Eden Hazard, black with a gold sole. Someone pointed out the incongruity of it to him. That was when we found out he'd been buying them on eBay.

It's a world that's changing fast. Where once it was about television spots, about paying for space in magazines and newspapers, it's now about followers. How many people have you got on Twitter, how many on Insta? Two million followers buys you a lot of sponsor attention. Too much shameless pushing of products loses you followers faster still. If all the tweets are, 'Wot a day for a drive in my new Sport Ranger Elite X9' and 'no probz on icy roads with the exclusive DynaGrip TM traction control on the Sport Ranger Elite X9' it gets dull fast. '#luvmyrangerelite #yeahbabyelitecru'.

You also hope you'll never do anything that haunts you, that's so bad that the whole world can see that haunting look in your eyes. I'm guessing Michael Owen did his infamous promo for Dubai tourism because Dubai's vast wealth as a city state was reflected in the fee. If you've seen it you'll know what I mean. If you haven't, you're in for a treat. It's almost too painful to watch, both for the viewer and for Michael, except for the bits that are too funny to watch. There is a 15-minute director's cut. It deserves to become an instant classic.

HOTELS

There is a moment, as a footballer staying in a hotel for a protracted period during a tournament, when everyone starts to go a little stir-crazy. That point with England under-21s came when I was walking back from lunch one afternoon along the corridor towards my room, and Jermaine Pennant and Jermain Defoe burst out of the room they were sharing, completely naked except for England socks and football boots. 'Crouchie! Two-man wall!' They stood there in the corridor, hands protecting private parts. I had to pretend to bend a free-kick over them. They had to jump in unison in an attempt to block the invisible ball. If I scored I could move on. That's team hotels.

With your club side in the Premier League you're usually only in a hotel the night before a game. With England you can be away for ten days at a time. When Wembley was being rebuilt and we were playing home games at Old Trafford and Anfield, we would stay at the Lowry in Manchester; when the new stadium was finished, we would be at the Grove in Hertfordshire. At both the vibe could be strange. We would have our own floor cordoned off from the rest of the guests, which meant that players would be bowling about the corridors in their pants, going from massage room to bedroom as if they were in a Parisian men's spa. There was a break-out area with sofas and a table of magazines, which felt like the bit of the spa where you fill in a form stating allergies and preference for herbal tea.

You were never allowed to go down to the main part of the hotel, to explore the hidden delights of the small foyer shop, the three PC terminals of the business centre, the bowl of highly polished apples on the concierge's desk. The one escape was golf, should the next match be sufficiently far away. Fabio Capello, surprisingly for an Italian, was obsessed with the game. He would play a round every day if he could, which meant he would have to let us play too. He would form a three-ball with one of his Italian assistants and Ray Clemence. You'd hear him a few holes ahead, shouting angrily whenever he missed a putt and blaming it all on Ray. Perhaps he felt the goalkeeping coach should have a superior understanding of the pace and angle of grassed areas.

You have your own breakfast area. You eat dinner away from all the other guests. One lad will always bring his PlayStation from home and set it up in his room as a communal games hub. Everyone brings a Bluetooth speaker and blasts their own music through it. As you walk down the corridor you'll hear different genres leaking out from underneath each door. It's like being in a big elongated club – this is the R&B room, this is the house room, here's the chill-out room, here's someone in their pants who's got carried away.

But it can actually be quite a lonely place. You train in the morning, have lunch at midday and then have nothing whatsoever to do for the next six hours. You're banned from going out. You can't even go for an aimless drive. You might go to the treatment room, just to hang out with the injured players and have a chat. Wayne Rooney could never sit still in his room. He was the closest we had to Gazza playing three sets of tennis in the afternoon sun the day before England's semi-final against West Germany at Italia 90. He was like a chunky ghost of the corridors.

In such circumstances the desire for self-improvement kicks in. Being a footballer it ends shortly afterwards. I tried learning the guitar but wanted to be an expert straight away and gave up to play *FIFA* instead. I whacked out 70 quid on the Rosetta Stone 'Learn Spanish' course and used about a fiver's worth. From a distance I admired Leighton Baines, who used to bring his acoustic guitar along and fill the empty hours by working on his finger-picking.

You see so many hotel rooms that you wake up in the middle of the night with no idea where you are. You also have no idea where the bathroom might be, which means you either guess based on the configuration of the standard hotel room or, as I do now, leave a dim light on in the bathroom, so that when you need a pee in the middle of the night you stagger towards the light like a lanky moth, hoping that the light coming under the bedroom door from outside doesn't mean you end up in the corridor naked while your door clicks shut behind you.

You are unlike any other guest. You don't choose where you stay and you can't give any feedback on TripAdvisor. You will stay in some amazing places in France and Italy and some in eastern Europe that are like dormitories and you have to treat them just the same. You never check in. Your key is always waiting for you when you arrive, you are never asked to leave a swipe of your credit card and all the minibars are cleared out before you get there. The odd time a player finds his minibar still stocked it gets raided by the team within seconds. None of us ever pay for it.

Our hotel in Baden-Baden during the 2006 World Cup was high on a hill above the spa town below. No other guests were allowed to stay. If you went to bed late the deserted corridors made it feel like *The Shining*.

Far better was when we travelled to Berlin, staying in a hotel right on one of the main squares. We were high up, looking down on the thousands of England fans drinking and partying down below from the window of the treatment room. We had been spotted early on, and as each player went to the window the hordes would erupt and start chanting their name. David Beckham tried it, uproar. Rooney tried it, deafening chants of 'Roo-ney! Roo-ney!'

Gary Neville gave me a nudge. Come on, Crouchie, you've got to give them the Robot. So I went to the window, looked out and rocked it – and the whole square followed suit. Thousands of England fans, all Roboting round. It must surely have broken world records for the most simultaneous Robots ever performed in one place. It's one of my all-time favourite England memories.

Four years later in South Africa we would barely see a single fan at our base in Rustenburg, away on the bushveld in the north-west of the country. It was beautifully equipped but felt rather like a luxurious prison. We played a lot of darts. We made up a lot of darts-related nicknames: 'Deadly Dart' Hart, Glen 'One-Dart Dartford' Johnson, a tribute paid to Jonno's Kent birthplace. I had the extended little finger of a darts superstar but not the skills to match. Gareth Barry was outstanding, James Milner predictably excellent, as he is at golf, cricket, table-tennis – any sport he chooses.

It used to be that you roomed in pairs. A small room, two single beds, not a massive amount of privacy. Not any more; we're kings of our own suites, and I slightly miss the camaraderie of the old days. Rafa Benítez used to put you in with someone in your position or a related one, assuming that you would want to talk tactics late in the night. When I was in with Jermaine Pennant that could be taken care of in the time it took to dump your bag in the corner and stick your washbag in the bathroom: 'Early ball back post please, mate, I'll get a run on the last defender.' 'Yeah, cool.'

Rafa did want to talk tactics all night, so he couldn't understand why others didn't. He would greet Jermaine at breakfast and ask him what he thought of the match the previous evening. The culture clash was amazing to witness.

Pennant, yawning: 'What match?'

Rafa, surprised: 'The Champions League.'

Pennant: 'Oh, who was playing?'

Rafa, shocked: '"Who was playing?!"'

You travel so much as a footballer. You travel so much and you see so little. You can genuinely forget where you are and where you've just been, because your entire experience is reduced to the same basic blocks: plane, bus, international hotel, set food, football match, bus, hotel, home. You fly into a private terminal. You get on a private coach. You have that private wing of the hotel. You want to go out and explore but it's not why you're there and it's not what they want you to do. People will ask you if you've been to a particular country. You'll think and say, no, don't think so. And then you look in your passport and realise you have. You're not a tourist, unless you're 17-year-old Theo Walcott at the 2006 World Cup, yet to play for your club Arsenal in the Premier League, taking a video camera everywhere you went. I don't blame Theo. It wasn't his fault, but he wasn't ready for anything more than a holiday.

Only on pre-season trips do you get to take in your hotel's surroundings, and only then because you're usually running up every hill for miles. With Liverpool, Rafa took us to Évian in France – flying into Geneva, training on the mountains, cooling off in a river. You could even drink the local water.

It's when you stay as a resident that good hotels turn bad. When I spent three months at the Belfry having signed for Aston Villa, I became a footballing version of Alan Partridge. I was on first-name terms with the staff. I ate in the on-site carvery so often it was as if every day was like Sunday. There is a nightclub in the resort. Some evenings I would go and sit at the bar with a pot of tea, just to hear loud dance music rather than having to watch bad TV in my box-room. I then went on loan to Norwich, stayed in a different hotel for three months and felt even more like Partridge. I was a big plate away from the full Alan. I became friends with a couple of builders who were also lodging there long-term. We used to console each other in the hotel bar.

It never seemed to work out very well. Upon signing for Liverpool I stayed at the Hope Street Hotel. On reception was a girl so good-looking I couldn't quite believe she was smiling at me all the time. Every time I walked through the lobby she looked delighted to see me. She would wave, smile, give me the occasional 'Hi, Peter!'

I told the lads in training. 'Honestly, she's beautiful. I think I've got a shout here.' Jamie Carragher listened carefully to my story and called a few of the other senior players over. 'Tell them again, Crouchie.' So I did. 'She's all over me. I'm on fire.' Carra again, all interest. 'What does she look like?' 'Amazing. Dark-haired. Spanish-looking. I'm in there, I'm telling you.'

It turned out she was Xabi Alonso's partner. She was just doing a bit of work to practise her language skills. He was very nice about it. So was she. Carra, less so.

Now we all stay in the same places. You play Manchester United, you stay in the Lowry. You play City, you're at the Radisson Edwardian. In Newcastle we all used to stay at the Malmaison; we're now all at the Marriott by the racecourse. Chelsea, the Royal Garden Hotel in Kensington. Arsenal and Spurs, the Landmark on the Marylebone Road. The staple that goes with them is the pre-match walk. It's as if you can't stay in the hotel all morning before a game. Even if it's just around the car-park, the team will leave the hotel together, trudge about for a bit, try to avoid being recognised and slope back to the hotel. You want to escape them but as soon as you do you can't wait to go back. Us footballers are creatures of habit.

And the team hotel, because you are there so often and for long, becomes the stage for some of your favourite moments. At Portsmouth, Sean Davis, Marc Wilson and David Nugent in particular used to wind manager Harry Redknapp up. His favourite player, even more than me, was Sylvain Distin – model pro, a man who led by example – but even he could bring the manager to despair. We were in South Africa for a mid-season training break, flying home early the next morning, when Harry gave us permission to reward ourselves for all our hard work by having a few beers. 'We're leaving at 6am sharp. Get in by midnight latest, and don't be in a state.'

We all rolled into reception at 5.55am. Tracksuits on, at the bar ordering one final round as Harry comes down with his suitcase. He went bananas. How could you do this? It's not an end-of-season piss-up. You're a disgrace. Why can't you be more like Sylvain? Sylvain would never let himself down like this.

And then Sylvain bowls through the hotel doors, three sheets to the wind, not even in his tracksuit. Harry takes one look and clutches his head. 'Sylvain? NOOOOO ...'

SOCIAL MEDIA

Of all the things I've done in my career – scoring in the World Cup finals for England, the flick-up and volley against Manchester City, the hat-trick at Anfield against Arsenal – I fear that I'll most be remembered in some quarters for a picture I posted on Twitter of me feeding two giraffes.

'Summer for me is about time with family.' The caption was the work of a moment, the impact a little larger: 150,000 retweets and counting, 330,000 likes.

I say this not to boast, but to underline how I think footballers and social media should mix. I liked Bradford City and Hull legend Dean Windass's first ever tweet to the world ('How you doing mate are you okay') almost as much as I liked his second ('Yes I'm fine thanks') but too many players get the approach all wrong.

You want real. You want a direct line to the player's thoughts. You want a lightness of touch, and the occasional hapless mistake. What you don't want is the generic, the ghosted, the fake. 'Fans were fantastic, big game Tuesday, we go again.' Honestly.

If there's stuff being written about you that isn't true, straighten it out. You could go through a journalist, but your point might be lost or twisted, or changed by the wrong headline or picture.

On social media you can have a proper run at it, and be who you really are too. For a player the whole point is to do it yourself. Don't ask your agent, don't get a company to roll out an organised campaign. The whole point is that you can interact with supporters. If you're getting grief, come back at the assailant. A bloke tweets a picture of a long TV camera boom being carried out of a stadium, wrapped in black plastic. 'RIP Peter Crouch. Cruel way to go.' Three crying-with-laughter emojis to rubber-stamp it. You don't kick off, you retweet it with your reply: 'It's only funny because I wasn't seriously injured.'

Step forward Louis Saha. 'Take a tomato and put sugar on it. Taste it if you never tried. It taste like strawberry.'

Suddenly we're with Louis in his kitchen, possibly late at night, face lit by the glow of the fridge's internal light. He's bored, or perhaps curious, and has already made three passes at the fridge without quite finding the snack he desires. And then, on its own in the bottom salad drawer, he spots a lonely tomato, and a wonderful culinary journey begins.

I was a little wary of Twitter at first. I thought it would be nastier, that there would be more idiots. I find it quite enlightening that it was actually relatively pleasant. My late arrival also allowed me to observe some of the early tribulations of others, like my former England team-mate Wayne Rooney.

'Hi rio do you want picking up in the morning pal'. In many ways that's textbook. Okay, Wayne is yet to work out the difference between a text and a tweet, but we get a glimpse into his daily life – busy with the kids in the evening and so with only enough time to dash a quick message off to Rio Ferdinand, rather than check the exact format used; generous enough to think of his team-mate's needs ahead of his own the following day; organised enough to think ahead 12 hours to what might be required to get everyone safely to Manchester United's training ground.

Now, of course, footballers are all over social media. There is competition in clubs over who has the most followers on Twitter. There is an obsession with Instagram, although I don't understand why you'd want to show the world what you're having for lunch or what you're doing with your family.

Unless you're Cristiano Ronaldo or Leo Messi you do not need your own website. WhatsApp can be useful, particularly for teams. The England senior squad has its own WhatsApp group, with its own brutal logic: get called up and you're added to the group, get dropped and suddenly the message is there on everyone's phone: 'Peter Crouch has left this group.' There can be the official ones, the one that the coaches see, and the players-only unofficial one, where the real talk goes on.

We have advisors come in to tell the younger lads how to navigate through some of the choppier waters – how a rogue comment can be taken the wrong way, how one man's idea of a joke might be an insult to another. They might also have to tell the younger lad's entourage. I recently saw a 16-year-old come into Stoke to talk about an academy contract. I assumed the five people with him were his family – parents, big brother, uncles – keen to have a look around, take a few photos, meet the manager. It turned out they were his 'team'. Quite possibly including a social media advisor.

It gets taken too seriously. Make it fun, not formal. Don't use it only to promote gear you're wearing or to go fishing for free gifts. 'Thinking of getting a new top-end coffee machine, any advice?' Then 24 hours later: 'Wow, thanx to Acme Espresso for the amazing new XJ5 bean-to-cup system #baristababy #coffeeswag #uwantchocolateonthat.'

Don't overdo it, deluging someone's timeline with every thought that appears in your brain. Pick your moment, choose your words. England's under-17 team beat Brazil to get through to their World Cup final to play Spain. 'Youngsters these days have no regard for tradition. We don't get to the finals of World Cups. How dare they.'

It gets misused. You'll see lads in training who haven't got a sweat on in three months, who jog their way listlessly through a session and then a few hours later are posting videos of themselves on Insta running up the stairs or out in the garden dragging weighted sledges. Hashtags like #betterneverstops and #4daluvofdaclub, the fans looking at it thinking, look how hard this lad is training, it's criminal that he's not getting picked for the first team, if only every player had his attitude. Except he's actually spent the afternoon on the sofa playing *FIFA* on his PlayStation, getting up only to film himself briefly jumping up the stairs or chopping wood like Rocky.

I enjoy following footballers who have something different to say, a unique perspective. You can rely on Jon Walters to make you spit out your tea or Robert Huth to get you wondering if he has no barriers between his personal and public spheres.

I like the instinctive, the unfiltered. Former Newcastle, Spurs and Watford defender Sebastien Bassong and his breathless 'working really hard #cleanshit'. I know that central defenders are supposed to tidy up at the back, but that's outstanding work.

I like the surprising. Who knew that Gary Lineker was funny before he joined Twitter? 'Messi makes me realise how shit I was.' The appropriate pause for comic effect, and then: 'Soldado makes me realise I wasn't that shit.'

Social media enlightens you. It reveals characters. It shows you that there is more to footballers than over the moon and great three points and there's no easy games at this level.

And then there is the disastrous, as exemplified by Victor Anichebe in the moments after his team Sunderland had conceded a last-minute winner away at West Ham.

'Can you put something like ... Unbelievable support yesterday and great effort by the lads! Hard result to take! But we go again!'

In less than 140 characters, the whole illusion stripped away. Modern football laid bare. Something that should dismantle the barriers between players and fans instead opening up fresh chasms. You don't get that with photos of giraffes. Trust me.

To be fair to Victor, he did later take the mickey out of himself in the days that followed. But all this change, of course, has come from the smartphone. I've been around football long enough to remember when a mobile was so big you needed a bag dedicated solely to its transportation. The mobile bit referred only to the lack of cables rather than the weight and size. When I was breaking into the QPR first team they were just starting to have an impact, and I wasn't always a fan. In place of the chat at the training ground you would have 20 blokes all complaining about their lack of battery.

There was a lot about Harry Redknapp that made you laugh. Even as smartphone technology advanced at pace, he retained the same massive Nokia he had owned for years. It was so big you could read his texts from ten paces away as they came in. They were usually about bets that had come off.

I used to fight text-speak. The younger the footballer, the looser the attitude to grammar and punctuation. The older you get the more resistance to emojis. I've tried to embrace the future. Don't fight progress, roll with it. It's good old-fashioned email that I still find troubling. An email is serious, an email is work. A text is a relationship, a joke, the start of a night out. I don't understand why you have to send an email. Can't you just text?

There are rules in place now. Phones away an hour and a half before kick-off. If you're at the ground earlier, the cut-off may fall then. But there are ways round it. Everyone has their music on their smartphones, and if you're listening to that music 15 minutes before kick-off, your phone is out and in your hand and you're locked away with it in your own secret world, so what's the difference anyway? You'll see a player whispering back to his music, and you hope he might be singing along, and then you glance at his screen to see he's FaceTiming his girlfriend in the VIP seats.

It's not all bad. The presence of phones on long coach journeys has allowed pranks to be supersized – Jonathan Woodgate and Robbie Keane texting Jamie O'Hara, pretending to be a girl he'd met the night before, Jamie spilling all sorts of secrets and coming up with all manner of fibs about the free stuff he could get hold of and the salary he was on; Glenn Whelan at Stoke arriving at training so embarrassed to be driving a Vauxhall Corsa that he tried parking it in the staff car-park, only to be rumbled and filmed on a team-mate's phone for all the squad to enjoy.

Inevitably a manager has been halfway through his big pre-match team-talk when someone's phone has gone off, Dom Joly style. Usually the lads will break the frozen silence that follows with a big cheer, partly to defuse the situation and partly out of sheer relief that it's someone else's phone rather than theirs. The two managers you least want that to happen in front of? Roy Keane and Fabio Capello. I once saw Capello almost decapitate Emile Heskey during a team meal on England duty. Emile was queueing up to get his pasta when his phone suddenly went off. Capello wheeled around and shoved all the lids off the metal tureens of food, sending them clattering to the floor.

You can imagine the noise. The whole room froze. Capello with his face red and eyes wild – 'We have thirty minutes in the whole day to sit down and talk to your team-mates, and you can't do it?'

A valid point made in a dramatic way. Safe to say Emile didn't do it again, and so when out with friends we now try to follow the same general idea without the tureen abuse. All our smartphones go in the middle of the table. The first person to touch theirs pays for the meal. You can see who's calling, and you can see the dilemma on the diner's face: I need to take this call or I'll get in deep trouble, but is it worth picking up the entire bill for?

The advent of the smartphone changed another key part of the footballer's world: it shifted it from autograph to selfie. I'm fine with that; I'll always pose for a photo and a side of accompanying chat. It's the secret filming that grates. You'll be in a restaurant, and you know they're filming you because they keep glancing over and trying to hold their phone out surreptitiously, and then you're certain because they've inadvertently set the flash off and now they're panicking, staring at you in horror and blushing and knocking over the menus. It happens all the time – on the train, walking down the street. You hear the shutter noise, you look at the culprit, they know that you know, they can't maintain eye contact …

It's a shame. People complain that footballers are out of touch, but when every time you go out you get filmed, no wonder some stay in or seek out the refuge of private clubs and velvet ropes. It's like when Wayne Rooney was turned over in the tabloids for having a few drinks at a wedding taking place in the England hotel. He looked a little worse for wear, but consider these extenuating circumstances. Some of the lads had gone into town, yet he had stayed in the hotel. The guests had invited him in. He posed for photos with the bride and groom, when had he refused people would have decried him as an idiot. He had a drink with them, he danced, he smiled. Do you want an England captain who chats to England supporters, or one who locks himself away and refuses all contact?

It's the same when Roy Hodgson got in trouble for chatting honestly about Rio Ferdinand's international future with a supporter on the Jubilee line going to Wembley. Roy's the son of a Croydon bus driver. Conversation on public transport comes naturally to him. And then suddenly he's on YouTube, and everyone's criticising him for being indiscreet, and he doesn't even know what YouTube is. Everyone in football has become more guarded, because they don't want every conversation they have to end up on social media. And so one of the great pub conversations will die away: 'You'll never guess who I bumped into today ...'

I've had to embrace it. When you're 6'7" the odds of sneaking around under the radar do not fall in your favour. I was at an Arctic Monkeys gig at Finsbury Park when security asked me to watch from the balcony rather than the dancefloor because it was causing too much of a commotion. And then I get spotted, and the whole crowd turns round with their camera-phones on, chanting, 'Crouchie do the Robot, Crouchie do the Robot ...'

And so I roll with it. Dance-offs with Abbey while on holiday in Ibiza, stuck up on YouTube by some fellow clubber before we've got back to the bar. Crowd-surfing at a Kasabian gig, because you don't want to miss out on what your mates can do, and in any case I'd scored after 19 seconds against Arsenal earlier in the day, and getting home to see footage from four different angles all over social media, and then the newspapers, all the while wondering what the manager's going to say when I get into training on Monday morning.

I can't give up crowd-surfing. It's too much fun. I'm just getting started. So if you see me at a gig, get your phone out. You can fill your boots.

GERRARD

The first time I saw Steven Gerrard we were both 17. He was playing for Liverpool's under-19 team, me for Spurs. We were down on the bottom pitch at Spurs Lodge, the first team training on the good pitches.

I'll never forget the passage of play that introduced us to him. One of our players in their box, in space, about to shoot. From nowhere a red blur, and a tackle that absolutely smashes the player but somehow stays legal, and Gerrard has won the ball too, it's there between his feet as he gets up, and as he does so he shoves the player on the floor, bursts past an onrushing Spurs midfielder and sets off. A hand-off to the next opposition player, a swerve to beat another, over halfway and on – barnstorming past our floundering central defender, pulling his right foot and belting an absolute screamer from 30 yards – smack onto the crossbar and back out again, all before most of us had moved.

We all looked at each other, open-mouthed. 'What the hell was *that*?'

I'd never seen a tackle that hard. I'd never seen anyone run that fast with the ball. I'd never seen a ball struck so hard. It was like putting an experienced Premier League player in a youth match, but a Premier League player who had already won three man-of-the-season awards and was the hero of every kid under the age of 11. And their dads.

All around the pitch, players and coaches and spectators saying the same thing: 'Who *is* that kid?' Alan Sugar, at the time Spurs chairman, was watching. As we came off the pitch at the end of the game, he walked on, straight to Stevie. An arm round the shoulder, a word in the ear: come and be my new apprentice, I'll have the contract ready before you get on the bus home. That was another thing I'd never seen before.

You'd expect the Liverpool coaches to be outraged, to be telling Sugar into which part of his large business empire he could tuck his contract offer. But that's the thing about Alan Sugar: he's Alan Sugar. You can't. And if you did, he could just give you the famous pointed index finger, and you'd meekly obey it as if not in control of your own limbs.

Stevie made his full debut for Liverpool a few weeks later. I would play with him at England under-18s, but only for one game, before he got promoted to the under-21s, and he would only be with them for a couple of matches before the magic escalator carried him upwards once again. I wasn't really ready for the Premier League until I was 23. He was a man early. He was ready at 17.

I would watch his early games for the Liverpool first team, when he was playing at right-back and somehow dictating the game from there. He was more hot-headed then, just as we saw later with the young Wayne Rooney. There was a level of aggression that you didn't get with young players who grew up in more comfortable London. He was different.

I heard how he would deliberately sit next to Gary McAllister on the Liverpool team coach so he could endlessly pick the veteran's brains about the secrets of midfield play. Later, when I signed for Liverpool in the summer of 2005, I saw that obsession myself. He and Jamie Carragher were on it all the time, talking about football, watching football, studying players, working them out, in full-blown love with the game in a way that went way beyond merely what was demanded by a professional contract. I thought you needed to switch off after training. Obviously you don't.

I half-knew him from my early days with the England squad when I went to Liverpool. It helped me prepare for the footballing initiation that awaited me at my first training session. Our warm-up was my favourite, boxes, where one man goes in the middle of a circle and has to cut out the passes being made by the players round the edge. You felt Gerrard and Carra judging you on your very first touch. Later I would see multimillion pound signings written off by the two of them after just three touches. 'He's a waste of money, this one ...'

Rapid pass after rapid pass in your direction, expecting you to deal with it. Passes hit too hard, to test you out. Are you good enough for us? Try this. What's your other foot like? Lay this one off. Chest, head, thigh – are you up to it?

You are 30 seconds into your first warm-up in your first training session and you realise you are suddenly among the elite. I failed to deal with one grenade. Gerrard gave me a look of total disgust.

You either buckle or you think, right, let's have this. He rapped another one at me, and this time I killed it dead. Bang, get it down, bang, trap, move it on. You're not even thinking about the manager. All you want to do is please Stevie. It must have been an absolute dream for a head coach: your captain imposing the standards, your captain demanding the very best.

He and Carra didn't seem to enjoy anything. Me? I'm happy-go-lucky. When we won I wanted to go out and celebrate. I was full of adrenaline and excitement. Those two would get back to the dressing-room and it was over, match gone, on to the next one. It was the same with the big fish at England – Frank Lampard, John Terry, Rio Ferdinand. They all had the ability to walk off the pitch after a brilliant win and be as calm as if we'd just done a light training session. It takes me ages to come down after a game. If you've scored it's like drinking three espressos in a row. If you score a hat-trick you think you'll never sleep again. Gerrard could switch it on and off as he liked. A local kid, born a man, setting the standards, driving it all on. What a gift for a club to have.

I saw big players come in at Anfield and big players go under. The expectations and standards were too high, the demands from Gerrard too much for them. Djibril Cissé, Salif Diao, Jan Kromkamp. Álvaro Arbeloa went on to play more than 150 times for Real Madrid, but Stevie and Carra were on to him straight away. The two of them would walk away from that first little circle with their minds made up about new signings. 'This kid's not got it.' 'He's a donkey. Waste of money.'

I felt like I had achieved at Liverpool only when I had earned the respect of those two. I found myself trying to impress them more than Rafa Benítez, who had actually signed me. Rio and Darren Fletcher told me that Roy Keane was the same at Manchester United. If they were happy with me then I was happy, regardless of what the manager said.

And the skills Gerrard had! People would say to me, Xabi Alonso is the best passer of a football I've ever seen. I'd say, yeah, but Stevie is better. They'd tell me that Claude Makélélé was the best tackler. Yeah, but Stevie's better. Lampard is the best goal-scoring midfielder. Yup, Stevie's on a par with him.

He could play right-back and left-back. He could play centre midfield, he could play off the striker. He could play centre-forward and he could dominate totally from right midfield.

It's only when you train with a player that you realise quite how good they are. On match-day you would see Thierry Henry and Gianfranco Zola producing little miracles. With Gerrard they were a daily occurrence. He was by far the best player in England training, and that includes David Beckham, Wayne Rooney and Michael Owen. I never trained with Paul Scholes; our times in the national set-up did not overlap. But the Chelsea lads would say the same thing: Gerrard is the most naturally gifted player we've worked with.

As I began to get to know him as a man I initially found him a really guarded character. It made sense. He had been a superstar from the age of 17. He learned early on to give nothing away. When you socialised with him you saw the difference – a normal lad, a funny bloke, one who would welcome you inside his small circle.

And he didn't care what others outside that tight group thought. If we were out, he would be the one that random strangers most wanted to talk to. They would stand next to him giving it their big spiel, and he wouldn't twitch a muscle. You'd say he looked through them, but he never even acknowledged their presence. It was as if they were behind an invisible wall. The season he scored 25 goals from right midfield and won the PFA Player of the Year, we all accompanied him to the ceremony in London to watch him pick up the award. There was a queue to get into the after-party, and even though Stevie had the trophy in his hand, the bouncers wouldn't let us in. We were all outraged. Stevie couldn't have cared less.

All the talk around England before the 2002 World Cup in South Korea and Japan was about whether David Beckham could recover from his broken metatarsal bone in time. Arguably as big a factor in England not making it past Brazil in the quarter-finals was the 21-year-old Gerrard's absence after injuring his groin on the final day of the Premier League season. In 2010 he would score in England's opening group game against the USA as captain before that horrible defeat in the knockout stages to Germany, and in 2014, as captain again, he took England's failure to get out of the group stage hard, especially having fallen just short of winning the Premier League title a month earlier too.

But 2006 was the biggest disappointment. That was our team. That was our chance to really do something. The pair of us scoring as we beat Trinidad and Tobago, battling past Ecuador, and then that quarter-final against Portugal, a game that was all over the shop. Rooney getting sent off, Stevie missing his penalty, and Lampard his, and Carra too. We had the team, we had the belief. Those ones haunt you.

It was a rare failure for Gerrard at least. He is the only player in history to score in an FA Cup final, a League Cup final, a UEFA Cup final and a Champions League final. He won all four of them. That's the definition of a great player: not just reaching big finals, not just influencing them, but deciding their outcome.

He was born for it. That 2005 Champions League final in Istanbul might be the greatest edition of them all, and he was the night's greatest player. I was away with England in the US at the time, our summer tour due to be joined by the Liverpool lads once their tilt was over. We were in Chicago, Joe Cole and I wandering out of the hotel to find somewhere to watch it, Joe desperate for Liverpool to lose after Chelsea's controversial defeat to Luis

García's 'ghost goal' in the semi-finals, me with no inkling I would be off to Anfield shortly and so entirely neutral. At half-time, Milan 3–0 up, Cole beside himself with delight, we strolled back to the hotel knowing the game was done. In the short walk home it had become 3–2. By the time we'd made it through the lobby it was 3–3. We'd learned our lesson by then. We didn't move an inch until extra time and penalties and celebrations and poor old Joe in a right old grump.

People talk about Rafa's team-talk at half-time. Speak to the Liverpool players and they'll tell you that Stevie was heavily involved in it all, shall we say. The header of his that began the impossible comeback a few minutes later was a study in perfection: the run, the leap, the neck muscles on it, the direction. His run for the penalty that tied it up, his penalty never missing, him the heartbeat and soul of everything that happened.

Club insiders will admit to you that that Liverpool side was perhaps more about perspiration than inspiration. Djimi Traoré, in the season of his wonder own-goal in the Cup against Burnley, and the song that followed suit; Igor Bišćan and Vladimír Šmicer often in harness, Milan Baroš and Djibril Cissé. Jerzy Dudek is a great lad, but he was not in Pepe Reina's class.

The whole run to the final seemed inspired by Gerrard. None of it would ever have happened had he not smashed home that late beauty against Olympiacos to rescue them in the group stages on goal difference. To be three goals down to an Italian side, being battered, and win it? Without Gerrard in the team, history would have recorded a straightforward Milan win.

And then I signed for them. They might have been expecting Andriy Shevchenko, they got Peter Crouch. Gerrard never complained once.

I would see his influence on a big showcase first hand. I was raised on FA Cup finals more than European Cups. As a kid they were bigger than the league for me, and it was the same for my Chelsea-supporting dad. He used to make me watch the win over Leeds in the replayed final of 1970 on video. I'm named after Peter Osgood, scorer of Chelsea's first goal in the second game. In Liverpool's run to the 2006 final in Cardiff I scored the only goal against Manchester United in the fifth round, but every time I look at my winner's medal now I only think of Stevie.

It was his pass to Cissé for our first. It was him running on to my knock-down to smash home our second. His third? His third is everything you want to know about Steven Gerrard in a single moment.

I'd come off by that point, us 3–2 down with time almost up. He had cramp, limping around. Our bench saying he'll have to come off, he's a walking liability. And then the ball breaks, 30 yards out, bobbling, and he runs on to it like an Olympic sprinter and cracks the cleanest of strikes into the exact five inches of Shaka Hislop's net that he wanted. Most good players could make that shot one time in 20. With Gerrard a part of you wasn't even surprised.

He was a routine scorer of extraordinary goals, from his very first for Liverpool, against Sheffield Wednesday back in 1999, the kit hanging off his teenage frame, skinhead cut, looking like he'd run straight off the streets of Huyton and onto the pitch. Thrashing one in from outside the box to put England ahead for the first time as they took Germany apart 5–1 in the Olympiastadion in Munich in 2001, technically so perfect, a bouncing ball on the edge of the box, bodies in the way, and in it flies.

Long-distance raspers against Southampton and Aston Villa around the same time, crashing one up and over Fabian Barthez in the League Cup final of 2003. Astonishing far-out free-kicks against Newcastle and Villa again. Ridiculous thumping volleys against Manchester City and Middlesbrough.

Special days, special nights, the ones you'll bore your grandkids about. The team bus slowing as it got stuck in human traffic close to Anfield, fans banging on the side, flares going off. You thinking, whoa, this a big match and a big, big club, and you glance across at Gerrard, and he's totally calm and focused. I watched our 2007 Champions League semi-final win over Chelsea again recently. It still gives me goosebumps. The noise bouncing around, the cameras shaking with the vibrations and the cavorting and the madness of it all. Gerrard the skipper at the helm. Maybe I was the mast.

All those tests he gave you on the training ground paid off. Passes fired at you in big matches, a confident, practised touch and Gerrard there again to bury the lay-off, just as against Newcastle in 2005, just as on so many occasions for all of us who played with him. He'd done his learning as an eight-year-old at Vernon Sangster sports centre on Priory Road, working with the old Liverpool youth team set-up of Dave Shannon, Steve Heighway and Hughie McAuley. Twice a week, for an hour at a time, those coaches would work all that little squad, which also included Carragher, Rickie Lambert, Michael Owen and Jason Koumas, driving passes, curling and caressing them, smacking a ball at the wall, killing the rebound dead. All of it a competition, all of it demanding. A sloppy pass or piece of control and they would have to do it again.

The kid becomes a man and he takes those lessons with him. You sink or you swim. Until I got to that level, I never realised it was so cut-throat. Players like Gerrard trust you as a team-mate until they can't. You have to deal with what they hit at you or you shouldn't be there. I became a much better player as a result of that harsh influence.

For a player who was so expressive on the football pitch he could be shy off it. It sometimes got misinterpreted as rudeness. But he was just different. No tattoos, a nice car but nothing flash. Straightforward clothes, no time for soft things like hair gel. He and Carra thought it was for flash cockneys. It was only right near the end that they realised you could style your hair without betraying your soul.

He was never shy around football. He would be the first one in Rafa's office if he thought something at the club wasn't right. It was always hard to get a 'well done' out of Rafa. That year Steve won PFA Player of the Year, Rafa was still telling him how to use his left foot, still trying to improve him. It worked. Stevie was a model of angry focus. 'Right, I'll show him ...'

He was a working-class hero. No special peg in the dressing-room, no special seat on the Liverpool bus, as long as he was sitting next to Carra. With England it would be a little Scouse clique of him, Rooney, Owen and Carra, with me hovering on the edge. The Chelsea boys – Terry, Lampard, Cole – on another table. Ashley Cole, Rio and Ashley Young at the back, playing on their Game Boys. Becks and Gary Neville near the front, teacher's pets.

A lot of kids grow up infatuated with football. Quite a number have ability. Only an elite few have all the technical skills and an insatiable desire too.

Gerrard did. That was what took the shy boy from No. 10 Ironside Road on Huyton's Bluebell estate to the sacred turf of

Anfield, to impossible nights in Istanbul, to three World Cup finals. Talent, hunger and obsession.

And so, in a book entitled *How to Be a Footballer*, our perfect example. Not a list of crimes against fashion, taste and behaviour, but the model all young players should aspire to. A proper footballer.

ACKNOWLEDGEMENTS

This book is for everyone who has helped me along the way. My mum, dad and sister who I wouldn't have been here without. David, Jonathan, Melvin and Winston for your help and guidance.

I had knockbacks but I also had people that believed in me when I didn't even believe in myself – Des Bulpin, Pat Nolan, Andy Campbell, Mr Wareing, Gerry Francis, Graham Rix and Graham Taylor.

Rafa for taking a chance on me when many others wouldn't have. Harry Redknapp never stopped believing in me (or signing me). All the England managers who gave me the chance to live the dream.

My beautiful wife and best friend Abbey and gorgeous kids Sophia, Liberty and Johnny. They are why I still do it and why I still do it with a big smile on my face. I love you.

A big thanks to Tom Fordyce who put all these stories together and made the whole process good fun. He loved it anyway cos I treated him to dinner at the Holiday Inn in Stoke-on-Trent a couple of times. Laura Horsley, Andrew Goodfellow, Ian Allen and all the team at Ebury, plus David Luxton.

Finally the fans. I had to work hard to gain respect when I was younger, but having got there I feel I have a good relationship with all of my previous clubs' supporters. Wherever I go I meet people who have enjoyed something I've done in my career, whether that's an important goal, a great game or more likely the Robot or a comment made years ago. Oh – and I would have been a copywriter in an advertising agency, is the proper answer to that famous question if you're interested ...

PHOTO CREDITS